North Korea

Other books in the History of Nations series:

THE HISTORY OF NATIONS

North Korea

Debra A. Miller, *Book Editor*

Daniel Leone, *President*
Bonnie Szumski, *Publisher*
Scott Barbour, *Managing Editor*

GREENHAVEN
PRESS®

San Diego • Detroit • New York • San Francisco • Cleveland
New Haven, Conn. • Waterville, Maine • London • Munich

LIBRARY OF CONGRESS CATALOGING-IN-PUBLICATION DATA
North Korea / Debra A. Miller, book editor.
p. cm. — (History of nations)
Includes bibliographical references and index.
ISBN 0-7377-1853-6 (pbk. : alk. paper) — ISBN 0-7377-1852-8 (lib. : alk. paper)
1. Korea (North)—History. 2. Korea (North)—Politics and government.
3. Korea—History. I. Miller, Debra A. II. History of nations (Greenhaven Press).
DS935.N67 2004
951.93—dc21   2003044898

Printed in the United States of America

Contents

Chapter 1: Early Korean History

1. Korea's Ancient Beginnings
by Donald Stone Macdonald
The period of the Three Kingdoms of Korea lasted
from about the time of Christ until A.D. 668. By the
ninth century, the Koryo dynasty (from which Korea
took its name) emerged to unify the Korean peninsula. Finally, in 1392, the Choson or Yi dynasty began
Korea's longest period of independence and unification, lasting until 1910.

2. Japanese Colonialism
by Geoff Simons
In the late 1800s and early 1900s, imperial Japan went
to war with both China and Russia for the right to
control North Korea. Japan officially annexed Korea
in 1910, beginning four decades of oppression and
exploitation of the Korean people.

3. The Rise of Communism and Nationalism in Korea
by Takashi Hatada
The Japanese colonization of Korea inspired resistance,
leading to mass protests in 1919 and to new Japanese
cultural policies that sought to integrate Koreans and
Japanese. Between 1920 and 1945, Korean resistance
and nationalist movements developed, including a
Korean Communist Party and the emergence of guerrilla leader and nationalist Kim Il Sung, who later
became leader of Communist North Korea.

4. The March First Movement
by Kim Il Sung
The first organized Korean resistance to the Japanese
occupation of Korea occurred on March 1, 1919. It

consisted of peaceful marches by Koreans from all walks of life and all parts of the country.

Chapter 2: The Creation of North Korea

1. The Division of Korea

After Japan's surrender at the end of World War II on August 15, 1945, Korea's hopes for a unified independence were dashed when the United States and Soviet Russia occupied the country and failed in an effort to negotiate a plan for electing a new government for Korea. Instead, the country was divided into a Communist state in North Korea headed by Kim Il Sung and an elected government in South Korea led by Syngman Rhee.

2. The Soviets Select Kim Il Sung to Lead North Korea

Kim Il Sung was born to peasant parents in 1912 and became a guerrilla in Manchuria in the 1920s fighting the Japanese occupation of Korea. After World War II ended with Japan's surrender in 1945, Joseph Stalin chose Kim Il Sung as the Soviet Union's choice to head Communist North Korea.

3. Kim Il Sung's Return to Korea

After the defeat of the Japanese in World War II, Kim Il Sung returned to Korea from his exile in the Soviet Union to find Koreans excited about the Japanese defeat and hopeful about the possibilities for national unity.

Chapter 3: The Korean War

1. North Korea's Invasion of South Korea

The circumstances surrounding North Korea's invasion of South Korea on June 25, 1950, included North Korea's and the Soviet Union's misreading of the United States's mood, a lack of preparedness of the South Korean military forces, a test of the newly created United Nations, and the reluctance of the United States to become involved in a war that could escalate into a global nuclear confrontation with the Soviet Union.

Chapter 4: The Uniquely Korean Communist Nation

Chapter 5: Modern Challenges for North Korea

FOREWORD

I n 1841, the journalist Charles MacKay remarked, "In reading the history of nations, we find that, like individuals, they have their whims and peculiarities, their seasons of excitement and recklessness." At the time of MacKay's observation, many of the nations explored in the Greenhaven Press History of Nations series did not yet exist in their current form. Nonetheless, whether it is old or young, every nation is similar to an individual, with its own distinct characteristics and unique story.

The History of Nations series is dedicated to exploring these stories. Each anthology traces the development of one of the world's nations from its earliest days, when it was perhaps no more than a promise on a piece of paper or an idea in the mind of some revolutionary, through to its status in the world today. Topics discussed include the pivotal political events and power struggles that shaped the country as well as important social and cultural movements. Often, certain dramatic themes and events recur, such as the rise and fall of empires, the flowering and decay of cultures, or the heroism and treachery of leaders. As well, in the history of most countries war, oppression, revolution, and deep social change feature prominently. Nonetheless, the details of such events vary greatly, as does their impact on the nation concerned. For example, England's "Glorious Revolution" of 1688 was a peaceful transfer of power that set the stage for the emergence of democratic institutions in that nation. On the other hand, in China, the overthrow of dynastic rule in 1912 led to years of chaos, civil war, and the eventual emergence of a Communist regime that used violence as a tool to root out opposition and quell popular protest. Readers of the Greenhaven Press History of Nations series will learn about the common challenges nations face and the different paths they take in response to such crises. However a nation's story may have developed, the series strives to present a clear and unbiased view of the country at hand.

The structure of each volume in the series is designed to help students deepen their understanding of the events, movements, and persons that define nations. First, a thematic introduction provides critical background material and helps orient the reader. The chapters themselves are designed to provide an accessible and engaging approach to the study of the history of that nation involved and are arranged either thematically or chronologically, as appropriate. The selections include both primary documents, which convey something of the flavor of the time and place concerned, and secondary material, which includes the wisdom of hindsight and scholarship. Finally, each book closes with a detailed chronology, a comprehensive bibliography of suggestions for further research, and a thorough index.

The countries explored within the series are as old as China and as young as Canada, as distinct in character as Spain and India, as large as Russia, and as compact as Japan. Some are based on ethnic nationalism, the belief in an ethnic group as a distinct people sharing a common destiny, whereas others emphasize civic nationalism, in which what defines citizenship is not ethnicity but commitment to a shared constitution and its values. As human societies become increasingly globalized, knowledge of other nations and of the diversity of their cultures, characteristics, and histories becomes ever more important. This series responds to the challenge by furnishing students with a solid and engaging introduction to the history of the world's nations.

INTRODUCTION

I n January 2002 U.S. president George Bush declared that North Korea is part of an "axis of evil" that, along with Iraq and Iran, threatens the peace of the world by supporting terrorism and developing weapons of mass destruction. In October 2002 North Korea confirmed U.S. suspicions that it is developing nuclear weapons. This admission violates a 1994 antinuclear agreement North Korea made with the United States in exchange for aid following a similar threat of nuclear weapons development by the country in 1993.

Many believe that Kim Jong Il, North Korea's repressive Communist dictator, is practicing a risky foreign policy of brinksmanship and nuclear blackmail as a means to acquire critical foreign aid and assurances of peace from hostile foreign powers such as the United States, Japan, and South Korea. For the United States, this type of blackmail poses a difficult dilemma: Either appease North Korea or risk confrontation with the well-equipped North Korean military at the doorstep of democratic South Korea, where U.S. troops have been stationed since the end of the Korean War. These recent events appear to be but the latest attempt by North Korea to survive by resisting and manipulating larger, sometimes hostile world powers.

As the selections in this volume illustrate, the history of North Korea, and the entire Korean peninsula, is really a history of the Korean people seeking to survive domination by greater powers. For centuries, Korea resisted foreign invasions, first by the Chinese and later the Japanese. Most recently, the peninsula has been dominated by the interests of the Soviet Union and the United States. Indeed, the division of the peninsula that created the two separate countries of North and South Korea was not the desire of the Korean people but rather the direct product of Cold War rivalry between the Soviet Union and the United States that began after World War II and lasted throughout most of the latter twentieth century. Today, North Korea is struggling to overcome the obstacles and repercussions created by these outside forces.

The Korean Peninsula's History of Domination by Foreign Powers

Even at the beginning of their civilization, Koreans were dominated by outside powers. To a large extent, Korea's (and now North Korea's) fate has been shaped by geography. It is situated on a mountainous peninsula in Asia bordered by China to the northwest, Japan to the southeast, and Russia to the northeast. Surrounded by larger, more powerful countries such as these, Korea learned to fight for its independence against invasions by outsiders and to play the interests of larger powers against each other to survive.

The history of the Korean peninsula, for example, reveals a series of Chinese invasions followed by Korean dynasties that continued to follow Chinese traditions, philosophy, and religion. Although Korea has a number of conflicting myths concerning its founding and date, by about the fourth century B.C. the Chinese appear to have established the kingdom of Ancient Choson in northwestern Korea. This kingdom was replaced later by another Chinese invasion in 109 B.C. led by a Han Chinese emperor. Local Korean tribes opposed these early Chinese rulers, however, and in time, weakened and collapsed the Chinese administration.

This early Korean desire for autonomy from foreign invaders soon led to the growth of three separate, strong Korean kingdoms (Koguryo, Paekche, and Silla) and eventually a united Korea on the peninsula. Nevertheless, Chinese influence and attempts at control continued on the peninsula during this time, as each of the kingdoms fought Chinese assaults. Koguryo was the first kingdom to develop, in 37 B.C. in mountainous northern Korea. Successfully resisting various Chinese assaults, it formed from a group of hunting tribes into a strong and thriving state extending over much of the Korean peninsula as well as parts of Chinese Manchuria. In the southern part of the Korean peninsula, an area where agriculture flourished, Korean Han tribes (different from Chinese Han) developed into two other kingdoms: Paekche and Silla. Paekche, formed in about 16 B.C., was located on the western coast of the peninsula; it repelled numerous Chinese assaults but was finally invaded by the Chinese Tang dynasty in 663. Silla, founded in 57 B.C., developed in central Korea. Although Silla initially began as a weak kingdom, it eventually grew to overtake both Paekche and Koguryo, to defeat Chinese Tang forces seeking to invade the peninsula, and to form the first unified state in Korea. By the end of the seventh century, most of the Korean peninsula was ruled by one government—Silla. Although it fought Chinese control, Silla adopted a Chinese system of government and much of Chinese culture and thought, including Buddhism and Confucianism.

Silla fell in 936 due to internal problems and was replaced by the Koryo dynasty (from which Korea gets its name). The Koryo period, even more than the period of the Three Kingdoms or Silla, was known for its incorporation of Chinese influences, Confucianism, and especially Buddhism. Koryo eventually weakened from foreign invasions, including a Mongol invasion in 1231 and yet another Chinese assault, this time by armies of the Ming dynasty in China.

Eventually, Korea entered its only golden period, 518 years of peace, independence, and unity during the Yi, or Choson, dynasty. Koryo general Yi Song-gye made peace with the Ming Chinese in 1392 and founded this new dynasty, naming it Choson after Ancient Choson. The new Yi monarch successfully consolidated power and like many rulers before him adopted

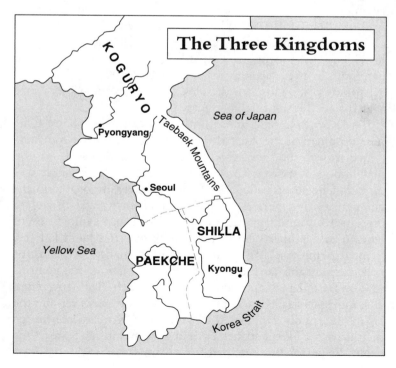

The Three Kingdoms

Chinese philosophy and politics, especially Confucian thought. The Choson dynasty was marked by many cultural and political achievements, and it adopted a policy of isolating itself from almost all foreigners. Later, it was weakened by political rivalries, Japanese invasions in 1592, and a Chinese Manchu invasion in 1636. Thereafter, the Manchus forced Koreans to be loyal to the Chinese Manchu emperor. The decline of the Choson dynasty in Korea was followed by four decades of brutal colonization by yet another country in the early twentieth century—Japan.

Japanese influence in Korea began in the late 1800s, when Japan, itself forcibly opened to Western trade by the United States in 1854, forced Korea to open to Japanese trade in 1875. Later, Japan emerged as the winner for control of Korea, after overcoming both Chinese and Russian interests in the peninsula. Japan first declared war on China over the issue of Korea and won, leading to the 1895 Treaty of Shimonoseki, which ended the war and declared Korea to be an independent, sovereign state. After the treaty was signed, the Korean king sought support from Russia, leading to a decade of squabbling between Russia and Japan over who would control Korea. Eventually, Japan went to war with Russia in 1904. This war ended with the 1905 Treaty of Portsmouth, mediated by U.S. president Theodore Roosevelt, in which Russia recognized Japan's right to control the Korean peninsula. In 1910 Japan formally annexed Korea, which became a Japanese colony for four decades, until Japan's defeat in World War II forced it out of the country in 1945.

The Korean people, after fighting for centuries against Chinese domination and after achieving a long period of independence, thus found themselves living under the rule of a brutal new imperialist power. Koreans never accepted the Japanese colonization, however, leading the Japanese to rely on force to maintain control. The period, therefore, was characterized by violent repression and military rule as well as by blatant exploitation of Korean land, property, workers, and culture. On March 1, 1919, in an amazing display of courage and nationalism, Koreans rebelled against the Japanese occupation in a nationwide demonstration for independence, known as the March First Movement. The movement failed to attract foreign support, however, and the Japanese brutally suppressed it. Thereafter, Koreans continued their drive for independence both in exile and inside Korea. One group of nationalists formed a government in exile in China called the provisional government, led by Syngman Rhee, who later became president of South Korea. Other nationalists included a Communist faction in Manchuria that produced anti-Japanese guerrilla leaders such as Kim Il Sung, who later became the leader of North Korea.

The Creation of North Korea—Korea Divided by Cold War Powers

After the Japanese were ousted from Korea in 1945 at the end of World War II, Koreans celebrated, believing they could now reestablish an independent, unified Korea. These hopes were dashed when Korea once again was occupied by foreign powers that controlled its destiny and eventually divided the peninsula into two separate and warring countries.

When World War II ended on August 15, 1945, with the bombing of Hiroshima and Nagasaki and the surrender of the Japanese, the Russians had already entered the northern part of Korea to fight the Japanese after the defeat of Germany. Shortly thereafter, the United States moved into the southern part of Korea. Although the Soviets and Americans had pledged in 1943 that Korea should become independent after the war, the matter was not given a high priority by either country and they instead imposed a trusteeship plan on Korea that called for elections to be held within five years. In the meantime, Korea was divided in half and subjected to a military occupation, with the Soviet Union occupying the area above the 38th parallel and the United States occupying the zone south of this dividing line.

The nationalist movement that had developed in Korea during the Japanese occupation blossomed after the Japanese were ousted, pressing for unity and independence. Nationalists in Korea and the surrounding areas were primarily Communist or left-leaning, supported by workers, students, and intellectuals. Following the division of the peninsula into northern and southern zones, the Soviet Union took advantage of this leftist sentiment in the north by quickly responding to economic and social needs, winning the support of the people, and organizing Koreans at the grassroots level along Communist lines.

In southern Korea, the United States imposed military rule on the Koreans similar to that used by the Japanese during Japanese colonization, a policy that did little to inspire popular support. The United States took such strong actions because it feared a Communist expansion in Asia and was concerned about the Soviet interest in Korea. The United States also felt compelled to oppose the popular sentiment for unification and independence because many nationalists in Korea at that time were Communists or leftists. As a result, the United States focused on maintaining order and eradicating Communists, backed the provisional government, and brought right-wing nationalist Syngman Rhee back to Korea.

Talks were held between the Soviet Union and the United States to establish an interim Korean government under the terms of the trusteeship, but the two distrustful superpowers failed to agree in negotiations and the trusteeship plan was never accepted by the Korean people. Finally, in August 1947, the United States referred the Korean question to the United Nations (UN), which established a commission to oversee elections on the peninsula. When the Russians refused to allow the commission into North Korea, the UN held elections only in South Korea, resulting in the creation of an independent Republic of Korea (ROK) in the southern part of Korea on August 15, 1948, with Syngman Rhee as the duly elected president. That same year, the Soviets in the north created their own Communist government, called the Democratic People's Republic of Korea (DPRK), headed by ex-guerrilla leader Kim Il Sung.

Korea thus became the battleground for the Cold War, resulting in a division between North and South that was contrary to the will of the Korean people. On June 25, 1950, the Korean War became the first battle in the Cold War, when North Korea invaded South Korea with Soviet support in an effort to reunify the Korean peninsula by military means. The United States, again in order to prevent Communist expansion in Asia, defended South Korea with UN support. U.S. intervention pushed the aggressors back northward toward Communist China. As a result, China entered the war on the side of North Korea, and the battle line in the war became the 38th parallel, close to the original partition line. Although the war dragged on until an armistice was signed in 1953, this border between North and South changed little as a result of the war, and today is known as the demilitarized zone (DMZ). In fact, it is not demilitarized; both sides maintain heavy troop concentrations in the area, including thirty-seven thousand U.S. troops currently stationed on the South Korean side.

This twentieth-century chapter of Korean history was perhaps more damaging than earlier foreign occupations of Korea. This

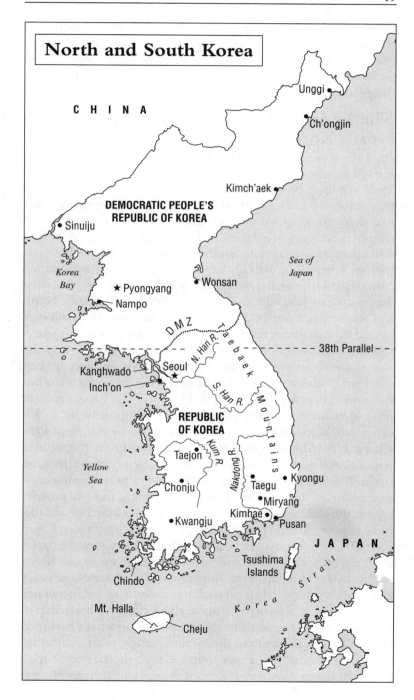

North and South Korea

CHINA

Unggi

Ch'ongjin

Kimch'aek

DEMOCRATIC PEOPLE'S
REPUBLIC OF KOREA

Sinuiju

Korea
Bay

Pyongyang

Nampo

Wonsan

Sea of
Japan

D M Z

N. Han R.

T a e b a e k

38th Parallel

Seoul

Kanghwado

Inch'on

S. Han R.

M o u n t a i n s

REPUBLIC
OF KOREA

Yellow
Sea

Taejon

Kum R.

Chonju

Naktong R.

Taegu

Kyongu

Miryang

Kimhae

Pusan

Kwangju

JAPAN

Tsushima
Islands

K o r e a   Strait

Chindo

Mt. Halla

Cheju

time the occupation resulted not only in foreign domination of the Korean people but also in a civil war that decimated the population and devastated the land, resulting in both a physical and an ideological division of the Korean people that continues to the present day.

The Legacy of the Cold War for North Korea

After the Korean War ended without unification of Korea, both sides faced massive economic reconstruction and problems of political instability. North and South Korea also remained technically in a war stance because although an armistice was signed, no formal peace treaty could ever be agreed on. Over the years, both countries have employed spies, and North Korea has made at least four attempts to assassinate South Korean presidents, has built numerous invasion tunnels under the demilitarized zone, and has conducted terrorist attacks against South Korean targets. Given the continuing hostilities and the vastly different ideologies, North and South Korea developed as totally separate countries, each supported by their respective superpowers and linked to their fates.

For South Korea, times were difficult immediately after the war. Economic reconstruction proceeded slowly in the early years amid political instability and controversy surrounding what became an unpopular Rhee dictatorship. Finally, in 1960, a student revolt overthrew the Rhee government, leading eventually to another pro-Western military government led by president Park Chung Hee. Although military rule continued to be unpopular, South Korea, with U.S. aid, made considerable economic progress in the 1960s, finally providing stability and improved living conditions for the population. The 1970s brought massive protests against the Park regime, and Park was shot and killed by an aide, only to be replaced by another repressive military ruler, Chun Doo Hwan. South Korea finally established a democratic government in 1992 under President Kim Young Sam. South Korea has maintained friendly relations with the United States and in recent years has acquired an even greater measure of independence and economic self-sufficiency under the democratic leadership of President Kim Dae Jung. In short, South Korea has developed along Western lines into a democratic nation with a thriving, modern economy, due largely to its ties with the United States.

North Korea, after the war, faced the same challenges of economic reconstruction and political stabilization as did South Korea. North Korea, however, relying on massive Soviet aid and a highly organized Communist structure, made a quick and successful economic recovery under President Kim Il Sung's 1956 Three-Year Plan. Later, when the Soviets reduced their support, North Korea emphasized a political philosophy of *juche*, or self-reliance, and learned to play the Soviets against the Chinese to reinforce North Korea's independence. Kim Il Sung also consolidated his political power, eliminated all opposition, built up the military, and followed the Communist, totalitarian model closely to create a dictatorship government that depends on military repression and isolation from the outside world to remain in power. Kim Il Sung called himself "the Great Leader" and created a cult of personality similar to that of Joseph Stalin in the Soviet Union.

North Korea's world changed with the end of the Cold War and the collapse of the Soviet Union in 1991. Its alignment with communism, helpful during the early years, now became a liability. The absence of aid from the Soviet Union contributed to a sharp economic decline, and China's policy of economic modernization and opening to the United States also undercut North Korea's centuries-old reliance on that country for protection and support. At this crucial time Kim Il Sung, the deified "Great Leader" of North Korea, died leaving the country to struggle under new leadership, that of his appointed successor and son, Kim Jong Il. These changes, plus natural disasters including floods and then drought, have left North Korea starving and even more isolated in a new global order, with a totalitarian and highly militarized government fearful of losing power. North Korea now faces a challenge to its very survival.

North Korea's Uncertain Future

By all accounts, modern North Korea is in crisis, suffering from widespread famine, an almost completely collapsed economy, and overspending on the military. The country continues to live as an isolated Cold War Communist state under a highly repressive totalitarian dictatorship concerned mainly with its own survival. It has been unwilling to loosen its grip on power or open the country to the world in order to respond effectively to the country's economic problems.

To survive, North Korea sells arms and pursues an erratic foreign policy that veers from diplomatic overtures seeking peaceful reunification with South Korea to aggressive military and nuclear threats. In 1993, for example, North Korea threatened to develop nuclear weaponry, spurring the United States to become involved in negotiations that resulted in the 1994 Framework Agreement, in which North Korea agreed to end its nuclear weapons program in return for foreign aid in building a light water reactor to produce badly needed electricity. In 1998 North Korea launched a medium-range, multistage rocket over Japan, threatening a longtime enemy. During the same approximate time period, however, North Korea pursued peace strategies with South Korea, culminating in a historic summit with South Korean president Kim Dae Jung in June 2000, and follow-up events such as North-South reunions for family members separated

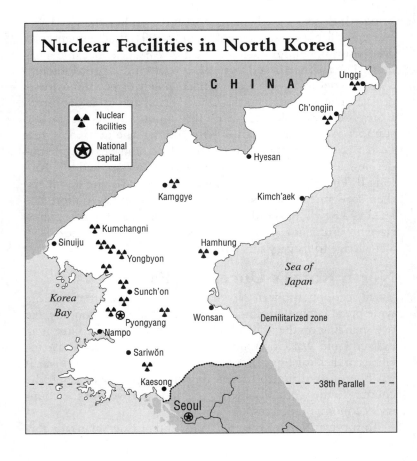

Nuclear Facilities in North Korea

since the Korean War. Throughout the 1990s, North Korea became one of the world's biggest purveyors of missiles to dangerous countries such as Iran, Iraq, Pakistan, and Syria; as recently as December 2002, a Korean ship loaded with missiles heading for Yemen was stopped by Spain and the United States.

In October 2002 North Korea began a repeat of its 1993 nuclear weapons scenario, announcing that it was restarting its nuclear weapons program while demanding new negotiations with the United States. This time, in the wake of U.S. president Bush's speech denouncing North Korea as being part of an "axis of evil," North Korea demands a nonaggression treaty to protect itself against potential U.S. military action .

Many have concluded that the country is pursuing a foreign policy of nuclear blackmail, in which it seeks to survive by extorting benefits from other countries by "rogue" threats. This view comports with the long Korean history of surviving by resisting and manipulating hostile world powers. Because it is no longer able to rely on its traditional Communist network for economic aid and protection, North Korea's regime may be playing the only cards that remain in its hand. It seeks more peaceful relations with its closest threat, South Korea, while extorting aid and assurances against military threats from its biggest enemy, the United States, using the best leverage available, nuclear weapons. Of course, there is one other option: North Korea could win over its enemies by changing its government and opening its economy to the world. However, this could mean a regime change and subordination to South Korea and the West, a prospect Kim Jong Il is unlikely to embrace.

The future of North Korea, as always, is not entirely up to North Korea. Although the decisions of North Korea's leader, Kim Jong Il, will be the determining factor, the actions of foreign powers, especially the United States and South Korea, but also perhaps China, Russia, and Japan, also will be of great consequence. How the United States responds to North Korea will be critical. Many think a hard-line policy could provoke a military confrontation in Korea. Similarly, although the recent election of pro-engagement candidate Roh Moo Hyun as president of South Korea suggests that South Korean policies of friendly negotiation and engagement with North Korea will continue, any changes in these policies could create a more threatening environment for North Korea and place greater pressure on the government of Kim Jong Il. Also, the degree to which China and Russia, now involved economically with South Korea, are willing or able to influence the actions of North Korea will be significant factors affecting North Korea's future. In addition, North Korea's relationship with Japan, Asia's leading economic power and now also a trading partner with South Korea, will surely influence North Korea's survival. In any case, the challenges for North Korea are whether it can overcome its Cold War legacy—a Communist government and failing economy—and how it will negotiate or survive the foreign power pressures of the twenty-first century.

THE HISTORY OF NATIONS
Chapter 1

Early Korean History

Korea's Ancient Beginnings

By Donald Stone Macdonald

The history of the Korean peninsula is one of invasions and influences from its larger, more powerful neighbors—China to the west, Japan to the east, and Russia to the north. The author of the following book excerpt on Korea's history, Donald Stone Macdonald, is now deceased but was a research professor of Korea studies at the School of Foreign Service at Georgetown University in Washington, D.C.; he also gained extensive knowledge of Korean affairs as a U.S. Army officer and diplomat. As his book reveals, the earliest Koreans lived in small fishing and hunting communities. Although nomadic Central Asian peoples were a constant threat, the first outside conquest of the Korean peninsula was likely by the Chinese, who attacked the kingdom of Ancient Choson in 109 B.C. Koreans, however, strongly desired independence, and the Chinese rule gave way to the formation of three separate, independent kingdoms—Paekche, Koguryo, and Silla. This period of the Three Kingdoms, from about the time of Christ until A.D. 668, nevertheless was heavily influenced by Chinese civilization, especially Confucian philosophy and Buddhist religion. Eventually, conflicts developed among these three states, with Silla emerging as the victor. Thus began a period of unity and self-rule on the peninsula that lasted until the 900s.

By the tenth century, the kingdom of Silla had declined, to be replaced by the Koryo dynasty, from which modern Korea takes it name. The founder of this dynasty successfully unified the Korean peninsula and continued Korea's adoption of Chinese culture. The Koryo dynasty gave way in 1392 to the Yi dynasty, which named its kingdom Choson after Ancient Choson and which again embodied Chinese philosophy and politics. The Yi or Choson dynasty lasted for more than five centuries, until the Japanese annexation of Korea in 1910.

Donald Stone Macdonald, *The Koreans: Contemporary Politics and Society*, edited by Donald N. Clark. Boulder, CO: Westview Press, 1996. Copyright © 1996 by Westview Press, A Division of HarperCollins Publishers, Inc. Reproduced by permission.

Peeople have lived in the Korean peninsula since the Pale-olithic period (about 60,000 years ago), but the origins of the first settlers have not been clearly established. Around the fifth millenium B.C., a Neolithic people entered the peninsula or nearby Manchuria. Korean tradition calls them Yemaek and regards them as the ancestors of present-day Korea. They must have come from the north and west, in small tribal groups, probably from the Yenisei river valley of Siberia. Such movement of related peoples continued into historic times. Links with Central Asia are suggested by the structural similarity of the Korean language to those spoken by Turkic, Mongolian, Tungusic, and other peoples who originated in East Asia north of China. There are also similarities between Neolithic Korean pottery and other remains, such as stone dolmens, and those found in Central Asia. The stylized fir-tree and reindeer motifs on ancient gold crowns found in Korean royal burial mounds also point to Central Asian origins.

Ancient Choson

The most popular Korean origin myth holds that the founder of the nation was Tan'gun, a man born of a bear at the bidding of a god. A tiger, also offered the opportunity, lacked the patience to wait the prescribed gestation period. The animals probably represented ancient tribal totem symbols. This event is dated 2333 B.C. and is celebrated in south Korea as Foundation Day (*Kaech'onjol*) on October 3. Another myth, with some basis in Chinese records, holds that Kija, a Chinese prince (Chinese: Qize), established Ancient Choson in 1122 B.C. In both myths, people are already present when the founder arrives.

By Neolithic times, the Koreans lived in small communities both by the sea and inland, fishing, hunting, and gathering fruits for their livelihood. Rice cultivation entered from China in the first millenium B.C. Chinese records establish that by the third century B.C., as China itself was becoming a unified empire under the Qin (232–208 B.C.) and Han (208 B.C.–A.D. 220) dynasties, tribes were moving from Siberia and Manchuria into Korea, bringing knowledge of bronze and iron. At the same time, Chinese influence expanded into the northwestern part of the peninsula, bringing with it new agricultural techniques and the use of metal. Partly in response to these pressures, the state known as Ancient Choson (Chinese: Chaoxian) emerged.

The nomadic peoples of Central Asia were a constant challenge to the Chinese empire from earliest times. Determined to crush their threat, the Han Emperor Wudi in 109 B.C. undertook a campaign to outflank them by conquering Ancient Choson. (This was about the time that Rome was demolishing Carthage in the West.) By the following year, he had destroyed Choson and replaced it with four military commands over large territories in the northern half of the Korean peninsula and southern Manchuria. However, the Chinese could not long maintain their hold on so much distant alien territory. A generation later, only one of the commanderies remained, known as Nangnang (Chinese: Lelang), with its capital at Pyongyang (now the capital of North Korea).

Controlling the northwestern part of the Korean peninsula, Nangnang endured four centuries, outlasting by one hundred years its parent Han Dynasty. Its ruling class was Chinese, and its culture was a replica of that at the Chinese capital; some of the finest remains of Han Dynasty culture have been found near Pyongyang. Nangnang was finally overwhelmed by the resurgent Koreans in A.D. 313 (roughly at the same time that the Roman Emperor Constantine established Constantinople as his capital). By that time, it had assured a permanent place for Chinese cultural influence in the Korean peninsula.

The Three Kingdoms

Outside the Chinese commanderies, the Koreans gradually came together into three kingdoms, Koguryo, Silla, and Paekche—a process doubtless helped by the influence of Nangnang. The Koguryo people were a hunting tribe that had settled the mountainous regions of Manchuria and northern Korea. They asserted their independence as the Chinese relinquished three of their four Korean commanderies and drew back into Nangnang in the first century B.C. Three hundred years later, Koguryo conquered Nangnang to complete its control of the northern part of the peninsula and part of Manchuria as well.

In the southern part of the peninsula, where conditions were more favorable for settled agriculture, the process of nation-building took longer. The tribal people there, called Han (not to be confused with the Han Dynasty), belonged to three broad groups, Mahan, Chinhan, and Pyonhan, which had no central authority. The divisions among the Han may have been the result of geography: A rugged mountain range, the Soback, isolates the southeast.

By the middle of the fourth century A.D., however, two states had arisen in the south: Silla in the east, and Paekche in the west. Paekche was probably dominated by a branch of the Puyo tribe that, like other peoples entering Korea, had come from the area of the Yenisei River in Siberia. The fluctuating division between Koguryo in the north and Silla and Paekche in the south was in the general vicinity of the 38th parallel—the line along which Korea was divided in 1945.

The Three Kingdoms period is traditionally dated from about the time of Christ to A.D. 668 (roughly contemporaneous with the rise and fall of the Roman Empire), but in actuality it probably covered no more than three to four centuries. It was characterized at first by Koguryo ascendency and by repeated wars between a militant Koguryo and its less warlike and less well organized southern neighbors. Nevertheless, Paekche was a prosperous and cultured state in the fourth century, trading with both China and Japan and calling upon Japan as an ally against Koguryo. Influenced extensively by Chinese culture, Paekche first encountered Buddhism, brought by a Chinese monk, in A.D. 384 (Koguryo was probably ahead of Paekche, both in Chinese influence and the adoption of Buddhism). Later, Paekche transmitted Buddhism as well as Chinese scholarship to Japan—which was then just beginning its own national development.

The kingdom of Silla, less affected by Chinese culture or outside conquest because of its geographic isolation, was at first weak and backward in comparison to the other two Korean states. It had a confederal rather than an autocratic political structure. The six major constituent tribes had an elite leadership strictly separated into hereditary classes known as "bone ranks." Silla also had groups of young warriors, known as *hwarang*; accounts of their training and esprit de corps are reminiscent of feudal Japanese or European fighting men. Their tradition, *hwarangdo*, is a source of patriotic inspiration for the modern Republic of Korea as well as a school of martial art.

As Silla matured in political organization, Chinese influence increased and may have been a factor in Silla's growing power. In the mid-sixth century, Silla and Paekche together crushed a smaller confederation of Han tribes in the south, known as Kaya (called Mimana by the Japanese, with whom Kaya had close relations); then Silla extended its territory at Paekche's expense. Meanwhile, China was reunited under the Sui Dynasty after three hundred years of internal division. As in previous periods of Chinese strength, the Sui emperors undertook campaigns to control the northern barbarians and again threatened Korea. This time, however, the Koreans were a match for the Chinese. Koguryo's defeat of the second Sui emperor's invasion attempt contributed to his overthrow by the succeeding Tang Dynasty in China. The hero of this campaign was General Ulchi Mundok, who is still acclaimed as a Korean national hero.

Unification Under Silla

China, however, tried to take advantage of the rivalries among the three Korean kingdoms as they sought allies in their struggles for hegemony. In 660, allied with Silla, a Chinese naval assault crushed Paekche. The victors then turned on Koguryo, and by 668 Silla alone remained to rule a united Korea; but it took eight years to push the Chinese out of the territories they had conquered and intended to hold.

By the end of the seventh century, most of the Korean peninsula was thus brought under a single government. The leaders in the unification effort, Silla Prince Kim Ch'un-ch'u (later King Muyol) and General Kim Yu-sin, brought many of the Koguryo and Paekche leaders into their ruling elite. Once it had rid the peninsula of Chinese power, Silla accepted a tributary relationship to China and utilized the Chinese political model in consolidating its own control. This was a brilliant period for East Asia, with China flourishing under the Tang Dynasty and Japan becoming a nation-state—while Europe was in the depths of the Dark Ages.

Notwithstanding Chinese influence on Silla, distinctive Korean characteristics endured. Notable among these were the "bone-rank" system of inheritance of political power, in preference to the Chinese merit examinations, and the survival of rigid class distinctions, with virtual serfdom among the peasants; some were slaves. Buddhism had more influence than Confucianism. Great Buddhist temples and shrines were erected with official patronage. One of the finer examples of the Buddhist art and architecture of the time is an artificial stone grotto on a mountaintop near the Silla capital of Kyongju, with a magnificent stone image of the Buddha.

The Koryo Dynasty

The kingdom of Silla fell in 936. Internal decay, encouraged by the tension between the indigenous culture and transplanted

Chinese institutions, had set in by the late eighth century. The cohesiveness of the ruling groups broke down; a king was killed, and members of collateral lines succeeded to the throne in rapid succession as various factions gained ascendency by force or guile. The peasantry rose in revolt or retreated into banditry. Inevitably rival leaders rose, carving out domains for themselves called "Latter Koguryo" and "Latter Paekche." A Latter Koguryo general named Wang Kon, from a trader family in the west-central port city of Kaesong, emerged supreme. Overthrowing the Silla Dynasty, but treating the fallen ruling class kindly, he proclaimed himself founder of the Koryo Dynasty, moving the capital to Kaesong (then called Songdo). Wang Kon's accession to the Korean throne thus followed Charlemagne's in the West by a little more than a century.

The new dynasty again drew from the Chinese model in organizing its political institutions, even modeling its capital city after the Chinese capital of Changan. However, it still differed from the Chinese in its aristocratic distinctions and in its patronage of Buddhism as a state religion. The status of women appears to have been higher in Koryo than in China. The Chinese examination system for entry into the bureaucracy existed, but in practice it was open only to members of the aristocracy. The extended family system was even stronger than in China. As time went on, the aristocracy gained more and more independent control over its landholdings, thus weakening the central government.

During its first century, Koryo successfully repelled invasion by a Tungusic Khitan tribe from the north and then pushed the northern frontier to approximately its present location (along the Amnok [Yalu] and Tumen rivers). Peace came a decade later, to be followed by thriving commercial, intellectual, and artistic activity. Then, like Chinese dynasties and like Silla before it, Koryo began to decay internally through weakness at the top, rivalry among court factions, growth of tax-exempt aristocratic landholdings, and indifference to the problems of the masses.

Koryo military officials, perceiving themselves discriminated against by civil officials, seized power in 1170, Korea's first military coup d'état. Three decades of civil war and revolt followed, ending with the assertion of power by a self-proclaimed administrator, Ch'oe Ch'ung-hon, reminiscent of the shoguns of Japan. His family held power for sixty years under impotent kings.

In addition to its internal troubles, the dynasty was constantly under external military threat from northern tribes. One of these, the Khitan, captured the Koryo capital in 1011 before being expelled. Such threats reached their peak in the Mongol invasion of 1231—Korea's share of the Mongol sweep through most of the known world. After a quarter century of struggle, the Koreans submitted; their kings, with titles and privileges reduced, were married off to Mongol princesses, and the sons were held hostage at the Mongol court at what is now Beijing. Mongol officials watched over the Korean administration, and Mongol culture strongly influenced the ruling class. Surviving elements of this influence can be seen in Korean cuisine and traditional military costume. The Koreans were mobilized to support the Mongols' unsuccessful attempts to invade Japan; meanwhile, the Koreans suffered repeated attacks by Japanese pirates.

The Koryo period was the zenith of Buddhism in Korea but also saw the growth of Confucian influence. Buddhism was, in

CONFUCIANISM IN KOREA

The Chinese influence on the Korean peninsula dates back to before the time of Christ and can be seen in the Koreans' adoption of Chinese Confucian thought.

Confucius, the Chinese sage who is assumed to have lived during the sixth century B.C., set up an ideal ethical-moral system intended to govern relationships within the family and the state in harmonious unity. It was basically a system of subordinations: of the son to the father, of the younger to the elder brother, of the wife to the husband, and of the subject to the throne. It inculcated filial piety, reverence for ancestors, and fidelity to friends. Strong emphasis was placed upon decorum, rites, and ceremony. Scholarship and aesthetic cultivation were regarded as prerequisites for those in governing or official positions. . . .

The date Confucianism became established in Korea is so early it cannot be even approximately pinpointed. No doubt, Confucian classics entered the peninsula with the earliest effect, the state religion. The temples and clergy were powerful and often wealthy; some temples had large landholdings and private armies. The oldest remaining wooden temple buildings in Korea date from the thirteenth century; many stone pagodas also survive from the Koryo period. The entire Buddhist scripture was codified and carved on wooden blocks early in the dynasty, though the blocks were destroyed by the Mongols. A second set of some 80,000 blocks, prepared as a penance early in the period of struggle against the Mongols, is still preserved at Haeinsa, a temple in southeastern Korea.

Graphic art and poetry flourished, particularly among the emerging Confucian literati, who often expressed themselves in Chinese-language poetry. The peasantry, also, had their *changga* (long poems) with accompanying song. Two important historical works date from Koryo: the *Samguk Sagi* (History of the Three Kingdoms), by Kim Yu-sin, and *Samguk Yusa* (Records of

specimens of written Chinese material well before the beginning of the Christian era. . . .

In Korea, Confucianism was accepted so eagerly and in so strict a form that the Chinese themselves regarded the Korean adherents as more virtuous than themselves. They referred to Korea as "the country of Eastern decorum," a reference to the punctiliousness with which the Koreans observed all phases of the doctrinal ritual. . . .

While Confucius' teachings may have disappeared as a basis for government and administration, after so many centuries of indoctrination in these tenets, Koreans could hardly be said to have discarded the customs, habits, and thought patterns derived from the system. On one hand, there is reverence for age, social stability, and a respect for learning and cultivation. On the other there is idolization of the past, social rigidity, and an abstract unworldliness that prefers to see things as they ought to be rather than as they are.

A Window on Korea: Confucianism in Korea, Sangji University.

the Three Kingdoms), a more anecdotal writing by the Buddhist monk Iryon. Internationally best known of Koryo's cultural achievements are the beautiful celadon bowls and vases. Printing with moveable metal type was developed (according to Korean sources) in 1240; a Paris museum houses an example of Koryo printing dated to 1377, greatly antedating Gutenberg's invention in the West.

With all its political and economic problems, the Koryo Dynasty could not long survive the collapse of the Mongol Empire in the mid-fourteenth century. The final blow came when a Korean general, sent by the Koryo court against the advancing armies of the new Ming Dynasty in China, realized the folly of the mission. Making his peace with the Ming, General Yi Songgye turned on his own government, seized control of it, and in 1392 proclaimed a new dynasty. He moved the capital to its present location, Seoul, and readopted the old name of Choson for the dynasty and the nation.

The Choson (Yi) Dynasty

The new Yi monarch (known by the posthumous title T'aejo, "Great Progenitor") promptly sought confirmation of his status by the Chinese court and eventually received it. T'aejo consolidated his power with great skill. He granted extensive privileges to his supporters ("merit subjects") but nonetheless established a governmental system closely modeled after the Chinese, including merit examinations for public service. He redistributed the land to ease the lot of the peasants. To dispose of the heavy Buddhist hand on the court, he banished the Buddhist priests to the hills, confiscated much Buddhist property, and established the neo-Confucianism of Ming China as a state philosophy. He made Choson a far more perfect embodiment of Chinese philosophy and politics than any previous Korean regime, adopting, among other Chinese institutions, the Ming administrative code. After six years on the throne, he wearied of the power struggles in his family, and abdicated in favor of one of his eight sons. Another son seized the throne four months later, setting the stage for the constant power struggles that characterized the dynasty thereafter.

The Korean adoption of the Chinese political system extended to society and culture. Within one to two centuries, Korea became recognized as a more perfect Confucian state than China itself. Court records were kept in Chinese; scholars composed excellent Chinese prose and poetry and were learned in the Chinese classics. The behavior of even the common people was governed by Confucian ethics.

Yet differences from China persisted. These differences included the strong aristocratic tradition, which limited examination takers to sons of the aristocracy; a marked tendency toward collective power at the expense of the king's authority; and a high incidence of factionalism, in which family, clan, and regional connections were factors. The Chinese institution of the Censorate, intended as a check on official misconduct and inefficiency, became in Korea an instrument for attack on the administration. The Korean state, smaller and less secure, was more strongly centralized than in China. Moreover, the Korean king was not the Son of Heaven but rather the vassal or licensee of the Chinese emperor.

The first century of Choson was one of notable cultural as well as political achievement. The fourth king, the great Sejong (1418–1450), and his court academy created a phonetic alphabet, *han'gul*, which is considered to be one of the best writing systems ever devised. Numerous works of literature and music were created by court-sponsored scholars. Rain and wind gauges were devised, as well as clocks, sundials, and surveying instruments.

The Decline of the Choson Dynasty

Toward the end of the fifteenth century, however, disagreements over the royal succession and other political and ethical points led to struggles for power and position among cliques of *yangban* (scholar-officials) at court. The struggles were bitter and bloody and they even ruined kings. For example, Yonsan'gun (1494–1506) lost his reputation during one wave of purges and was dishonored after his death. After the first series of purges around the year 1500, factional rivalries became a major motif of Korean politics, often taking precedence over the general welfare. By the late seventeenth century, the *yangban* were divided among four major factions and their adherents had their own economic base in agricultural estates, lived in separate areas of the capital, and jockeyed constantly to gain power.

In 1592, Hideyoshi, second of three great leaders who reunified Japan after a century of civil war, decided to invade the Asian continent through Korea. (This was fifteen years before the first permanent English settlement was established at Jamestown in what was to become the United States.) He was initially successful against weak and faction-ridden Korean government forces. However, he suffered a severe naval defeat at the hands of Korean Admiral Yi Sun-sin, who invented an armored ship (the famed "turtle ship") and used a flotilla of them to devastating effect. Volunteer bands called *Uibyongdae* (Righteous Armies), and even armed Buddhist monks, offered significant resistance.

In the end, the Japanese were made to abandon their adventure in 1598 by Chinese intervention and the death of Hideyoshi. Six years of devastation, however, had dealt Korea a heavy blow. Adding insult to injury, the retreating Japanese took with them many of Korea's best artisans and craftsmen. The Japanese ceramic and lacquer industries, for instance, owe their start in large part to the imported Koreans. The resentment of the Korean people that resulted from the war has never ceased. Nevertheless, peaceful relations were established with the leaders who succeeded Hideyoshi. The Japanese were given limited access and residence rights in a small area near the southeastern port city of Pusan, an arrangement that continued into the nineteenth century.

The strain of countering the Japanese invasion of Korea weakened China as well as Korea and facilitated the Manchu conquest of both countries. The Jurchen, or Manchus, descendants of the barbarian tribes that had conquered north China in the twelfth century, reestablished a Manchurian empire of their own in the sixteenth century. Before invading China and founding the Ch'ing dynasty, they invaded Korea in 1636 and forced the Koreans to pay them tribute and break off relations with the Ming. Submitting bitterly, the Koreans also instituted a rigid exclusion policy, authorizing no visitors except for officials from China and Manchuria, and traders from Japan at their enclave near Pusan.

The Japanese and Manchu assaults, together with continuing factional strife, weakened the Korean political and economic structure. The aristocratic class entrenched itself in privileged political and economic positions at the expense of the throne and the common people, upholding the rigid neo-Confucian order inherited from China against all attempts at social change.

In other areas, however, there were significant reforms. One of these was the philosophical movement now referred to as *Sirhak* (Practical Learning), which arose among aristocrats out of power in the seventeenth century. It was inspired in part by deteriorating social conditions and in part by new currents of thought in

China, including Christian ideas, brought by young members of the official tribute missions to China. At the same time, new agricultural techniques brought about the growth and concentration of wealth and the beginnings of a commercial economy, despite continuing aristocratic disdain for such activity. During the reigns of kings Yongjo and Chongjo (1724–1800), factional strife was brought under control by a policy of equal distribution of posts.

However, there was further decline in the nineteenth century. There were significant uprisings of peasants. At court, rival families jostled each other for power through their women relatives (reigning and previous queens, subsidiary wives, concubines), while a succession of boy-kings were put on the throne. Midcentury reform efforts by the regent T'aewon'gun (father of the boy-king Kojong, who ascended to the throne in 1863) failed to meet the country's needs. On the contrary, T'aewon'gun's rigid enforcement of the long-standing policy of excluding all foreigners made Korea all the more vulnerable when the nineteenth-century imperialists commenced their penetration of Korea. The ensuing struggle for hegemony ended with Japanese annexation in 1910.

The Choson Dynasty thus perished, but its long rule of 518 years had left a deep impression upon national attitudes and behavior that is still important. Chinese philosophy, ethics, and politics had become accepted as part of Korean culture.

Japanese Colonialism

BY GEOFF SIMONS

The Choson dynasty in Korea collapsed early in the twentieth century under the pressure of Japanese imperialism. The following excerpt explains the events that permitted Japan's colonization of the Korean peninsula. It is from a book written by Geoff Simons, a freelance author who has written approximately forty books on historical, political, and other topics. As Simons describes, as Asia was opened to the Western world, Japan became more aggressive toward its neighbors, including Korea. Japan's first step in controlling Korea came with the Sino-Japanese War of 1894–1895, when Japan ended Chinese influence over Korea. After the war, Japan declared Korea independent, paving the way for future annexation. From 1904 to 1905, Japan fought and won a war with Russia over the right to exploit Korea. Russia agreed, in the Portsmouth Treaty brokered by U.S. president Theodore Roosevelt in 1905, to recognize Japan's interests in Korea. The United States and Britain fully endorsed Japan's colonization of Korea, believing it would be an effective curb on Russia's power in Asia: The interests of the Korean people were not considered. Thereafter, Japan gradually disempowered the Korean government and officially annexed Korea in 1910. What followed for Korea was four decades of brutal oppression and exploitation, ending only after Japan was defeated in World War II.

I n the early twentieth century the Korean peninsula was absorbed into the expanding Japanese empire. At that time Korea was the imperial prize, offering natural resources, abundant human labour and a platform for further territorial expansion. For centuries the Korean people had been buffeted by powerful neighbours who sometimes stimulated cultural advance but as often brought repression and exploitation. Now the prospects for national independence seemed bleak, the search for sovereignty increasingly desperate.

Geoff Simons, *Korea: The Search for Sovereignty.* New York: St. Martin's Press, 1995. Copyright © 1995 by Geoff Simons. Reproduced by permission of Palgrave Macmillan. \

The Treaty of Portsmouth

The first steps towards the Japanese annexation of Korea were taken in the second half of the nineteenth century. It was already obvious that Japan was attaching increasing importance to the control she had established in the politically critical region of Manchuria, [described in a League of Nations document as] 'the meeting ground of the conflicting needs and policies' of three great nations, Russia, China and Japan. The Sino-Japanese Treaty of Shimonoseki (1895) forced China to pay an indemnity to Japan, ceded Chinese control of Taiwan to Japan, and recognised the independence of Korea, a necessary condition for its subsequent unopposed absorption by Japan. Pressure from Russia, France and Germany temporarily eroded these Japanese gains; but the likely incorporation of Manchuria and Korea into the Russian empire was prevented by the Russo-Japanese War, whereupon the US-brokered Treaty of Portsmouth (1905) served to consolidate and expand the familiar Japanese claims. Britain and the United States welcomed such developments. Russian ambitions would be blocked by an increasingly Westernised Japan; in this *realpolitik* world the welfare of Korea was of no account.

The British knew of, and approved, Japan's intention to create a protectorate over Korea. . . . President Theodore Roosevelt's Secretary of War, W.H. Taft, declared to Count Katsura, the Japanese premier and foreign minister, that 'the establishment by Japanese troops of a suzerainty over Korea . . . would permanently contribute to permanent peace in the East'. In a cable (29 July 1905), Roosevelt commented to Taft: 'Your conversation with Count Katsura absolutely correct in every respect. Wish you would state to Katsura that I confirm every word you have said'. In the Portsmouth Treaty (Article II) Russia agreed 'not to interfere or place obstacles in the way of any measure of direction and protection, and supervision which the Imperial Government of Japan may deem necessary to adopt in Korea'. For its part, Korea vainly hoped that its nominal independence would survive, but without powerful foreign protectors the government was powerless in the face of Japanese ambition.

Japanese Pressure on Korea's Emperor

In October 1905 Japan increased the pressure on the Korean emperor and his advisors to allow complete Japanese supervision of Korean affairs, including control of the country's foreign rela-

tions. On 15 November Marquis Ito Hirobumi announced to the
Korean emperor that the Korean department of foreign affairs
was to be abolished; that future diplomatic affairs were to be han-
dled by a council in Tokyo; that the Japanese minister in Seoul
was to be termed the 'General Superintendent' or 'Director'; and
that the Japanese consular representatives in Seoul and in the Korean ports were to be termed 'Superintendents'. The Korean emperor, dismayed at the proposals, reminded Ito that Japan had
formerly pledged to 'preserve the independence and integrity of
Korea'; and declared the proposals 'beyond my slightest appre-
hension'. Japan, ignoring this response, assumed direct control of
Korean affairs, formalising and expanding the three Articles proposed by Ito.

A Japanese financier . . . had now assumed control of the Korean finance ministry. Japanese control was established over the
entire Korean telegraph and postal systems, while the Japanese
Army had already taken over large areas surrounding Seoul, dis-
placing 15,000 Korean families in the process. A Japanese corporation . . . acquired all Korean 'waste lands', comprising more
than half of all the national territory, including all the underde-
veloped mineral resources. Japanese agents, enjoying military protection, scoured the country to discover and seize valuable properties on the pretext that they were needed by the Japanese
armed forces. Japanese money-lenders set up their trade in every
Korean city, lending money at 12 per cent monthly interest rate
and confiscating property in the event of default. Already, Koreans were abused by Japanese soldiers, forbidden access to particular areas, and subjected to summary military justice. There were
already some years to go before the formal annexation of Korea.

In June 1907 the Korean emperor sent a secret mission to an
International Conference being held at The Hague [a city in the
Netherlands used as a meeting place for international courts] to
complain about Japanese policy on his country and to request
Western support. When this initiative became known, the Japanese response was predictable. Japanese delegates managed to block
Korean access to the conference chamber, and there were urgent
calls in Tokyo for 'decisive measures', including a demand from
the influential gangster Toyama Mitsuru, 'asserting and confirm-
ing' that the sovereignty of the Korean emperor 'should be del-
egated to our nation'. It was now time to force the abdication of
the Korean king.

On 16 July the Japanese government publicly announced that it was determined to 'go along with the opinion of the people' and adopt 'a strong line of action' towards Korea. The next day, Viscount Hayashi, the Japanese minister of foreign affairs, journeyed to Korea to consult with Ito; while, before his arrival, the pliant Korean cabinet called upon the emperor to sign with his own seal the proposed Articles (formalised 17 November 1905) to which he had still not agreed (five of the eight-strong cabinet had signed). The Korean cabinet also suggested that the emperor accept the appointment of a regent, and that he go to Tokyo to apologise personally to the Japanese emperor. Such moves, it was thought, might serve as an alternative to abdication. On 19 July 1907 the Korean emperor, still stubbornly refusing to agree to the Articles, abdicated in favour of the [Japanese] crown prince. Evidence that he acted under duress is perhaps his statement to the contrary: 'In abdicating my throne I acted in obedience to the dictate of my conviction; my action was not the result of any outside advice or pressure.'

Japan Takes Over Korea's Government

The Japanese were now in a position to tighten their grip still further. With the Korean imperial authority now nominally in the hands of an inept crown prince, said by some to be feeble-minded, there was little difficulty in securing imperial assent for a total restructuring of Korean-Japanese relations. On 24 July 1907 a new seven-clause agreement was signed, removing from the Korean government any last vestige of power to make independent decisions or to exercise government functions. The earlier Japanese moves had merely placed Japanese officials in every sphere of Korean government and administration, with Koreans allowed to operate under condition of 'advice'. Following the 24 July agreement the functions of government were placed squarely in Japanese hands. On 29 November two-thirds of the offices of the Korean royal household were abolished, with a separate accounting bureau established for royal affairs. A Japanese Directorate of Police was set up for the entire country, and all provincial forces were run by Japanese officers. Korean soldiers, regarded as mercenaries, were not seen as 'a perfect instrument of national defence' [as stated by M. Frederick Nelson]; and so, on 1 August 1907, the Korean army was disbanded. . . . The total Japanese control of Korea, already a *de facto* reality, now only waited on what could be represented as a *de jure* solution to the 'Korean question'.

Formal Annexation

In August 1910 the Korean emperor effectively abolished the monarchy, so bringing to an end the reign of the Yi Dynasty that had lasted from 1392. The treaty of annexation—to extinguish Korea as an international personality—was signed on 22 August, after approval by the [Japanese Emperor] Meiji and the Korean emperor, by Viscount Terauchi and Yi Wan-yong, the Korean prime minister. The members of the Korean royal family, now with no vestigial shred of power, were granted annual allowances sufficient for their life-styles, with the Japanese committed thereafter to awarding peerages and grants to those non-royal Koreans deemed meritorious. . . .

The Effect of Annexation on Koreans

The impact of the annexation was devastating for every aspect of Korean life. The currency was converted; transport and communications were controlled in their entirety by the Japanese government; and all Korean farmlands became the property of the Japanese Oriental Development Company, which at the same time retained the ancient system of feudal land-tenantry. Korea was now a helpless captive state. The Korean people, long accustomed to oppressive rule, were now forced to confront yet more decades of naked exploitation on an unprecedented scale.

Japan moved swiftly to impose a brutal military regime on the entire peninsula. Opposition movements, if not crushed, were forced into exile: one faction based in Manchuria, later to be headed by Kim Il-sung; another in Hawaii under Syngman Rhee. In Korea the Japanese took over land and property, vastly increasing the levels of poverty and homelessness. Thousands of Koreans voluntarily migrated to Japan in the search for work; or, even more pitifully, were forced to go there as virtual slave labour. Koreans, whether in their own land or in Japan, were regarded as racial inferiors and possessed none of the political rights enjoyed by the Japanese; and, as a subject people, were forced to endure a thorough programme of enforced 'Japanisation'. Harsh measures were undertaken to wipe out the indigenous Korean culture, with Japanese pronounced the official language in the 1930s. Korea and Taiwan now provided the most obvious examples of Japanese colonialism and would serve as models for the other lands to be occupied with the expansion of the empire in the years to come.

Japanese historians and archaeologists conducted projects in the peninsula with the aim of demonstrating that Korean history was a part of Japanese and that there was an evident Korean backwardness that only Japan could rectify. . . .

The Japanese authorities made it clear that any move of the Korean people towards independence would be met with 'severe punishment'. According to statistics published in the *Annual Statistical Bulletin* of the Japanese Governor-General of Korea, between 1911 and 1918 there were 330,025 cases of summary conviction under the military regime. . . . Even the churches, seldom a hotbed of nationalist fervour, were monitored by the Japanese for any sign of ideological deviation. . . .

Japanese Exploitation

The Japanese seizure of Korean land had resulted in the impoverishment of much of the Korean population. There was now a substantial number of large-scale Japanese landowners, with a number of pliant Korean landowners of the former privileged *yangban* class allowed to maintain their positions. Most of the peasants were now no more than marginal tenant farmers, having lost any rights to eventually own the land they worked. They typically worked at subsistence level on minuscule plots, often compelled to work as well on the land of others. According to figures supplied by the Japanese Governor-General, 44.6 per cent of all farm households, some 1,273,326 out of 2,728,921, were unable to earn enough to live on. Near to half of the entire Korean population, mostly unable to secure loans, were starving to death, forced to eat roots or the bark of trees in order to survive. Even the Japanese authorities conceded that at times more than a half of all Korean farm households were starving. . . .

The exploitation by the Japanese of Korean farmers was paralleled by their treatment of Korean industrial workers. Koreans had been driven into mines and factories in Korea and Japan through the 1930s and early 1940s as forced labour required in the mounting war effort. By 1944 there were 350,000 Koreans in Korean mines and 600,000 in the factories, all under close Japanese supervision and with no industrial rights. Nearly a half of factory workers and more than a third of mine workers toiled for more than twelve hours a day, while Korean workers typically received less than a half the pay of the equivalent Japanese workers, themselves exploited by a semi-feudal employment system. Similarly Korean women and children were paid less than half their Japanese counterparts, making it difficult to achieve even the most basic subsistence levels. In these circumstances the workers were often diseased or disabled, subject to common industrial accidents where there was no legal worker protection.

Korea was ravaged as a captive state for nearly four decades. The Korean people, repressed and brutalised, were stripped of much of their culture while their land was stolen and their buildings confiscated. Driven from their farms, the peasants either starved in a near-subsistence economy or were coerced into mines and factories to swell private wealth or to fuel Japanese imperial ambitions. . . . [Ultimately,] the Japanese failed to extirpate Korean culture, and were eventually evicted from the peninsula; but not before long decades of struggle and the deaths of countless martyrs to the independence cause.

The Rise of Communism and Nationalism in Korea

By Takashi Hatada

The book excerpt below was written by Takashi Hatada, a scholar and history professor from Japan with a specialty in Korean and modern Chinese history. Hatada describes how Koreans resisted Japanese colonization of Korea in the early 1900s. Landowners, capitalists, intellectuals, and men from all segments of Korean society participated in 1919 in the March First Movement, a mass popular uprising against the Japanese. The leaders of the movement appealed to foreign governments to allow independence for Korea. The movement failed when foreign support did not appear and the Japanese military suppressed it. The resistance, however, caused the Japanese to switch from a policy of military suppression of Koreans to one of cultural rule, in which Koreans were coerced to integrate with the Japanese.

Thereafter, Korean nationalist resistance continued but took other forms, such as tenant and labor disputes, student organizations, and ideological campaigns. These nationalist movements included the creation of a Korean Communist Party and resistance groups based outside of Korea. One such group was based in Manchuria and led by guerrilla fighter Kim Il Sung, who later became leader of Communist North Korea.

[I]n 1919, nine years after the Japanese annexation,] a serious disturbance took place in Korea. This was the March First movement, significant in the history of the Japanese administration of Korea and in the history of the development of the Korean nationalist movement. It is also sometimes known as

Takashi Hatada, *A History of Korea*, edited and translated by Warren W. Smith Jr. and Benjamin H. Hazard. Santa Barbara, CA: American Bibliographical Center—Clio Press, 1969. Copyright © 1969 by ABC-CLIO, Inc. Reproduced by permission.

the *Manse* (10,000 years, i.e., Long live Korea) incident. After the Japanese annexation, Korea's society rapidly disintegrated. The Japanese land survey [a survey of Korea by the Japanese to establish modern land ownership rights], other reforms, and the importation of Japanese goods into what had previously been a barter economy, caused many farmers to go into debt and lose their land, and in some cases even brought about the ruin of members of the *yangban* [civil and military government officials] class. New economic opportunities sufficient to absorb these impoverished persons were not available. Farmers who had been badly off in the past became desperate, and crowds of wretched people without means of livelihood appeared in farming villages. The number of those who abandoned their homes and wandered about unemployed increased. They went into the mountains and practiced fire-field agriculture or, in many cases, drifted off to Manchuria, Siberia, and to the United States, China, and Japan.

Opposition to the Japanese rule burned fiercely among the Koreans in spite of the fact that manifestations were severely suppressed under the Japanese military administration. Just at that time, the First World War ended and revolutions occurred in Russia and other countries. The doctrine of national self-determination, proclaimed by President Wilson of the United States, spread among the oppressed peoples throughout the world. The doctrine appealed especially to the Korean people who had lost their fatherland. The independence movement first developed among Koreans living abroad and gradually extended to the masses in Korea itself.

The March First Movement

In January 1919, the former ruler of Korea, Yi T'aewang (Kojong) died, and it was rumored that a Japanese physician had poisoned him. The death of Yi T'aewang, a symbol of the former Yi Dynasty in Korea, galvanized the independence movement into action. The first day of March, 1919, two days before his funeral, was chosen as the day for the public announcement of an independence proclamation. Landowners, capitalists, religious representatives, intellectuals, well-known men from every walk of life signed the proclamation. It stated that Korea, through the kind help of the powerful nations of the world, hoped to gain independence. The proclamation did not call for a violent struggle. In fact, the movement had recourse to only two methods in its efforts to achieve independence, namely to make petitions to foreign powers and to shout in the street "Long live the independence of Korea." There were no plans for an armed uprising. The leaders of the independence movement believed that through the good will of foreign nations alone independence could be gained. On March 1, the leaders advised the Japanese authorities by telephone that the movement was about to begin and asked them to deal with the matter calmly. The leaders were quickly arrested, but the independence proclamation was announced in Seoul and other cities, and demonstrators marched shouting *manse* (a cheer, pronounced *banzai* in Japanese). The Japanese military police used gunfire against the demonstrators and called even the army and navy for help. From the Japanese point of view, the fact that the Koreans even shouted for independence was considered insubordination, and the use of large mass parades was adjudged the height of rebelliousness. Vicious fighting broke out between the Koreans and the Japanese in the cities, and soon in the country also, to which the movement rapidly spread. Throughout the nation people joined the movement and took part in the mass parades—old men, young men, women, and children of all classes. In March and April, when the movement was at its height, it is estimated that about 500,000 people actively joined in the demonstrations, and the members of the movement numbered over a million. All over Korea resounded the cry: "Long live independence."

There were disturbances at 618 places and a total of 848 such instances altogether. Forty-seven township offices, three military police posts, and twenty-eight regular police stations were damaged, as well as seventy-one post offices, court houses, customs houses, schools, and other public buildings. The number of dead and wounded were: 166 Japanese officials and military police; 29 Japanese civilians; and 1,962 Korean rioters. Held for investigation were 19,525 persons, including 471 women, and 10,441 persons, including 186 women, were prosecuted. The independence movement was not limited to Korea, but developed also in Harbin and Chien-tao (Manchuria), in Hawaii, and in any place where a Korean colony existed. In Chien-tao, Manchuria, in particular, it was strong; there, Koreans attacked the Japanese consulate.

But even this surprisingly large independence movement was suppressed and ended in failure. The foreign support on which the leaders had counted did not materialize. The "calm meeting"

with the Japanese had been out of the question. Shouts of *manse*
were no match for Japan's military power. . . .

The March First movement failed, but it had engendered
enormous nationalistic feeling in Korea and had inspired the
people to more and braver action than could have been expected
by its leaders. It served to awaken the Japanese to the enormous
force which was threatening them and was being held in check
only by their military might. Though the movement was crushed
this time, the Japanese realized that in the long run their military
administration would be unequal to the task. Therefore the
Japanese changed their policy. They replaced the Governor General and adopted a "cultural rule policy." At first this was rather
limited in scope, but the fact that it was established at all was due
to the force of the March First movement. . . .

Life Under Japanese Rule

The March First movement brought about a change in Japanese
administrative policy in Korea from a military administration to
one based on a so-called cultural policy in which the integration
of Koreans and Japanese was advocated. From this time onward,
the Korean economy, society, and culture made surprising progress
at the strong insistence and pressure of the Japanese. Especially
following the Manchurian Incident in 1931 [a railway bomb incident that Japan used as a pretext to occupy Manchuria], the Korean economy changed completely as it was adapted to growing
military demands. While Korea was experiencing its "industrial
revolution," changing from an agricultural to an industrial economy, the integration of Korea with Japan was proceeding apace
through the development of such activities as the Japan and Korea Unification movement. But what did the Korean people actually obtain from Japanese rule over Korea?

Without doubt, the government, the society, the economy, and
the culture of Korea developed extraordinarily during the period
of Japanese domination. In place of the former *yangban* rule, an
organized government of civil servants was established. In areas
which previously had not been opened up, large-scale industries
were established. Vast agricultural estates with excellent irrigation
facilities came into being. Modern communication and transportation services were set up, and large cities developed. Schools
were built everywhere, the magnificent Imperial University was
established, and an excellent palace of fine arts and museum were

constructed. In particular, the enormous hydroelectric generating facilities constructed in north Korea were impressive. When one considers all these things, it would seem natural even today, after Japan's defeat in the Second World War, that there would be people in Korea who would acknowledge the benefits of the Japanese administration. Actually, it is highly questionable whether Koreans profited from these excellent facilities, and whether the living standards of the Koreans were raised by them. One must not forget the great numbers of destitute persons during the period when Japan was in control. In January 1934, at a consultative meeting of the principal leaders of the rural village reconstruction movement, Governor General Ugaki Issei spoke of the fearful misery of the Korean peasantry. He stated that every spring the number of wretched farmers lacking food and searching for bark and grass to eat, approached 50 percent of the total peasant population. These were the words of the Governor General, so the real situation was worse; even the Governor General was forced to recognize the terrible plight of the Korean farmer.

Large numbers of destitute persons existed also during the Yi Dynasty, and the Japanese administration was unable to change this situation. But, worse than that, the development of Korea under the Japanese constantly created a new destitute population. Words in current use at the time such as the "spring and autumn poor," "uprooted wanderers," "stowaway," "fire-field agriculturists," and "dwellers in earth mounds" indicate the seriousness of the conditions. As the words signify, there were constantly people suffering from starvation, groups of Koreans who in desperation crossed over to Japan and Manchuria, peasants who penetrated mountain forests and practiced a primitive fire-field agriculture, and persons who lived in earth caves on the outskirts of large cities like Seoul. By 1939, when Korean industry had made great strides forward, there were 570,000 chŏngbo [one chŏngbo equals 2.4 acres] of fire-fields, and 340,000 households or about 1,870,000 persons living off fire-field agriculture—a really extraordinary fact. The rapid capitalist development of Korea had thus created a large number of primitive agriculturalists. And these victims, born of the progress of Korea, were the foundation upon which such progress was first built. . . .

The Japanese administration introduced much that was new in Korea and built a great deal. In doing so, it made victims of many in the very heart of society. It produced a small number of Koreans who depended on Japanese power and, at the same time, a large number of Koreans who disliked Japanese control. The Japanese tried through the Unification of Japan and Korea and the Transformation into Imperial Subjects to take away from Koreans their national consciousness, but they could not remove the resentment from their hearts. The resistance movement of the Koreans against the Japanese continued to be strong, up to the time of Japan's defeat and withdrawal from Korea in 1945.

Korean Nationalist Movements

The nationalist movement in Korea, which had died down for a while after the failure of the March First movement, gradually grew up again in a new form. It differed from the March First movement, which had been simply a demonstration for national independence, relying on the aid of foreign nations, for now they developed into movements associated with socialism and the class struggle. The leaders of the March First movement had included landowners and capitalists, while now the main supporters of the new movement were workers, farmers, students, and intellectuals. These organizations did not include any active nationalistic capitalists, such as often appeared in other colonial countries, because there was little opportunity for such a group to develop under Japanese control. The few small Korean capitalists who did establish themselves were able to exist only on Japanese sufferance. Tenant and labor disputes, student organizations, ideological campaigns, incidents involving the Communist Party, and similar organizations, events, and activities characterized the new nationalist movement.

These movements reached their high-water mark about 1930. In 1920 there were 15 tenant disputes involving 4,040 persons; in 1923, 176 disputes involving 3,973 persons; in 1930, 726 disputes involving 13,012 persons; and in 1931, 667 disputes involving 10,282 persons. Labor disputes followed the same pattern. Originally Korean labor consisted mainly of miners and construction workers, and there were few factory workers. This was especially true before the Manchurian Incident; due to paternalistic control, labor organization was impeded. In 1917 there were only 8 strikes involving 1,148 persons, but in 1920, 81 strikes involving 4,599 persons, and in 1923, 72 strikes involving 6,041 persons. After 1925 labor disputes intensified and became organized. Major labor disturbances took place, such as a general strike in Wŏnsan in 1929 and a general strike in Seoul the following year.

Communist Influence in Korea

The labor disputes were not simply spontaneous occurrences, but were politically motivated as part of the Korean struggle against Japanese imperialism. Immediately following the March First movement, some of the Korean nationalists in Shanghai became dissatisfied with the old movement and approached the Russian Communist Party. In 1920 they established in Shanghai a Korean Communist Party *(Koryŏ Kongsandang)* which opposed the Provisional Government of the Republic of Korea *(Taehan Minguk Imsi Chŏngbu)* that had been formed there from among the supporters of the March First movement. This new trend in political thought occurred not only in Shanghai but spread among the Korean younger generation within Korea and abroad, and, in place of the former nationalists, the Socialists and the Communists became powerful. In 1922, the Seoul Young Men's Association *(Seoul Chŏngnyŏn Hoe)* was formed, and in 1923 the North Star Society *(Puksŏng Hoe)* was founded among Korean students in Tokyo, both of which were active in fostering Socialist and Communist ideas. Shanghai and Tokyo became the two main centers for the ideological movement of the Koreans, and from these two centers revolutionary ideas were introduced into Korea until, in 1925, the Korean Communist Party *(Chosŏn Kongsandang)* was established in Korea itself. With this a revolutionary movement within Korea began in earnest, reaching its height in 1930. The previously mentioned tenant and labor disputes were encouraged as an important aspect of this movement.

In 1925 the Peace Preservation Law was put into effect to oppose this movement and, in the same year, the first Communist Party members were arrested. On June 10, 1926, the Communist Party tried to stage a new March First movement and to instigate a nationwide independence march on the occasion of the death of Yi Ch'ŏk (Sunjong), the last king of the Yi Dynasty. Before the demonstration could take place, however, it was discovered and occasioned the second arrest of Communist Party members. After this, too, the Communist Party was struck hard blows, for in March 1928, the third wholesale arrest of its members took place, and again a fourth round-up of Communists was carried out in August of the same year. After each police action, however, the Communist Party was reconstituted, and continued to encourage and lead tenant and labor disputes.

One group of Communists formed the New Foundations Society *(Sin'gan Hoe)* in 1927 which was made up of writers and educators, including Korean nationalists and reformers. This society was legally organized and provided a broad united front. Laborers, students, and intellectuals were deeply influenced by it. The large-scale student disturbance of 1929 was the greatest product of its efforts. This was triggered by a clash between Japanese and Korean high school students on commuter trains in Kwangju, South Chŏlla Province. This dispute developed into a nationwide movement of students who demanded the abolition of colonial discriminatory treatment. The movement continued through 1930, and grew into a huge disturbance in which 54,000 students participated involving 194 schools. This was the largest nationalist uprising since the March First movement, but its character was different in that it was carried out by students explicitly as a protest against Japanese imperialism.

Labor and tenant disputes occurred constantly, encouraged by this student movement. This was the period around 1930 when Korean popular movements reached their apogee and during which all Korea was gripped by an air of tension. The struggle for national independence, bound now to the daily problems of the people, extended throughout the whole of Korea. This was the time, too, when Korea became enveloped in the wave of the world financial panic, when farm villages which had become producers solely of rice suffered hard times, and when depressed economic conditions, characterized by emigration, legal and illegal, and unemployment, became prevalent. Under these circumstances leftist movements spread and grew strong. To counteract these, the authorities, on the one hand, sponsored rural village reconstruction and self-help movements, and on the other, severely suppressed leftist organizations, rounded up and imprisoned Communists and instigators of labor disputes, and did not hesitate to close schools in which there were serious strikes.

With the outbreak of the Manchurian Incident in 1931, the strategic importance of Korea increased. The measures adopted for dealing with labor disputes and radical movements became more stringent. It was no longer possible for political opposition to express itself publicly as had been allowed earlier. Also the trend toward thought control in order to resist communism was accentuated. Among the Koreans themselves, divisions and differences appeared, and in 1931 the *Sin'gan Hoe* was dissolved. An underground group of Communists, however, involved largely with the peasantry and labor, continued its activity. Futhermore, the rapid advance of industry from this period on caused a great increase in the number of industrial workers, from 250,000 in 1933 to 300,000 in 1935, to 520,000 in 1937 and to 690,000 in 1938. After the China Incident in 1937 [Japan invaded China in an attempt to annex it] and the outbreak of the war in the Pacific in 1941, the number of Korean workers again took a sharp upturn. This increase broadened the base for Communist activity, but agitation was quickly suppressed by Japanese military force. There was no possibility of organizing resistance, for at the slightest sign of danger all disturbances were nipped in the bud. Despite this, Korean opposition to Japanese rule burned more strongly than ever.

During this period Korean political activities were carried on by groups outside Korea. They included the Northeast Anti-Japanese United Army *(Tongbuk Kangil Yŏn'gun)* of Kim Ilsŏng, which was based on support from Koreans in Manchuria; Kim Ku's nationalist party, the United Association of Movements for the Revival of Korea *(Han'guk Kwangbok Undong Tanch'e Yŏnhaphoe)* which was allied with the Chinese Nationalist Government *(Kuomintang)* in Ch'ung-ch'ing (Chungking); and Syngman Rhee who had American backing. The anti-Japanese movement in Manchuria of Kim Ilsŏng was the strongest of these. The vast majority of Koreans who were outside of Korea lived in Manchuria. From the latter years of the Yi Dynasty, displaced Koreans had gone to Chien-tao, Manchuria, but during the period of Japanese administration of Korea the number of Koreans migrating there had greatly increased. In 1936 there were approximately 870,000 Koreans there. This group had strong anti-Japanese feelings, and frequently caused major disturbances after the March First movement. The Chien-tao area became the base for ceaseless anti-Japanese activity and was looked upon by the Japanese as a den of "rebellious Koreans." Kim Ilsŏng organized these Koreans living in Manchuria, armed them and, throughout the entire Second World War, kept up a struggle against the Japanese. To Koreans who could not carry out anti-Japanese activities within Korea itself, this movement was considered most courageous. This made it possible for Kim Ilsŏng to become the leader of North Korea at the end of the war.

The March First Movement

BY KIM IL SUNG

In the following selection taken from his memoirs, Korean leader Kim Il Sung provides a firsthand account of the March First Movement, a widespread Korean resistance movement begun March 1, 1919, aimed at overthrowing Japanese rule in Korea. Kim Il Sung, who was eight years old at the time of the March First uprising, describes how the Japanese soldiers attacked unarmed Korean marchers with swords and rifles, killing and maiming them, and suppressing the uprising. He states that the lesson of the failure of the movement was that Koreans themselves must fight for independence rather than relying on peaceful demonstrations and the help of foreign nations.

It was freezing cold on the day when Father left home. . . . Not long after my father's departure, the March First Movement erupted on March 1, 1919. All the pent up angers and sorrows of living under the Japanese imperialists for ten long years exploded on that day. In ten years after the annexation, Korea had become a gigantic dungeon, no better than those of the Middle Ages. The Japanese colonists used naked military power to suppress the Korean people's aspiration to become free again. The Japanese took away our freedom of press, freedom to hold meetings, freedom to form organizations, and freedom to march. They took away our human rights and properties. The Korean people formed secret organizations, independence fights, mass enlightenment activities, and had built up considerable potential energy against the decade of plunder and exploitation by the Japanese.

Catholics, Protestants, Buddhists and other religious leaders, patriotic teachers and students had planned and executed the March First Movement. Our nationalistic feelings were subli-

Kim Il Sung, "Long Live Korean Independence!" www.kimsoft.com, Korea Web Weekly. Reproduced by permission.

mated and ripe for kinetic explosion, like a volcano letting out the pressure built up over the years. Thus, at noon, March 1st in Pyongyang, church bells rang out in unison to signal the start of the march. Several thousands students and citizens gathered at the front yard of Sungduk Girls School located at Jang-dae-jae. Declaration of Independence was read aloud and it was solemnly proclaimed that Korea was a free nation. The crowd began the march shouting "Long Live Korean Independence", "Out with the Japanese and their army". They were joined by tens of thousands of citizens.

The villagers of Mangyong-dae lined up in a file and marched into Pyongyang and joined the crowd of marchers already there. We got up early on that day and ate our breakfast; all of us joined the march. When we left the village, there were only a few hundred of us, but by the time we reached Pyongyang, our rank swelled to several thousands. We beat on drums and gongs and marched toward Botong Gate, shouting "Long Live Korean Independence!" at the top of our lungs.

The Japanese Response

I was only eight years old at the time, but I joined in the march wearing my worn-out shoes full of holes. I shouted and shouted with the marchers and reached Botong Gate. The marchers rushed inside the castle past the Gate; I could not keep up with them in my tattered shoes and so I took them off and ran after the marchers as fast as my little legs could move. The enemy mobilized mounted police and army troops to stop our march. They slashed and shot the marchers indiscriminately. Many of the marchers fell spilling blood. But the marchers marched on and fought the enemy with bare hands.

For the first time in my life, I witnessed people killing people, Korean blood staining our own land. My young mind and body was enraged. After the sunset, the villagers from Mangyong-dae went to Mangyong Peak and held a rally at the summit. Torches were lit and bugles blared. We beat drums and metal pans, making enough noise to wake up the dead. We shouted hurrah for our independence. This continued on for several days. Mother and her sister took me along when they joined the crowd at the summit. Mother was busy carrying drinking water and burning oil for the torches to the protesters at the summit.

The marchers in Seoul were joined by the people who were

in Seoul to attend King Kojong's [the king of Korea before
Japanese rule] funeral. Several hundreds of thousands of people
joined the march. Hasegawa, Governor General of Korea, ordered the 20th Infantry Division garrisoned at Yongsan to squash
the movement. The Japanese soldiers attacked unarmed marchers
with swords and rifles, turning Seoul into a sea of Korean blood.
But the marchers stayed their course; when the vanguards fell, the
next in line took the lead. The marchers pushed on stepping over
their fallen comrades. People marched in all major towns and
cities in Korea on that day.

Young school girls marched holding up Taeguk-gi [the national flag of Korea]. When their hand holding up the flag was
cut off by the Japanese, they picked up the flag with the other
hand. When both hands were cut off, they marched on until they
dropped, shouting "Long Live Korea!" Even the most hardened
Japanese savages were afraid of such determined opponents. The
mass uprising in Seoul and Pyongyang soon spread to all of the
thirteen provinces of Korea by the middle of March. It had
spilled over to Manchuria, Shanghai, Siberia, Hawaii and other
foreign places. The uprising was a true pan-national movement,
of all Koreans, all overseas Koreans, irrespective of their gender,
age, religion and vocation. Every one was welcome to join. Even
the lowly women servants and entertainment maidens (kisaeng),
the bottom echelon in the feudal society, formed their own formation and joined the march.

For over a month or two, the Korean peninsula resonated with
shouts for independence. Spring passed and Summer came, and
the ardor of the uprising gradually subsided. Many Koreans mis-
takenly assumed that the Japanese would get out, if they marched
for several months shouting slogans. They were sadly mistaken;
the Japanese were not about to leave Korea on account of mere
marches. Japan fought three major wars over Korea. . . .

The elite of Korea who organized and led the March First
Movement failed to see this lesson from history. The March leaders erroneously opted for non-violent marches, totally ignoring
the people's burning desires for action. All they accomplished was
to publish a declaration of independence, that gained precious
little for the Korean people. They did not want the people to go
beyond peaceful demonstrations.

Some of the leaders believed that Korea could be freed by
sending petitions to other nations. They took and swallowed US

President Woodrow Wilson's "Doctrine of Self Determination" and expected the United States and other Western Powers to pressure Japan into freeing Korea. They wrote petition after petition, becoming laughing stocks of the imperialists. Kim Gyu Sik [a leader in the March First Movement] and associates begged and pleaded with representatives of the imperialist nations, who were more keen on grabbing more colonies for themselves than freeing any colony.

It was a mistake for those Korean leaders to take Wilson's self-determination doctrine at its face value. The so-called doctrine was nothing but an American ruse to counter the October Revolution in Russia and to dominate the world. The American imperialists used the doctrine to stir up divisive forces in the Soviet Union and prevent it from assisting colonies fighting for independence. The doctrine was also a scheme to take over colonies of the nations defeated in World War I.

Early in the 20th century, the United States signed the Kazra-Taft Treaty whereby Japan was given a free hand in Korea. To expect America to pressure Japan to give up Korea was ludicrous. There is no record of any strong nation helping a weak nation, presenting its people with freedom and independence. A nation's nationhood can be maintained or regained only by the people. This is a truth proven throughout the history. During the Russo-Japanese War . . . , King Kojong dispatched emissaries to the United States and pleaded US help in keeping Korea independent. The fact of the matter is that the United States sided with Japan during the Russo-Japanese War and did everything it could to ensure Japanese victory. After the war, the United States in effect negotiated on behalf of Japan and injected issues favorable to Japan. US President Theodore Roosevelt refused to accept King Kojong's letters claiming that they were not "official" documents.

King Kojong dispatched secret envoys to Hague Peace Conference [an international peace conference held in 1907]. Kojong declared that the Korea-Japan Ulsa Agreement of 1905 was illegal, void and null. He appealed to the world conscience and humanitarianism, believing that Korea would be helped doing so. The Japanese countered Kojong's moves with false propaganda and other world powers ignored the King's pleas. The emissaries suffered tearful rejection after rejection by the delegates. Because of the secret emissaries, Japan forced King Kojong to abdicate and his son Sunjong ascended the throne.

The Hague emissary fiasco was a loud warning bell that shook the very foundation of Korea's feudal ruling class, rooted deep in toadyism. Lee Jun, Kojong's secret emissary, cut his stomach open at the Hague Peace Conference and stained the conference hall red with his Korean blood; it is a tragic lesson that Korea should not count on other nations for independence, because they did not care. In spite of this sad lesson, some of our nationalist leaders clung to the naive notion that the United States, with its "doctrine of self determination" would free Korea; it shows how toadish they were; how deep-rooted their pro-Americanism was.

The failure of the March First Movement showed that the Korean bourgeoisie nationalist leaders could not lead our anti-Japanese independence movement. The social class mix of the march leaders was such that they were not totally opposed to the Japanese rule of Korea. Their objective was to extract concessions from the Japanese authorities so as to protect and enhance their class standing in the Korean society. The fact that many of the leaders became after the march pro-Japanese collaborators and social reformists under the Japanese rule supports the above assertion.

At the time, Korea had no progressive elements that were strong enough to counter reformism. There was no major industrial proletarian class consciousness that could fight against bourgeois reformism at the time. Our toiling mass was still untouched by Marxism-Leninism and lacked organized leadership. It would be years before Korea's working class had at last a vanguard that fought for and protected its class interest; it had to make a long hazardous journey. In the aftermath of the failed March First Movement, the Korean people came to realize that a strong leadership was needed to gain independence. Although millions of Korean people joined the movement, there was no people's organization or class-root leadership and the movement was hampered by divisiveness and ineffectual spontaneity.

The failed March First Movement taught us that in order to win our fight for independence and freedom, we must have effective revolutionary leadership and organizational structures; we must use the right tactics and strategies; and we must debunk toadyism and build up our strength on our own.

The March First Movement, even though failed, showed to the world that the Korean people did not wish to be slaves of other nations, that they were strongly self-reliant and self-deterministic, that they were willing to die for their country. The March First Movement shocked the Japanese imperialists into imposing harsh martial laws and brain-washing indoctrination policies.

The March First Movement put an end to Korea's nascent bourgeois nationalist movement and the Korean people's struggle for independence entered a new stage. . . .

It was not until the Fall of that year when Father returned home to take us with him. . . .

The Nationalist Movement Becomes a Communist Revolution

Father told us about the demonstrations by the people in northern border regions and we told Father about the heroic activities of the villagers during the March First uprising. I still remember my father saying: "An armed robber in your house will not spare your life, just because you plead for your life. Other armed robbers standing outside will not rush inside to help you no matter how loud you scream. If you want to live, you must fight off the armed robber yourself. Armed robbers must be fought with arms."

I could see that Father's mind was set on a new course for Korean independence activities. I learned later that during the March First uprising, Father observed the events unfolding in Korea from various locations in the northern border regions and southern Manchuria. His thoughts were on changes in the class structure in Korea. The March First Movement taught us that you cannot free your country by merely shouting and marching around. The march turned Korea into a gigantic Japanese prison, buried under forests of Japanese guns and bayonets and it would take superhuman efforts to fight the Japanese. We must learn from the Russian revolution and mobilize and arm the people of Korea, in order to free our nation and build a new Korea of equality, freedom and justice for all. This is the gist of Father's new way of thinking—proletarian revolution.

Father saw that the Korean independence movement was not going anywhere; all it had done was to leave bloody tracks of meaningless sacrifices; he realized that a new strategy was called for. Father saw hope in communism in light of the Bolshevik revolution in Russia. The March First fiasco convinced him that we must change our nationalist movement into communist revolution. . . .

Father's belief in communist movement provided much needed nourishments for my growth.

THE HISTORY OF NATIONS
Chapter 2

The Creation of North Korea

The Division of Korea

By Han Woo-Keun

After colonizing Korea in the early twentieth century, Japan continued an aggressive pattern of imperialist conquests that eventually brought the country into World War II. Japan's defeat in that war led to the liberation of Korea from Japanese control. This selection, an excerpt from a book by Han Woo-Keun, a professor of Korean history in South Korea, describes the events following Japan's defeat on August 15, 1945, that resulted in the division of the Korean peninsula into North and South Korea. As this selection explains, the United States and the Soviet Union occupied Korea intending to create a five-year temporary trusteeship that would pave the way for eventual elections and independence for the country. This plan ultimately failed, due largely to Cold War ideological divisions between Communist Russia and capitalist United States. Korea was partitioned into a Communist state in North Korea headed by Kim Il Sung and an elected government in South Korea led by Syngman Rhee. Shortly thereafter, the Korean War began when the North attacked the South, in an attempt to force unification.

While intensifying her oppression of Korea, Japan was beginning the series of military conquests that brought her into World War II and finally resulted in her defeat and Korea's liberation. Deliberate military provocation [by the Japanese] in Manchuria in 1931 resulted in the setting up in the following year of the puppet kingdom of "Manchukuo" under Japanese rule and also in placing the leading militarists in complete control of the Japanese government. Clashes with China increased until a state of all-out war was reached in 1937. Taking advantage of the preoccupation of the Western powers with the threat of war in Europe, Japan began to move into Southeast Asia, and when France fell in 1940 occupied French

Han Woo-Keun, *The History of Korea*, translated by Lee Kyung-shik and edited by Grafton K. Mintz. Seoul, Korea: The Eul-Yoo Publishing Company, 1970. Copyright © 1970 by Han Woo-Keun. Reproduced by permission of the publisher.

Indochina and Siam, threatening British positions in Burma and Malaya. Then began the farce of the "Greater East Asia Co-Prosperity Sphere," with Japan posing as the liberator of the Asian peoples from Western colonialism while treating those she conquered just as badly and sometimes worse than ever the Westerners had. The nationalist movements that were about to break out on every land in Asia were ignored or suppressed.

Japan's Aggression and World War I

In 1940 Japan took another step toward world war by concluding a military alliance with Germany and Italy. At the end of 1941, frustrated in her attempts to obtain American sanction for her conquests and angered by the United States' refusal to continue supplying her with war materials, Japan took the fateful step of provoking war by the attack on Pearl Harbor, Hawaii, December 7, 1941. The United States Navy was badly hurt, and at first Japan swept all before her. In 1942 the Americans were driven out of the Philippines and the British strongholds of Hong Kong and Singapore fell. Japanese troops fanned out to northern New Guinea and most of the adjacent smaller islands and took the strategic American base on Guam. There seemed no stopping them.

The Allies' Defeat of Japan

But the turning point had already come, with the battle of Midway Island, in June 1942, from which a severely mauled Japanese navy limped home in secrecy. Japanese expansion in the Pacific was stopped at that point, and in the following year the tide began to turn. One by one, the conquered islands were retaken and the Japanese forces pushed back. Meanwhile, the dictator [Benito] Mussolini was overthrown in Europe and Italy surrendered to the Allies. With prospects of victory good in both theaters of war, the leaders of the United States, Great Britain and China met at Cairo at the end of November 1943, to confer on strategy and post-war policy. In the Cairo Declaration which embodied the results of this conference, they announced that the war would continue until Japan surrendered unconditionally, that all Japanese territory acquired since 1894 should be returned to its previous owners, and that Korea should in due time become a free and independent nation.

In 1944 came the [Allied] invasion of Normandy, opening the

last chapter of Hitler's mad career in Europe. Germany surrendered in May of 1945, and the Allied Powers turned their full attention to Asia. On July 26 the leaders of the United States, Great Britain, the Soviet Union and China met at Potsdam and issued the Potsdam Declaration, again demanding the unconditional surrender of Japan. The Japanese, determined to struggle to the bitter end, refused. On August 6 the first atomic bomb obliterated Hiroshima, and on August 9 another fell on Nagasaki. Russia declared war on Japan on August 9, and within five days was in full control of northeastern Manchuria and northern Korea. Japan finally surrendered on August 15.

Japanese Oppression of Koreans

The war in the Pacific involved great suffering for Korea, especially in its later stages, for as Japan's defeat drew nearer her exactions and oppressions increased. Korea began being used as a supply base with the outbreak of war with China in 1937. In addition, as Japanese rice production fell because of a manpower shortage, more and more Korean rice went to Japan. Between 1917 and 1938 Korean rice exports rose tenfold, finally reaching over fifty million bushels. In addition, cattle were confiscated for meat and metal objects of all kinds, including scrap iron, brass pots and dishes, and even metal spoons and chopsticks were seized for the munitions factories. Japanese soldiers were everywhere. There were 46,000 of them in 1941 and 59,000 in 1943. By 1944 they had increased to 68,000, and in the disastrous year of 1945 the number leaped to 300,000.

A Japanese general, Minami Jiro, was appointed Governor-General in 1936. In 1937 the notorious "assimilation" policy was put into effect. Henceforth all educational institutions were to use the Japanese language exclusively. In 1940 the leading Korean-language newspapers were suppressed and in 1942 the last two literary magazines in Korean disappeared. In October of 1942 most of the members of the Korean Language Society were arrested and imprisoned on the pretext that they were secretly fomenting a nationalistic movement against Japanese rule. Scholarly and literary groups were dissolved.

From then on, all meetings and ceremonies in Korea began with an oath of allegiance to the Japanese Emperor, and Koreans were compelled to worship at Japanese Shinto shrines. In 1939 the assimilation movement reached a height of absurdity when all

Koreans were ordered to change their names to Japanese ones. As the war extended, Japan ran short of manpower and Korea was forced to supply the need. In 1938 a "volunteer" system, which was anything but voluntary, began conscripting Korean youths. In 1939 the Japanese began using forced Korean labor in mines and factories and military construction abroad. By the end of the war 2,616,900 persons were engaged in forced labor in Korea, while 723,900 had been sent abroad. Japanese patriotic societies were set up and Koreans forced to join them. In 1942 Korean men began being drafted into the Japanese army. As the strain on Japanese resources reached the breaking point and defeat loomed over her, the actions of her government in Korea become more and more desperate and cruel.

Korea's Hope for Independence

Korean reactions to this oppression were many and varied. One of the most important was that of the Christians, many of whom refused to obey the order to worship at Japanese Shinto shrines. In 1937, the year this order was promulgated, the minister and many members of a Presbyterian church in P'yongyang were arrested for refusing to obey. In 1939 all Christians who would not worship the Shinto gods were imprisoned, and many of them were tortured. In 1940 a number of Christians were accused of campaigning against the war and put in prison, and in March of 1941, even before the United States entered the war, several dozen British and American missionaries were arrested and secretly interned in a remote area of Kangwon Province.

Many Korean youths attempted to evade conscription, and were sent to the coal mines and munitions factories when caught. Many who were conscripted deserted at the first opportunity. As the situation worsened it became increasingly clear even to many Japanese that the defeat of Japan was inevitable.

The Japanese takeover of Manchuria in 1932 had greatly hampered the activities of patriot groups there. Many of them retreated into China proper, where some joined the forces of the Provisional Government [a government in exile set up by resistance leaders during Japanese rule], while others were won over by the Communists. In 1940 the Provisional Government removed to Chungking, where the Chinese government was then operating, and brought a great many Korean patriot groups under its control. In 1941 it organized a single military force from these, with Yi Pom-sok, a patriot fighter from Manchuria, as commander. At the same time, Korean units were set up within the Chinese Communist forces, which were based at Sian in the northwest. All these forces fought the Japanese side by side with the Chinese, and one Korean unit was even dispatched by the Chinese leader Chiang Kai-shek to aid the the British in Burma.

After the Japanese attack on Pearl Harbor brought the United States into the war, the Provisional Government began to make diplomatic contact with the Allied Powers with a view to ensuring Korea's independence after the war. As the Japanese suffered defeat after defeat, hope and joy rose in the hearts of Koreans both at home and abroad. The day of liberation was surely coming soon.

Driven back from all her Pacific conquests, pounded by perpetual Allied bombing raids and appalled by the tremendous destruction of the atomic bombs dropped on Hiroshima and Nagasaki, the Japanese at last surrendered unconditionally on August 15, 1945. The provisions of the Cairo and Potsdam declarations immediately came into force, and after forty years of struggle against the oppression of rulers who had tried to obliterate her very identity, Korea was free once more. For about three weeks, the Korean people lived in a state of happy confusion, and for many of them it was an emotional experience too deeply felt to be adequately described. Their happiness was soon overshadowed, however, by domestic political differences and the collision of the United States and Soviet Russia.

Tens of thousands of political prisoners came out of the jails as the Japanese relinquished control, and political and social organizations appeared in bewildering variety. The chief differences were between the Nationalists, who were awaiting the return of the Provisional Government leaders, and the Socialists and Communists, who wished to set up a Socialist state. All the differences which had rent the independence movement in the past and even divided the Provisional Government on occasion reappeared in aggravated form once independence became a reality.

Russia and the United States Occupy Korea

Meanwhile, arrangements made among the victorious Allies were developing in such a way as to have the gravest consequences for Korea. One of the agreements reached after Russia's entry into the war against Japan had been that, upon a Japanese surrender, Russian troops should occupy Korea north of the thirty-eighth parallel, while those of the United States should occupy the area south of it. On the part of the United States, at any rate, this was thought of as a purely temporary arrangement, until such time as a Korean government could be formed and national elections held under the supervision of the United Nations. It was soon to become clear that the Russians saw it differently.

With the Russian forces already occupying the north, the troops of the United States Eighth Army under the command of Lieutenant General John R. Hodges began to arrive at Inch'on on September eighth. On the following day the Japanese forces officially surrendered in Seoul. The Governor-General was dismissed and the Japanese flag hauled down from the Government-General building. General Archibald V. Arnold was appointed military governor and a military government was organized. The American authorities made it clear from the outset that freedom of political activity was guaranteed and that they would observe strict neutrality in all arrangements made by Koreans in the process of organizing a government and holding elections.

In the north meanwhile, the Russians hastened to set up a Communist government led by Koreans. Cho Man-sik at first headed the Council of People's Commissars, but was soon replaced by Kim Il-song, who then began his long dictatorship. The Korean Provisional Council of People's Commissars was then set up and a Russian-style Communist regime organized. The nature of its rule could easily be judged by the fact that tens of thousands of people fled to the south, accompanied by every Japanese soldier or resident who could escape. Their numbers increased daily, and as the Russians guarded the thirty-eighth parallel more closely their efforts became more desperate.

Members of the Provisional Government now began to arrive in Seoul. Syngman Rhee returned in the middle of October, after a thirty-three-year absence from his homeland. In the latter part of November President Kim Ku and other important leaders arrived. All the nationalist groups supported them, and the people were anxious for the promised elections which were supposed to end the division of the country. They had to declare that they had returned in the capacity of private citizens, however, for the American military government recognized neither the Provisional Government nor the People's Republic which had been set up in the south.

Immediately upon his return, Syngman Rhee said in an interview, "When I heard there were some sixty political parties in Korea while I was preparing to return, my heart ached." He added that the first task for the Korean people was to unify the country and terminate the American and Russian military governments as quickly as possible. As soon as he could, he contacted General Hodges and Military Governor Arnold to urge upon them the importance of a free and united Korea.

The Trusteeship Plan

The division of the country was widely resented, and many of the political parties pressed for an end to it. One of them, the People's Party, even sent a resolution to [U.S.] general MacArthur demanding its abolition. But the Koreans were in for worse trouble. In October came the shocking news that the Allied Powers had decided that Korea was to be ruled by a trusteeship system for a maximum of five years. A provisional government was to be formed under the trusteeship of the United States, Britain, the Soviet Union and China. A conference of the foreign ministers of the United States, Britain and the Soviet Union was to be held in December in Moscow, and two weeks later the American and Russian commanders in Korea should proceed to carry out the arrangement.

Resistance was instantaneous and practically unanimous. After all the years of longing and fighting for independence, the Korean people simply could not accept the idea of even benevolent foreign rule. All the political parties agreed on this point and issued public statements opposing trusteeship. Demonstrations were practically continuous during the last months of 1945, and the press encouraged them in every paper that appeared. The trusteeship arrangements continued, however, and on the last day of the year the streets were still filled with angry people and the shopkeepers had closed their stores in protest.

Then on January 2, 1946, the Communist groups in Korea, doubtless on Russian instruction, suddenly changed their attitude and came out in favor of trusteeship. Well-rehearsed demonstrations in favor of trusteeship were held in north Korea and leftist groups in the south dutifully fell into line, while the nationalists stubbornly maintained their opposition.

In the midst of the continuing political turmoil, preparations went on for a Russo-American conference to organize a provisional government and a House of Representatives was appointed with Syngman Rhee as speaker, to act in a consultative capacity to the U.S. military government. This helped solidify the nationalist groups while the leftists were still trying to organize opposition to them. The trusteeship issue thus had the effect of creating a clear division between left and right.

After several preliminary meetings, the formal conference was held at Toksu palace in March, and almost immediately reached an impasse. The Russian side insisted that no political group or leader that had participated in the anti-trusteeship movement should be allowed to take part in forming the new government, hoping in this way to exclude the nationalists and set up a leftist government which they would be able to control. The American side refused to accept this provision and insisted that, to be truly democratic, the new government should consult all leading groups and shades of opinion. After weeks of fruitless argument, the conference was suspended *sine die* on May eighth.

The American Efforts and the Rise of Syngman Rhee

[U.S.] General Hodges and his staff had not expected to rule a whole nation for any length of time, and despite their goodwill they faced problems with which they were ill prepared to deal. Japanese exploitation and concentration on munitions industries during the war had left the Korean economy a shambles, and in any case most of the nation's heavy industry was in the north and so controlled by the Communists. In addition, some 2,000,000 refugees had poured into the south, mostly from the north but many from China and Japan. Many of what factories there were stood idle because of lack of technical or administrative skills.

The American authorities did what they could, taking control of mines, reforming farm rents, and prohibiting the buying and selling of Japanese property. But they lacked detailed knowledge of civil administration and economics, and their regulations were made on a trial-and-error basis and frequently changed, creating more confusion. The political uproar over trusteeship and the Russo-American Conference was a constant and perplexing problem.

The political situation did clarify somewhat. The Korean

People's Party led by Syngman Rhee pushed strongly for national unification and withdrawal of the trusteeship plan. The Korean Independence Party under Kim Ku and other members of the former Provisional Government wanted a national assembly elected and cooperation of all parties against trusteeship. A middle-right group led by Kim Kyu-sik and a middle-left group led by Yo Un-hyong both tried to heal the rift between left and right. But the left, especially the Communists, refused to give up support of trusteeship and demanded that the Russo-American Conference be resumed. When warrants were issued for the arrest of leading Communists on criminal charges, they went under ground and began fomenting strikes and riots, the most serious of which were the railway strike in Pusan and the riot of workers in Taegu.

In December of 1946 the Interim Legislature was formed under the American Military Government. Of the forty-five elected members the majority were from the Korean Democratic Party and the People's Council, which was led by Syngman Rhee. An additional forty-five were appointed by the Military Government, mainly from the groups led by Kim Kyu-sik and Yo Un-hyong. It was to propose urgently needed legislation in consultation with the Military Government.

During its first year, the American Military Government used a dual system with joint American and Korean heads of each department. When this proved ineffective, the Americans were changed from heads of departments to advisers. In February 1947, An Chae-hong was appointed Civil Governor, the highest post. In June the military government was officially designated the south Korean Interim Government. A committee on government reorganization was established. A little later So Chae-p'il, who had supported Korean independence fifty years before, returned to offer his services as adviser, and was of great help in establishing a civilian administration. But the Interim Government was subject to many strains and stresses, and there were many problems with which it could not cope. It became daily more obvious that the formation of an independent Korean government was a necessity for the welfare of the people.

U.N. Involvement

The Russo-American Conference meetings were resumed in Seoul in May 1947, at which time the leading political parties presented to it in writing their suggestions for the formation of a provisional government. These suggestions differed so widely and contradicted each other in so many ways that the Conference could find no common ground on which all of them could be included. Moreover, the Russians renewed their insistence that all groups which had opposed the trusteeship plan must be excluded, a position which remained unacceptable to the United States. No real discussions were held, the two sides simply issuing statements from time to time.

Judging that negotiations must be held at a higher level if any progress was to be achieved, the United States proposed calling a foreign ministers' conference of itself, Britain, China and the Soviet Union for the settlement of the Korean problem. When Russia officially refused to accept this proposal, the United States placed the Korean question before the United Nations on September 17, 1947. The United Nations agreed, despite Russian objections, to attempt a solution.

The committee appointed to work on the problem laid before the General Assembly a plan which called, first of all, for general elections throughout Korea under U.N. supervision. When a Korean government had been formed, both Russia and the United States were to withdraw their troops. At the same time, the United Nations Committee for the Unification and Rehabilitation of Korea (UNCURK) was to be organized to advise and consult with the new government. Over continuing Russian objections this plan was accepted by the General Assembly with some slight alterations.

UNCURK began to function in January 1948 and immediately found itself excluded from north Korea by the Russians. In February it was decided to hold elections in the south in accordance with the U.N. resolution. These were held on May 10, when 198 representatives were elected to the National Assembly, 100 seats being left vacant in case of possible future elections in the north. The Assembly held its first session on May 31, and declared that from henceforth the official name of the nation was Taehan Minguk (freely translated as the Republic of Korea) and then set about drawing up a constitution, which was promulgated on July 17. Under this constitution, the Assembly elected Syngman Rhee as the first president of the Republic, and he immediately formed a government. On August 15, 1948, the third anniversary of liberation, the newly formed Republic of Korea was proclaimed to the world. It soon received diplomatic recognition from the United States and about fifty other countries. In December the United Nations proclaimed it the only legitimate government on the Korean peninsula.

The Formation of Communist North Korea

While these events were going forward the last feeble gesture toward peaceful unification ended in failure. Having founded the Korea Council of People's Commissars as a step toward establishing a permanent Communist regime, the north Koreans proposed negotiations between representatives from north and south Korea at P'yongyang in April of 1948. This turned out to be simply a brain-washing operation on the part of the north Koreans, and nothing was achieved. Matters had gone too far for Korea to be unified through negotiations. For the time being, however, there was no overt conflict. The Russo-American Conference was dissolved and by June 1949, both Russian and American troops had been withdrawn.

In defiance of the U.N. resolution the so-called People's Republic of Korea was formed in September 1948. Almost immediately it began harassing guerrilla raids on the south, together with a propaganda campaign and fomenting of riots. Behind the scenes, serious military preparations were pushed forward as fast as possible.

In the south, the new government was having a difficult time. Communist-inspired strikes and riots were frequent, and so much money had to be spent on maintaining public order that shortages of essential goods and inflation followed. A majority of the Assemblymen elected were without political party affiliations, a clear sign of public disenchantment with the politicians. And the Republic's armed forces, which possessed no tanks and no warplanes, were far inferior in strength to the north Korean forces.

North Korea Attacks the South: War Begins

The Republic of Korea immediately protested to the United Nations. In response, the Security Council passed a resolution ordering the Communists to withdraw to the thirty-eighth parallel and encouraged all member nations to give military support to the Republic. United States troops soon began to arrive, and were subsequently joined by those of many other nations, including Britain, France, Canada, Australia, the Philippines and

Turkey. Under the command of [U.S.] general Douglas Mac-
Arthur they began to take the initiative, and after the surprise
landing at Inch'on pushed the Communists out of south Korea
and advanced into the north. Some units reached the Yalu River,
and it seemed unification would at last be realized.

But in October the Communist Chinese intervened. Chinese
troops appeared in such large numbers that the U.N. forces were
compelled to make a strategic retreat, and Seoul once again fell
into Communist hands on January 4, 1951. The U.N. forces re-
grouped and mounted a counter-attack which re-took Seoul on
March 12. A stalemate was reached roughly in the area along the
thirty-eighth parallel, where the conflict had begun.

The War Ends in a Divided Korea

At this point the Russians called for truce negotiations, which finally began at Kaesong in July of 1951 and were transferred to
P'anmunjom in November of the same year. These talks were
once suspended and dragged on for over a year before agreement
was finally reached on July 27, 1953. Against the will of the Republic of Korea, it was agreed that each side should pull its forces
back behind a demilitarized zone that was to follow the battle
line at the time the armistice went into effect. Prisoners were exchanged and a neutral Supervision Committee was set up to ensure that both sides abided by the agreement. The three years of
struggle had resulted in nothing but loss of life and property for
both sides, and unification had been rendered virtually impossible without a radical change in the world situation.

The casualties and damage inflicted by the war were heavy. On
the U.N. side 150,000 people were killed, 250,000 wounded,
100,000 kidnapped to the north, 200,000 missing and several
million homeless. Precise figures are not available for the Communist side, but it is probable that their casualties were far greater.
Taken and retaken four times, Seoul lay in ruins, as did most of
the other cities of the south. More than half of all industrial facilities were inoperative, countless numbers of roads and bridges
were destroyed and whole villages had been wiped out in many
areas. But the gravest damage was to the Korean dream of unification. This was no longer a matter only of Korean concern, but
had become an issue in the world conflict known as the Cold
War. Once again Korea was compelled to suffer from the clash of
powers greater than herself.

The Soviets Select Kim Il Sung to Lead North Korea

By Andrei Lankov

In this excerpt from a book written by Andrei Lankov, a Russian scholar and author who has written much about North Korea, Kim Il Sung's path is traced from his birth to his position as North Korea's Communist dictator. Born to peasant parents, Kim Il Sung moved with his family to Manchuria during the time of Japanese occupation. Later, he became a guerrilla fighter in Manchuria with an anti-Japanese militia set up by the Chinese. The guerrilla unit fled Manchuria for the Soviet Union in 1940 after a crackdown by the Japanese army. While in exile, Kim Il Sung was recruited by the Soviet Union to be an officer in charge of a Korean battalion in the Soviet military. After World War II ended with Japan's surrender in 1945, the Soviets chose Kim Il Sung to become the Communist leader of North Korea. According to author Lankov, Kim Il Sung found himself the leader of North Korea almost by accident and was initially frustrated that he was chosen for the political appointment. Lankov also confirms that the Soviets largely controlled North Korea during the first several years from 1946 to 1949. Thereafter, however, Kim Il Sung took charge of the country and ruled for the next forty-six years, ultimately ensuring the regime's dynastic survival by the succession of his son, Kim Jong Il.

Not much is known about the family background and the childhood years of Kim Il Sung. Although North Korean propaganda has published countless volumes on this subject, it is difficult to separate the truth from later falsifications.

Andrei Lankov, *From Stalin to Kim Il Sung: The Formation of North Korea: 1945–1960.* London: Hurst & Company, 2002. Copyright © 2002 by Andrei Lankov. Reproduced by permission.

Kim Il Sung's Beginnings

Kim Il Sung was born Kim Sŏng-ju on 15 April 1912 in Mang-yŏngdae, a small village near Pyongyang [the modern capital of North Korea]. His father Kim Hyŏng-jik (1894–1926) changed occupations many times during his short life. In the biographical references on Kim Il Sung published in the Soviet press, his father was usually called a 'village teacher', which, for a Soviet editor, sounded respectable since teaching is a noble vocation and also an 'appropriate' occupation for the father of a Communist leader. It was not untrue: Kim Hyŏng-jik did sometimes teach in primary schools, but on the whole the father of the future Great Leader belonged to the world of the Korean petty intellectual, semi-modern and semi-traditional, not always poor but seldom affluent, who earned his living either by teaching or by doing office work, or in some other way. Besides teaching, Kim Hyŏng-jik also practised traditional herbal medicine.

The family of Kim Il Sung was Christian. Protestantism, which had come to Korea in the late nineteenth century, was spreading in the North of .the country throughout the colonial period. Christianity was often perceived in Korea as an ideology of modernisation and, partly, of modern nationalism. Kim Il Sung's father attended a missionary school and maintained life-long connections with Christian churches and missions. Until recently, the fact that the parents of Kim Il Sung were not just Christians but Christian activists had not been mentioned by Pyongyang publications, while their contacts with religious organisations were explained away by an imputed intention to find a legal cover for their alleged revolutionary activities. The mother of Kim Il Sung, Kang Ban-sŏk (1892–1932), was the daughter of a local Protestant minister. Besides Kim Sŏng-ju, the future Kim Il Sung, there were two other sons in the family.

Like the majority of rural intellectuals, the Kim family hardly managed to make ends meet. According to North Korean historiography, the parents of Kim Il Sung, particularly his father, were prominent leaders of the national movement. From the late 1960s onwards, the official propaganda even insisted that Kim Hyŏng-jik was the principal figure in the entire anti-colonial resistance. This is far from being the truth, although the family's attitude to the Japanese colonial regime was, in all probability, indeed hostile. Some documents from Japanese archives indicate that in 1917 Kim Hyŏng-jik did play a rather active role in an underground nationalist group organised by the students of his school. Some of his fellow-members eventually became prominent Communists, although this happened later. North Korean publications maintain that Kim the elder was even arrested and spent some time in a Japanese prison, but it is not clear to what extent this assertion is true.

Apparently, for both political and economic reasons, the parents of Kim Il Sung, like many other Koreans, moved to Manchuria in about 1920. There little Kim Sŏng-ju attended a Chinese school. As a child he mastered Chinese, which he spoke fluently till the end of his long life: it was said that in his later years his favourite reading was classic Chinese novels. At some point he returned to Korea to stay with his grandfather for a while, but soon left his homeland again to return there only twenty years later. In Manchuria the situation of the family did not improve and in 1926 Kim Hyŏng-jik died at the age of thirty-two. Kim Sŏng-ju was just fourteen years old.

Fighting the Japanese

In Jilin, while a high school student, Kim Sŏng-ju joined an underground Marxist group, created by a local youth organisation of the Chinese Communist Party. The group was almost immediately discovered by the police and the seventeen-year-old Kim, the youngest of its members, was imprisoned for several months in 1929. As could be expected, the official North Korean propaganda maintains that he was not just a member but the founder and leader of the group—an assertion fully disproved by documents. He was soon released, but his life radically changed: without apparently even having graduated from school, the young man joined one of many guerrilla bands then active in Manchuria. He went to fight against the Japanese and their local collaborators for a world more just than the one he saw around him. At the time it was a choice made by many young and honest Chinese and Koreans who refused to adapt to the occupation regime or make a career and fortune in what they saw as the world of injustice and repression, both national and social. It was, however, important that for these young revolutionaries national goals were often seen as more important than social ones. After all, the worst acts of social injustice were perpetrated by foreign exploiters, so the national struggle fused with the social.

The early 1930s were a time when the anti-Japanese movement was gathering momentum in Manchuria. Among its members and leaders there were both Koreans and Chinese, people of all political inclinations, from Communists to extreme nationalists. Young Kim Sŏng-ju, who since his school years had been connected with the Communist resistance, joined a Communist guerrilla unit. Not much is known of this period of his life. According to the official North Korean propaganda, from the beginning Kim Il Sung headed the Korean People's Revolutionary Army which was said to have been created by him and which, although maintaining some contacts and co-ordination with units of the Chinese Communists, on the whole acted independently. This version has nothing to do with reality. No Korean People's Revolutionary Army ever existed. This 'Army' was first mentioned by Korean propaganda in the late 1940s and finally established itself in the official North Korean historiography a decade later. From the late 1950s onwards, North Korean propaganda has tried to present Kim Il Sung first of all as a national Korean leader and thus tried to conceal or downplay his early contacts with China and the Soviet Union. For instance, the North Korean press never mentioned his membership in the Chinese Communist Party (from 1932) or his service in the Soviet army during the Second World War.

Around 1935 Kim Sŏng-ju also adopted a *nom de guerre* [war name] under which he was to remain in history—Kim Il Sung. The young guerrilla must have shown himself to be a good soldier, because his career progressed fast. In 1935, soon after guerrilla units acting near the Korean-Chinese border were amalgamated into the second division, itself part of the United North-Eastern Anti-Japanese Army, Kim Il Sung became the political commissar of the 3rd detachment, about 160 strong. Two years later, the twenty-four-year-old fighter occupied the post of commander of the 6th division, usually known as the 'division of Kim Il Sung'. The term 'division' should not mislead: in this case it meant a guerrilla unit numbering, at most, a few hundred soldiers. Nevertheless, it was a measure of his success, showing that the young man had some military talent, as well as leadership skills.

The best known of his operations was a successful raid on Poch'onbo, after which Kim Il Sung even acquired some international fame. In the early morning of 4 June 1937, about 200 people under his command crossed the Chinese-Korean border and made a sudden attack on the small town of Poch'onbo. They destroyed a local police post and some Japanese offices and withdrew after a few hours. Although modern North Korean propaganda has blown the scale of this operation out of all proportion, adding it to the activities of the mythical Korean People's Revolutionary Army, this episode was indeed of some importance. In the 1930s, the guerrillas almost never succeeded in crossing the strictly guarded Korean–Manchurian border and penetrating into Korean territory. Following this raid, the news of which quickly spread all over Korea, Kim Il Sung started being taken seriously as a military leader. The press wrote about the raid and its organiser, while the Japanese police force included him into their lists of particularly dangerous 'Communist bandits'.

In the late 1930s Kim Il Sung met his wife Kim Chŏng-suk, the daughter of a farmhand from North Korea, who herself had joined a guerrilla unit at the age of sixteen. It is likely that she was not his first but his second wife; his alleged first wife, Kim Hyo-sun, had also fought in his unit but in 1940 she was taken prisoner by the Japanese. Later, she lived in the DPRK and occupied various middle-level administrative positions. At this stage it is difficult to say whether this information about Kim's first marriage is correct. According to an official version, the first wife was Kim Chŏng-suk, the mother of Kim Chŏng-il, future heir and successor to Kim Il Sung. According to the recollections of N.G. Lebedev, who met her in the 1940s, she was a small, quiet woman, not particularly well educated, but friendly and life-loving. Kim Il Sung lived with her through the most turbulent decade of his life, during which he rose from a commander of a small guerrilla unit to the ruler of North Korea.

Exile in the Soviet Union

By the late 1930s, the situation of the guerrillas had radically worsened: in 1939–40 significant Japanese forces were concentrated in Manchuria to suppress the armed resistance. The guerrillas suffered serious defeats. By then Kim Il Sung had already become the commander of the 2nd operational region of the 1st Army, with the guerrilla units in the province of Jiandao subordinated to him. His fighters occasionally managed to inflict considerable damage on the Japanese, but time worked against them. By late 1940, of all the top leaders of the 1st Army—the commander, the commissar, the chief of staff and the commanders of three operational regions—only Kim Il Sung remained alive, and the Japanese launched a hunt for him. The situation was becoming desperate. In late 1940, together with a dozen of his fighters, he fought his way to the north and crossed the frozen Amur river. His exile in the Soviet Union had begun. . . .

Kim's forced defection to the Soviet Union was not unusual. From the mid-1930s, Manchurian guerrillas often crossed over into Soviet territory. After 1939, when the Japanese radically increased the scale of their anti-guerrilla campaign, the exodus of the remnants of the defeated guerrilla forces to the Soviet Union became massive. On their arrival the guerrillas were submitted to security checks. If they passed the checks well, their lives could take very different routes. Some joined the Red Army, some were recruited by Soviet intelligence services, some were found suspicious and sent into prison camps, while others, having adopted Soviet citizenship, lived ordinary lives as peasants or, rarely, as workers. Like others, Kim and his soldiers were for some time interned in a 'filtration' (investigation) camp. However, Kim's name had already become known, at least to those who 'had to know', so the security check did not last long. According to G.K. Plotnikov, Kim received some training at the Khabarovsk infantry officer school where he studied until the spring of 1942; however, no other source has confirmed this fact so far. It was the first time in a decade of wandering, hunger and exhaustion that he could rest and feel safe. His life went well. In February 1942 (according to some sources, in February 1941) Kim Chŏng-suk gave birth to a son who received a Russian name, Yura, a short form of Yuri. He was to become the 'Dear Ruler, the Great Successor of the *Chuch'e* Revolutionary Course, Marshal Kim Chŏng-il'.

Kim Il Sung in the Soviet Military

In the summer of 1942 the Soviet military decided to form a special unit from the former Manchurian guerrillas. This was the 88th Independent Brigade, which was located in the village of Viatsk (Viatskoe) near Khabarovsk. The young captain of the Soviet army Kim Il Sung (who in those days was more often called Jin Ri-cheng, according to the Chinese pronunciation of his name's characters) was sent to this unit. Zhou Bao-zhong, a prominent Manchurian guerrilla leader, by then a lieutenant-colonel in the Red Army, became the commander of the brigade. He was assisted, advised and, one might presume, also controlled by several Soviet officers. The brigade consisted mostly of Chinese, so training was conducted in Chinese. The brigade contained four battalions, a total, according to different estimates, of 1,000 to 1,700 people, of whom about 200–300 were Soviet personnel attached to the brigade as instructors and ideological indoctrinators. Korean guerrillas, most of whom had fought under the command of Kim Il Sung in the 1930s, served in Kim's first battalion. According to the estimations of Wada Haruki, the battalion had a strength of between 140 and 180 (much smaller then a 'normal' Red Army battalion was supposed to be).

The life of a military unit located far behind the front line during the war was monotonous and fairly difficult. As is clear from the evidence of people who served with Kim Il Sung at the time or had access to the materials of the 88th Brigade, it was not a special-purpose unit despite its specific contingent. In its weapons, organisation and training, it did not differ from the ordinary units of the Soviet army. Yet from time to time some servicemen from this brigade were selected to carry out various intelligence and sabotage operations in Manchuria and Korea. The training for these operations was not conducted in Viatsk and Kim Il Sung himself during the war never left his brigade, nor was he ever in Manchuria or Korea.

Kim Il Sung, who had been involved in action since he was eighteen, seemed to have liked the difficult and dangerous but orderly life of a professional officer; it seems that he was satisfied with his new position and that his superiors did not complain about him. During their life in Viatsk, Kim Il Sung and Kim Chŏng-suk had two more children: a son named Shura (short for Alexander) and a daughter. Children were given Russian names, which might indicate that at the time a return to Korea did not look very likely to Kim and his wife. According to eyewitnesses, Kim had a clear vision of his future: service in the army, a military academy, then command of a regiment or maybe even a division. Had history taken a different turn, Kim Il Sung, as a retired colonel or major-general of the Red Army, might have lived out his days in Moscow, with his son Yuri working in some Moscow research institute and in the late 1980s participating enthusiastically in the pro-democracy rallies. . . .

The New Leader of North Korea

Soon after the end of the war the 88th Brigade was disbanded and its soldiers and officers received new appointments. . . . The largest Korean city then under Soviet control was Pyongyang, and logically Kim Il Sung, who had the highest rank among the Koreans of the 88th Brigade, was appointed deputy *kommendant* [commander] of the future North Korean capital, and went there together with some soldiers of his battalion. A first attempt to reach Korea by land ended in failure as a railway bridge on the Chinese-Korean border was damaged, but in late September 1945 Kim arrived in Korea aboard the steamship *Pugachev* via Vladivostok and Wonsan. Recently, it has been reported in the South Korean press that the role of Kim Il Sung as the future national leader had been determined before his departure for Korea during his meeting with Stalin which supposedly took place in early September 1945. Though not entirely impossible, these assertions look very doubtful. It is probable that at the moment of Kim Il Sung's arrival in Pyongyang neither he nor those around him had any particular plans for his future.

However, the arrival of Kim Il Sung was timely. By the end of September, the Soviet command had realised that its initial attempts to rely on the local nationalists headed by Cho Man-sik were doomed to failure. In early October the Soviet military and political leadership started to look for a figure who could head the emerging regime. Due to the general weakness of the Communist movement in the North, it was impossible to rely on local Communists: there was hardly anybody among them who enjoyed any popularity in the country. In this situation a young officer of the Soviet army, whose guerrilla past was relatively well known in Korea, appeared to be the best candidate for the still-vacant post of 'leader of the North Korean progressive forces'. A few days after his arrival in Korea Kim Il Sung was invited (or rather ordered) to deliver a short greeting at a pompous rally to honour the 'Liberating Soviet Army' (14 October). His appearance at the rally was the first sign of his political ascent. Several days earlier, he was included in the North Korean Bureau of the Communist Party of Korea, although at the time he was not yet the formal leader of the Communists in the North. Another step to power was his appointment as chairman of the North Korean Bureau of the Communist Party of Korea in December 1945; then in February 1946 the Soviet authorities made him head of the North Korean Provisional People's Committee, the country's provisional government.

Thus in early 1946 Kim Il Sung formally became ruler of

North Korea. Although in retrospect much has been said about his cunning and ambitions, V.V. Kovyzhenko, who often met Kim in late 1945 and 1946, insists that he was rather frustrated by the turn of events and took his political appointment without much enthusiasm. At the time Kim Il Sung might have preferred a career as a Soviet army officer to the strange and complicated life of a politician. V.V. Kovyzhenko, then head of the 7th Department of the political administration of the 25th Army, who often met Kim, says: 'I remember very well when I visited Kim Il Sung after he was invited to become the head of the people's committees. He was very frustrated and told me: "I want [to command] a regiment and then—a division. What is this for? I don't understand anything and don't want to do this."'

Thus Kim Il Sung found himself at the top of the power structure in North Korea almost by accident. Had he arrived in Pyongyang a few weeks later or been sent to another large city, his fate would have been different. However, in 1946 and even in 1949 he was hardly the real ruler of Korea. The Soviet military authorities and the apparatus of advisers had a decisive influence on the life of the country, and in the first years of the DPRK Kim was only nominally ruler.

Kim Il Sung's Return to Korea

By Kim Il Sung

In this memoir by Kim Il Sung, the leader of North Korea remembers his return to Korea in 1945 from his exile in the Soviet Union. Kim Il Sung recalls the excitement among Koreans following the defeat of Japan at the end of World War II and what he calls his "grand welcome" home. He also discusses the speech he gave on October 14, 1945, in Pyongyang at a welcoming rally organized for him, and Korean hopes at that time for national unity.

In August 1945, Korea was aflame with the joy of liberation. In the wave of excitement that enveloped the whole land of Korea, the people were waiting impatiently for the triumphal return of the national hero General Kim Il Sung. The ancient city of Pyongyang, where the leader of the nation was born, was astir even at night waiting for the arrival of General Kim Il Sung, who left his home in a snowstorm in 1925. When would he come back, tomorrow or the day after tomorrow? The four hundred thousand Pyongyangites were all waiting for him.

In Seoul, . . . leading figures of the national liberation struggle organized the preparatory committee to welcome General Kim Il Sung. Every day the Seoul railway station plaza was crowded with tens of thousands of people who were waiting for him. The hearts of thirty million people were throbbing in expectation of the moment of General Kim Il Sung's triumphal return home.

Japan's Surrender and Korean Hope

At the news of Japan's unconditional surrender, the KPRA [Korean People's Revolutionary Army] men at the training base were seized with excitement, preparing to return home. I also wished

Kim Il Sung, "The Triumphal Return," www.kimsoft.com, Korea Web Weekly. Reproduced by permission.

to return home as soon as possible, for I had lived in foreign lands going through storm and stress for 20 years. But we had to put off our return for some time, repressing the yearning for our motherland and native place. We knew how eagerly the people in the homeland were waiting for the triumphant return of the KPRA.

However, we did not hurry our departure. We wanted to make better preparations before going to the homeland. We needed to prepare for the building of a new country. Now that we had carried out the strategic task of national liberation, we had to draw up a schedule to hasten the building of a new country.

On September 2, 1945, on board the USS *Missouri*, which was at anchor in Tokyo Bay, an international ceremony was held to legally confirm the unconditional surrender of Japan. That day, on behalf of the Japanese government and military authorities, Foreign Minister Shigemitsu and Chief of Staff of the Japanese army Umez signed the instrument of surrender. When he was Japanese Minister to China, Shigemitsu lost one leg in a grenade attack by Martyr Yun Pong Gil. Umez, too, was a notorious Japanese militarist. He was the Commander of the Kwangtung Army from the autumn of 1939 to the summer of 1944. Approximately a dozen persons were in command of the Kwangtung Army in succession, and Umez was the last one. Under his command, the enemy launched a large "punitive" operation against the KPRA under the high-sounding name of "special cleanup campaign for maintaining public peace in the southeastern area".

With Japan's surrender, the Second World War, which had thrown mankind into immeasurable miseries and agony, resulted in the victory of the anti-fascist forces. When our sworn enemy Umez signed the instrument of surrender and drank the bitter cup of defeat, we were preparing to return home as the heroes who had triumphed in the anti-Japanese revolution and made a new history of national liberation. The end of the Second World War opened the prospect for different countries in Europe, the cradle of communism, and in Asia, the forefront of the national liberation struggle, to build a new society on a democratic basis. The situation in the motherland was good.

Immediately after liberation, people's committees were organized in many parts of our country. Party organizations and mass organizations were formed everywhere centering on the revolutionaries who had been involved in the homeland Party organizations and the resistance organization members. Literary men and artists at home and abroad gathered in Pyongyang, Seoul and other major cities, cherishing a new hope for building national culture. Workers formed armed guards and protected factories, enterprises, coal and other mines, ports and railways of their own accord. Our people's enthusiasm for national salvation, which had been displayed in national resistance, was converted into enthusiasm for nation-building with the liberation.

From the viewpoint of both the immediate task of the Korean revolution and its ultimate objective, the situation was very optimistic. However, we could not relax in the least. Though the Japanese imperialists had been defeated, the reactionaries did not give up their offensive against the revolution. Even after the Japanese Emperor had declared an unconditional surrender, the remnants of the defeated Japanese army continued their resistance.

The New Occupation of Korea

Pro-Japanese elements, traitors to the nation and the representatives of the exploiting class were hatching a plot underground to disturb the building of a new country. Traitors to the revolution, heterogeneous elements and men of political ambition concealed their true colors and infiltrated Party organizations and people's government organs. When we were in the Soviet Far East region, we heard the news that the US army would be stationed in Korea south of the 38th parallel. This meant that the troops of two big powers would be stationed in our country at the same time. It was a bad omen that the armies of two countries would be stationed in our country, which was not a defeated nation, no matter what excuse they might make or how they might justify it.

During the peasant war of 1894, Japan and China dispatched their armies to Korea. But the Korean people did not benefit at all from them. The dispatch of the two armies culminated in the Sino-Japanese War that devastated our country.

The stationing of the Soviet and US armies might have turned our country into an arena of confrontation between socialism and capitalism, and our national force was liable to be split into left and right, patriots and traitors to the nation. If factional strife prevailed and factions conspired with foreign forces it would end up in the ruin of the country. In these circumstances, we had to strengthen the motive force of our revolution in every way in order to defend the independence of our nation and speed up the building of a new country.

A Revolution for a New Korea

By the motive force of our revolution I mean the force of our own people. Since the first day we set out on the road of revolution, we made every effort to educate, organize and mobilize the people who were to undertake the anti-Japanese revolution. Millions of people in the ranks of resistance who took part in the final battle for national liberation were not people who turned out spontaneously to the battlefield but the organized masses whose forces we had built up for many years.

We never hesitated to walk a hundred miles to win over a man for the revolution. We became human bombs and plunged even into the heart of the fire to protect the people. The whole process of the anti-Japanese revolution was a history of love and trust with which we held up the people as the makers of history, awakened them to political awareness and organized them to stand in the forefront of the liberation war. It was also a history of struggle and creation, in which the people demonstrated themselves as the dignified makers of history, shedding their blood and sweat.

These people and the fighters of the People's Revolutionary Army were the motive force of our revolution that would build a new country. In the crucible of the anti-Japanese revolution we found a valuable truth: that when we believe in the strength of the people and fight relying on them, enjoying their love and support, we can overcome any trial whatever and emerge victorious in any adversity. After liberation, some people said that liberating the country was difficult, but building a society after liberation would not be very difficult. But I considered that nation-building was indeed a difficult and complicated undertaking.

Just as our people had carried out the anti-Japanese revolution by their own struggle, so they had to build a new country by their own efforts. We resolved to build the Party, state and armed forces, and also the national economy, education and culture, and develop science and technology by relying on our people's strength. In order to rouse the people to build a new country, we needed the staff of the revolution and state power which would educate, organize and mobilize them, as well as an army which could protect the building of a new society with arms.

With this in mind, I convened a meeting of military and political cadres of the KPRA at the training base on August 20, 1945, and set forth the three major tasks of building the Party, the state and the armed forces new strategic tasks for strengthening the motive force of our revolution. We discussed the specific ways and methods for carrying out these tasks, and made necessary arrangements. We formed small teams for implementing these tasks and designated the places where they would be sent. . . .

Kim Il Sung Comes Home

As I was returning home after 20 years, leaving my blood relations, friends and comrades buried in a foreign land, I was overcome with mixed emotions of joy and sorrow, which were beyond words. We arrived at Wonsan [a port in North Korea] on September 19, 1945. The members of the headquarters of a Soviet army unit stationed in Wonsan greeted us at the port. . . .

Because the Soviet army had kept our coming a secret, there was no crowd of people at the port to greet us. . . .

On September 20, 1945, I left Wonsan by train for Pyongyang, together with my comrades who were to work in the west coast area. The representative of the Soviet army headquarters in north Korea came down as far as Puraesan station from Pyongyang to meet us. He grasped my hands warmly, congratulating me on my return home. . . .

On the day I entered Pyongyang, together with my comrades-in-arms, I set about carrying out the tasks of building the Party, state and army. That was one of the busiest days after liberation.

In the homeland, too, I worked mainly among the people, among the masses. While visiting factories, rural communities and streets to meet people on the one hand, on the other I met various visitors from at home and abroad in my office and lodgings, sharing bed and board with my comrades as I had done on Mt. Paektu. . . .

After visiting the Kangson Steel Works on October 9 and founding the Communist Party of North Korea, I gave my first address to the people in the homeland at the Pyongyang City mass rally to welcome me.

The fact is that I had never intended to meet the people at a grand welcoming rally. But the important persons in the homeland and my comrades-in-arms insisted on holding such a grand ceremony.

On the day when I first revealed my real name to the public

at a meeting, instead of my assumed name, Kim Yong Hwan, someone proposed to hold a national mass rally to welcome my triumphal return. The whole meeting hailed the proposal. Preparations for the welcoming ceremony had been under way behind the scenes, under the sponsorship of the South Pyongan Provincial Party Committee and People's Political Committee. On the eve of the ceremony, a pine arch and makeshift stage were erected in the public playground at the foot of Moran Hill.

Kim Il Sung's October 14, 1945, Speech

I had told Kim Yong Bom not to arrange a grand ceremony. But the people of the South Pyongan Provincial Party Committee were so stubborn, that they put up posters in every street and lane announcing that we had entered Pyongyang and I would meet the people in the public stadium on October 14.

About noon on October 14, 1945, I went by car to the Pyongyang public playground, the venue of the ceremony. I was amazed at the sight of the surging crowds filling the squares and streets. The playground, too, was already full of people. There were even people in the trees around the playground, and the Choesung Pavilion and the Ulmil Pavilion were covered with people. Going through the waves of welcome I raised my hand in acknowledgement of the cheering crowds.

General Chistyakov, commander of the Soviet 25th Army, and Major General Rebezev were present at the mass rally. Many people made speeches that day. Jo Man Sik took the floor. I still remember a passage of his speech which triggered laughter among the audience. He said in a merry voice that at the news of liberation he pinched himself to see if he was not dreaming and he felt pain. He even showed how he had pinched his arm.

When I mounted the platform the shout "Long live the independence of Korea!" and the cheers of the crowd reached a climax. As I listened to their cheers, I felt the fatigue that had accumulated for 20 years melting away. The cheers of the people became a hot wind and warmed my body and mind. Standing on the platform amidst the enthusiastic cheers of more than 100,000 people, I felt happiness that defied description by any flowery language. If anyone asked me about the happiest moment in my life, I would reply that it was that moment. It was happiness emanating from the pride that I had fought for the people as a son of the people, from the feeling that the people loved and trusted me and from the fact that I was in the embrace of the people.

It may be said that the cheers of the people resounding in the Pyongyang public playground on October 14, 1945, were the acknowledgement of and reward for the arduous struggle we had waged for the first half of our lifetimes for our country and fellow countrymen. I accepted this reward as the people's love for and trust in me. As I always say, no pleasure can be greater than that of enjoying the love and support of the people.

I have regarded the love and support of the people as the absolute standard that measures the value of existence of a revolutionary and the happiness he can enjoy. Apart from the love and support of the people, a revolutionary has nothing.

Bourgeois politicians try to lure the people with money, but we obtained trust from the people at the cost of our blood and sweat. I was moved by the people's trust in me and I considered it the greatest pleasure I could enjoy in my life.

The gist of my speech that day was great national unity. I appealed to the whole nation to build a prosperous independent state in Korea, united as one those with strength dedicating strength, those with knowledge devoting knowledge and those with money offering money.

The crowd expressed their support with thunderous applause and cheers. The Pyongyang Minbo, a newspaper of those days, wrote about the sight of the Pyongyang public playground on that day under the title "Cheers of 400,000 People Shake Korea, A Lovely Land".

> Pyongyang has a long history of 4,000 years and a large population of 400,000. Has it ever had such a large meeting as this? Has it ever held such an important meeting? What gave historic significance to this meeting and turned it into a storm of emotion, was that General Kim Il Sung, the great patriot of Korea and a hero whom Pyongyang produced, was present in person there, and extended joyful and warm greetings and words of encouragement to the people. . . . As soon as General Kim Il Sung appeared on the platform, the hero whom the Korean people hold in high respect and have been looking forward to seeing, a storm of enthusiastic cheers arose, and most of the audience

were deeply moved to silent tears . . . , as he touched the hearts of the masses with steely force their thunderous cheers seemed to voice their determination to fight to the death together with this man.

We can say that the mass rally was the start of a great march of our people towards building a new country.

THE HISTORY OF NATIONS
Chapter 3

The
Korean War

North Korea's Invasion of South Korea

By Michael Hickey

Korean War veteran and historian Michael Hickey, in the following excerpt from his book on the Korean War, describes the circumstances surrounding North Korea's June 25, 1950, invasion of South Korea and the U.S. decision to defend the South against communism. The differences between South and North Korea's military readiness just prior to the start of the Korean War were striking. The United States had not made much progress training the South Korean military. Much of the army's time had instead been spent repelling numerous guerrilla raids from the North. Meanwhile, North Korea was fortified with Soviet expertise and equipment, and was training frequently. By mid-1950, the North Korean army numbered almost one hundred thousand, with backup from police, a coast guard, and a small air force.

As Hickey explains, North Korea's Kim Il Sung and his Soviet backers misread the mood of the United States, believing that it would accept a Communist invasion of South Korea since American troops had been withdrawn. With only the poorly prepared South Korean army left to defend the South, Soviet leader Joseph Stalin felt comfortable authorizing a military invasion. Not surprisingly, the South was crushed, and by June 28, 1950, the North had captured Seoul, the capital of South Korea.

The United States was reluctant to become involved in a war that could lead to a confrontation with the Soviet Union and China. Nevertheless, the Americans slowly warmed to the idea of defending South Korea. With the United States leading the way, the United Nations (UN) passed a resolution condemning the invasion and calling for a cease-fire by the North Koreans. On June 27, 1950, the UN passed a second resolution calling for member states to help South Korea repel the attack. Ultimately, U.S. president Harry S. Truman decided it was necessary to

Michael Hickey, *The Korean War: The West Confronts Communism.* Woodstock, NY: The Overlook Press, 1999. Copyright © 1999 by Michael Hickey. Reproduced by permission of the publisher and the author.

challenge this expansion of communism, and he committed America com-
pletely on June 30, with an authorization of ground troops as well as a
naval blockade of North Korea.

The planners in Pyongyang [the capital of North Korea] were almost certainly lured into the attack of 25 June 1950 by a misreading of the mood in Washington. It seemed that the Americans had accepted, however grudgingly, the communist victory in China and, from the pronouncements of numerous eminent politicians and service chiefs, that they would also accept the subjugation of the Republic of Korea, now that American troops had been withdrawn. On 12 January 1950, when [U.S. Secretary of State] Dean Acheson made his notorious National Press Club address in Washington defining American Far Eastern policy, he had added that there was no longer an intention to guarantee any areas on the Asiatic mainland against military attack.

[North Korean leader] Kim Il-sung, encouraged by these pronouncements, aired his plans to Stalin who at first held back, knowing that it would be fatal to risk all-out war with the United States until the Russian nuclear weapon, first exploded in 1949, had been tested and put into production. But after the American troops had left Korea . . . he felt safe in giving his tacit approval for an invasion, now that there was only the poorly rated ROK [Republic of South Korea] army to deal with.

South Korean Military in Disarray

The ROK army was not in a position to offer much more than token resistance as the summer of 1950 drew on, despite the optimistic pronouncements of KMAG's [Korean Military Advisory Group, U.S. Army] senior officers. Their ROK army training directive for the year called for four three-month training periods. It was hoped that battalion programmes would be complete by the end of March, and that formation training and full manoeuvres would follow. The task was enormous, for at the end of 1949 only 30 out of 67 battalions had completed company-level training and 11 had still not completed even their platoon training programme. The American M1 Garand semi-automatic rifle was now being issued but only 28 battalions had satisfied KMAG as to their proficiency with it. Some progress had been made in other directions; each infantry division now had its own combat engineer battalion and signals and ordnance companies. There were as yet few artillery units and only half of them had fired a range course. In order to spare the army the continuing burden of anti-guerrilla operations, 10,000 police were to be formed into 22 combat police battalions. With an increase of border incidents in the first months of the year had come a significant rise in the number of guerrilla attacks on police posts and other targets in the south. Since the risings on Cheju and the mainland in October 1948, trained guerrillas and sabotage experts had been infiltrated across the 38th parallel by sea and land to link up with guerrillas and mutineers from the former constabulary. By the end of 1949 the ROK army was having to mount an average of three anti-guerrilla operations a day. Although some training value was obtained from these, they were not good practice for general war, and unit training suffered badly. The situation was made worse by the rapid expansion of the army from 65,000 to over 100,000 men in 1949.

After three months, KMAG was forced to admit that the ROK army training programme was in disarray. A new schedule was patiently drawn up and ROK army commanders urged to adopt it. It was too late; by the middle of June only the supposedly élite Capital Division had finished its battalion-level training, together with seven battalions of the 7th Division and a solitary battalion in the 8th. A further 30 battalions had struggled through their company training programme but 17 still had not even completed platoon exercises. KMAG was obliged to postpone the target date for battalion training once again, to 31 July, while regimental training was to be complete throughout the army by the end of October. . . .

Strength of North Korea's Military

In North Korea, things were very different. When the Red Army departed in 1948, it left behind some advisers as instructors, and much of its weaponry and equipment. After 1949 the formation of a field army went ahead rapidly. Conscription was introduced, and the army was formed around the trained cadres of men with wide operational experience in the Chinese Communist Forces or the Red Army. Many of the pilots and technicians in the new air force had been trained in the Soviet Union.

In March 1950 there was a further infusion of Russian equipment, following [Soviet leader Joseph] Stalin's tacit permission to invade. This enabled the North Koreans to equip eight full-strength infantry divisions, two at half strength, an independent infantry regiment, a motor cycle reconnaissance regiment, an armoured brigade and five brigades of border troops. The Russians promised to deliver enough piston-engined reconnaissance, ground attack and light bomber aircraft to guarantee air superiority for the attackers. North Korea had developed a considerable industrial base and a thriving armaments industry was producing large quantities of munitions. Unlike the ROK army, the NKPA [North Korean People's Army] had completed its battalion training in good time and had been staging frequent regimental and divisional exercises since early in the year.

On the eve of war the ROK army was 95,000 strong, backed by 48,000 lightly armed National Police, 6,100 in a coast guard slowly growing into the makings of a navy, and 1,800 in the embryonic air force which, the Americans having declined to issue combat aircraft, possessed only ten Harvard trainers and a dozen light observation planes. . . .

North Korea's Successful Attack

At 4 A.M. on Sunday, 25 June, after ninety minutes of preliminary bombardment, elements of the North Korean 6th Division began to attack the ROK army positions.

The attack spread from west to east across the 38th parallel. . . . At Kaesong, the keystone of the ROK 1st Division's defensive area, only one of the KMAG advisers was in residence, the others having gone to Seoul for the weekend. Woken by the dawn cannonade, he went outside in his pyjamas and got into his jeep to drive round the town as ROK army personnel ran aimlessly around the streets. A train had pulled into the railway station from the north and was disgorging a battalion of North Korean infantry who immediately set about anything that looked like opposition. The American prudently headed south, as bullets cracked about his jeep. Further east, the ROK 6th Division, whose commander had retained his men in post over the weekend, rushed to arms and began to fight resolutely in and around the important town and communications centre of Chunchon. In the Chorwon area, however, where a regiment of the ROK 7th Division had been posted to guard the Kapyong-Pukhan valley route to Seoul, resistance folded before troops on leave could be recalled to their units. Over on the east coast the 8th Division resisted staunchly to begin with, until rumours, followed by confirmation, informed the divisional commander that numerous landings were being made along the coast up to fifty miles to the south.

The United States ambassador in Seoul, John Muccio, heard the news at 9.30 A.M. An inspired choice for this difficult job, he had been in Korea for several years, spoke the language fluently and knew his way around the political labyrinth surrounding [South Korean president] Syngman Rhee. He could hear explosions as the first air raids took place, and brought out the evacuation plan for American and other foreign nationals, the only fully prepared American contingency plan for Korea. Codenamed Operation 'Cruller', it was activated by the codeword 'Fireside', broadcast that evening by the local American Forces Network station. This was the cue for all American nationals to make their way at once to Inchon, where shipping had been commandeered. Muccio, having conferred with the head of KMAG, signalled Tokyo for an immediate airlift of ammunition for the ROK army, adding that it would be catastrophic were the South Koreans to be defeated simply because the United States had failed to provide enough basic military resources.

Doubts were now raised over the status of KMAG. Should its members take up arms and fight alongside the ROK army, or should they be evacuated with the American and other civilians? Muccio even proposed at one point that they should all claim diplomatic immunity, the advisers and their families taking refuge in the American embassy. It was decided in Tokyo, however, that the whole mission should leave Korea, and aircraft were sent to Kimpo airfield to lift the Americans out in between the frequent unopposed air raids. The North Korean air force had effortlessly achieved immediate air supremacy and could do what it liked. During 26 June most of the American and other civilian evacuees were put aboard an overcrowded Norwegian ship at Inchon—700 of them on a cargo vessel with accommodation for 12 passengers. All praised the ship's crew who coped philosophically with this unexpected contingency.

On Monday the 26th, Kim Il-sung broadcast to the Korean people from Pyongyang. He told them that the southerners had invaded the north, but that the NKPA was now counter-attacking successfully across the 38th parallel. He called for increased guerrilla activity in the south, for its workers to go on strike, and for the peasants to call for immediate land reforms; he also demanded the restoration of the People's Committees suppressed by Rhee's government. Despite vociferous claims from Kim and other North Korean leaders that the south had initiated the war by invading the north, sets of operation orders recovered from the war ministry in Pyongyang later in the year provided evidence to the contrary. They were written in Russian, and translations were taken after the originals had been photographed; these mysteriously disappeared and have never been seen again.

Meanwhile the ROK army, temporarily deprived of its

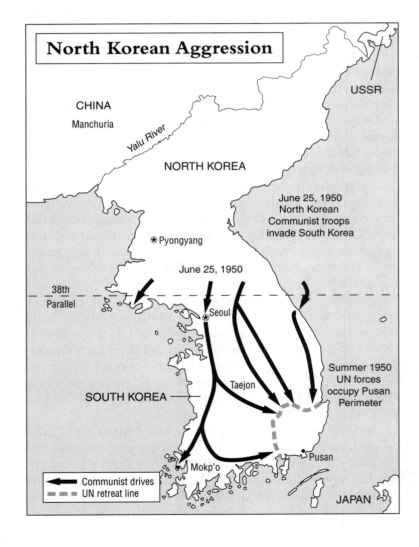

KMAG advisers, was faring badly against a ferocious and well-executed North Korean assault. A powerful armoured and infantry column was sweeping all before it on the main route south through Uijongbu, heading straight for Seoul. Far out to the north-west in their isolated positions on the Ongjin peninsula, after losing an entire battalion, Colonel Kim [Chong-won]'s remaining troops managed to embark on their landing ships and sailed south. On the 26th, the ROK 2nd Division was ordered to launch a counter-attack in the area of Uijongbu in an effort to stem the armoured tide; only part of the force turned up on the start-line and the divisional commander could not make up his mind what to do, eventually beating a disorganized retreat. On the central front the ROK 6th Division held its ground at Chunchon but was finally forced to retreat on the 28th, when the units on its flanks collapsed. It saved most of its transport and guns and had inflicted heavy casualties on the NKPA 2nd Division. Elsewhere, many ROK units stood and fought courageously against overwhelming odds. With almost no anti-tank guns, the ROK infantry adopted suicidal tactics in their efforts to stop the rampaging T-34 tanks which threatened to overrun them, climbing on to their turrets with explosive charges or hurling themselves as human bombs on to the tanks to detonate satchels of explosive tied to their bodies. Many ROK army artillery units stood by their inadequate M3 howitzers until shot down at their guns, after inflicting heavy casualties on their assailants over open sights. With the return of thousands of men off weekend leave the forward units regained a degree of cohesion; but the high command was wanting and direction from the army headquarters in Seoul inept. By last light on the 28th the leading North Korean probes had reached the northern suburbs of Seoul. . . .

Muccio and the remaining staff of the American embassy pulled out of Seoul on 27 June after destroying their diplomatic radio station. With him were the few remaining KMAG personnel including its senior officer, Colonel Wright. Later in the day, without reference to KMAG, General Chae, the ROK army chief of staff, and his headquarters departed hurriedly from the capital, thereby depriving the ROK divisions in the field of their entire higher command. Colonel Wright set out in hot pursuit, to find ROK army headquarters setting itself up on the road to Suwon. The chief of staff, who maintained that he had been 'forcibly carried off by his staff against his wishes', was persuaded to return to Seoul with Wright. But irreparable damage had been done to the morale of the ROK military, as well as to the civil population, by the unedifying spectacle of the nation's top soldier cravenly fleeing the field.

The ROK army headquarters had only been back in Seoul for a few hours when they were off again, accompanied by thousands of terror-stricken soldiers and civilian refugees, jamming the approaches to the bridges across the Han. ROK army engineers now blew the main bridges, still packed with fleeing soldiers and civilians; an estimated 800 of these perished. Thousands of ROK soldiers were still marooned north of the bridges, together with Colonel Wright's KMAG headquarters, which drove out of the ancient east gate of the city, making for the next bridge upstream, eight miles away. This too had been blown, but KMAG got over on a raft with some of its vehicles including the precious radio truck, now the only reliable source of contact with Tokyo. Those members of Wright's staff for whom no places could be found on vehicles which got over to the south bank had to march cross-country for Suwon, some twenty miles away. As they set out, the first American fighter aircraft from Japan appeared overhead to attack the North Korean troops entering the northern suburbs of Seoul, and to challenge the brief North Korean command of the sky.

The United States Becomes Involved

With the International Date Line interposing, it was still late on the evening of Saturday the 24th when news of the invasion reached Washington in the form of Muccio's signal, hotly followed by confirmation from MacArthur's headquarters. Dean Acheson was among the first officials to be informed; he was at his country home after a busy Saturday in Washington but immediately returned to the office after informing Dean Rusk, now his Assistant Secretary of State for Far Eastern Affairs, who found himself pitched once more into the affairs of the countries whose frontiers he had so arbitrarily selected back in August 1945 off a school atlas and without any reference to geographical, ethnic, military or economic factors. Acheson's immediate reaction was to get the duty staff at the Pentagon and in the State Department to contact Trygve Lie [Secretary General of the United Nations] asking him to convene an emergency meeting of the UN Security Council as early as possible on Sunday the

25th. The call went through before midnight.

Acheson now started to ring round town; the President had to be told, but Truman was out of Washington that weekend in his home town of Independence, Missouri. As it would not be possible for him to get back to the Oval Office until the following afternoon, Acheson took it upon himself to make a number of crucial decisions that were constitutionally outside his power; he authorized at once the additional military aid for the ROK army sought earlier by Muccio, directed MacArthur to task the Far East Air Force to provide overhead cover for the evacuation of American nationals from Korea, and the US 7th Fleet to cruise between Formosa and mainland China in order to discourage any attempt by Mao to invade Chiang Kai-shek's unsteady stronghold (and equally to deter Chiang from attempting to invade China proper). All this was done without consulting the Joint Chiefs of Staff and before formal approval had been obtained from Congress. . . .

Acheson had long been one of the strongest advocates of 'containment': a strategy based on the principle that if any part of the globe appeared to be coveted by the Soviet Union or one of its surrogates, United States intervention was justified, on the pretext that democracy had to be offered as the only viable alternative to communism. He held no brief for wresting North Korea back from Kim Il-sung, but equally the invasion of South Korea was to him the spearpoint of world aggression by the communists; if the two Koreas were reunited on communist terms it would trigger the next stage, which would rapidly see the end of democracy in Japan, the Philippines and the rest of south-east Asia. He believed that it would be regarded as a sign of fatal weakness if the United States recoiled from this, the first test of its resolve in the Far East. As a convinced 'European' he believed that in the event of war, the great battleground would inevitably be in western Europe or the Middle East, but that events in the Far East should not be permitted to get out of hand and affect what he regarded as the final confrontation on the north German plain. Whilst the Koreans, north and south, always thought of the conflict as a civil war between two sides seeking unification, albeit on their own terms, Acheson saw no purpose in reunification under either Rhee or Kim Il-sung. His belief in 'containment' was shared by Truman, who compared South Korea's struggle with that enacted in Greece as the Greek royalist army fought for democracy against the Greek communists after

1945, under the military tutelage of the American General Van Fleet. As long as the ROK army could offer resistance the containment could be indirect; but as the ROK army disintegrated, Truman realized that direct American, then United Nations, assistance was urgently required. . . .

UN Resolutions

The UN Security Council met in New York on the afternoon of 25 June to consider a draft resolution hurriedly tabled by the United States calling for collective action against 'unprovoked aggression' and an immediate cease-fire by the North Koreans. Disagreement broke out among the delegates; the United Kingdom, France, Egypt, Norway and India argued that this appeared to be a civil war, that as there had been breaches of the peace for many months on both sides of the 38th parallel it could hardly be described as 'unprovoked', and that both sides should be ordered to stop fighting. This amendment, however, was rejected by Trygve Lie and Charles Noyes, the American delegate, and the original resolution passed by a 9-0 vote; the Yugoslav delegate abstained. Far more significantly, the Soviet representative Jakob Malik was not present; he was under orders from Moscow to boycott the Security Council in view of its continuing refusal—and that of the full Assembly—to admit communist China in place of Chiang's Formosan nationalist government. Had he been in attendance Malik would certainly have availed himself of the veto and the resolution would have been stillborn. In that case the Americans would have been obliged either to go to South Korea's aid alone or leave Rhee to his fate.

On the evening of 25 June, following the passing of the Security Council resolution, a top-level conference took place in Washington at Blair House. It was chaired by Truman, recalled to the capital from Missouri. Present were Acheson, Defense Secretary [Louis] Johnson, and the Joint Chiefs of Staff [JCS] under General [Omar] Bradley, who initially advised against the committal of American ground troops; in this he was motivated by the parlous state of the army following drastic rundown post-1945 and the certainty of overstretch if resources now earmarked for western Europe were sent to the Far East. The Chief of Air Staff, Lieutenant-General Hoyt Vandenberg, believed that air power alone could quench the invasion; he favoured attacking Soviet Far East air bases with nuclear weapons, and Truman at once issued instructions for plans to be drawn up for this drastic scenario. He called on the JCS to make an appreciation as to where the USSR might strike next. There was immediate consensus that Moscow's hand lay close behind the North Korean invasion.

Truman now agonized over the appalling implications of committing American armed forces, and especially launching a nuclear strike against the Russians. 'In the final analysis,' he wrote later, 'I did this for the United Nations. I believed in the League of Nations. It failed. Lots of people thought it failed because we [the US] weren't in it to back it up. OK, now we started the UN. It was our idea, and in its first big test we just couldn't let them down. If a collective system under the UN *can* work, it must be *made* to work, and now is the time to call their bluff.' The President's authority was given for the movement of elements of the 7th Fleet to mask Formosa from the mainland, and for the US Air Force to provide air cover for the evacuation of American and other civilians from South Korea, provided that this was limited to sea and air space south of the 38th parallel.

However, a group of experts went from Tokyo to Korea at once, headed by Brigadier-General [John H.] Church, to assess the situation on the ground. Church recommended the immediate insertion of American ground combat forces. UNCOK [UN Commission on Korea], still recommending negotiation as the proper solution, was ignored when the Security Council met again on 27 June to consider another US resolution calling on UN member states 'to furnish such assistance to the Republic of Korea as may be necessary to repel the armed attack and to restore international peace and security in the area'. The resolution was adopted, to visible relief in Washington; Britain, France, nationalist China, Cuba, Ecuador, Norway and the United States were in favour, whilst Yugoslavia was against and India and Egypt abstained. The Soviet Union was once more absent.

Tension mounted in America, haunted by a spectre of general war; even Acheson, at a meeting of the National Security Council on 28 June, advised that a very serious situation could arise if rapid success against North Korea was not achieved. The CIA was alerted to report the slightest hint that the USSR was preparing for global war, and the hawkish chiefs of the young United States Air Force, [Chief Hoyt S.] Vandenberg and Air Force Secretary [Thomas E.] Finletter, pressed for authority to attack North Korea at once. It was not forthcoming, for Truman feared

rapid global escalation if the USAF's strategic bombers on Oki-
nawa and the Marianas Islands were given their head. Aircraft of
the USAF based in Japan were, however, already ranging widely
across North Korea on MacArthur's orders, attacking road and
rail systems as well as industrial targets and any troop concentrations they found. A fresh directive had to be drafted for Mac-
Arthur, not yet appointed United Nations commander but already acting *de facto* as such. The National Security Council met
in Washington on 29 June to do this. . . .

U.S. President Truman Goes to War

Truman, a provincial with little knowledge of the greater world
who had begun his working life as a draper's assistant and had no
pretensions to intellectual ability, possessed considerable moral
courage and resolution when hard decisions had to be made. He
backed his worldly-wise Secretary of State to the hilt as the crisis unfolded. Whilst the use of American ground forces was still
withheld, naval reinforcements were ordered and a carrier group
cruising in the Pacific was ordered to steam for Sasebo, the Japanese naval base used by 7th Fleet. Congress was directed to approve
increased aid to the Philippines as well as to French Indo-China;
the Chinese nationalists on Formosa were ordered to abstain from
offensive operations against the mainland.

The military situation in Korea went from bad to worse. On
29 June the JCS signalled MacArthur, supplementing previous
directives. He was told to limit ground force participation to
communications and service units but authorized to deploy combat troops to secure an emergency exit port in the Pusan-
Chinhae area. . . . MacArthur was also admonished that the deployment of naval and air forces in Korean operations did not
constitute permission to wage war against the Soviet Union.
Should Russian forces enter the operational area he was to adopt
a defensive posture and report back to Washington.

Truman went a step further by authorizing the wider use of
American ground forces in Korea on 30 June with the rousing
words: 'We have met the challenge of the pagan wolves.'. . .

MacArthur knew that even the immediate commitment of
American combat troops would come too late, and had privately
to admit to himself that under his regime as commander of the
occupying army in Japan, its infantry divisions had lapsed into a
state in which they were unfit for action; yet they were all that

could be brought to bear. He informed Washington of his intention to move a regimental combat team—the equivalent of a British brigade—to Korea at once. He knew that it would not be enough, envisaging it as the nucleus of a two-division build-up which would enable him to go over to the offensive as soon as possible and drive out the invader. Truman immediately cleared the sending of the combat team, but only to secure the line of communication. MacArthur fumed at the hesitation in Washington and demanded that the President be woken so he could give permission to commit the combat team to the battlefront—which Truman did.

After an early breakfast Truman conferred again with his advisers. The JCS changed their minds and recommended the despatch of more combat troops. MacArthur was authorized to commit all four of 8th Army's divisions if necessary, subject only to the need to safeguard the security of the Japanese islands. The President also gave authority for a naval blockade of North Korea. Gone was any talk of negotiating a peace, or of holding back until other UN members had agreed to contribute ground forces. America was going in as the free world's champion.

The Soviet Union Supported North Korea's Aggression

By Kathryn Weathersby

In this article Kathryn Weathersby, assistant professor of history at Florida State University (Tallahassee) and researcher of Soviet policy on Korea, disputes North Korea's historical claim that the Korean War began as a military provocation by South Korea. The recent release of Soviet archival materials suggests that the 1950 North Korean attack was a military offensive authorized by the Soviet Union after a year of pleas from North Korean leader Kim Il Sung to reunify Korea by force. The Soviets agreed to back the offensive only because they believed, based on intelligence and speeches by American policy makers, that the United States would not defend South Korea or become involved militarily in Asia. Also, the Soviets wanted control over South Korea as part of a regional security plan. They did not want Japan to regain control over the peninsula or use it as a staging ground for invasions into Soviet territory, as had happened in the past.

The new documents also reveal that although Stalin ordered Kim Il Sung to acquire China's consent before invading South Korea, China was not involved in planning the attack and was reluctant to enter the war to help North Korea. Finally, the documentation shows that Soviet support for North Korea was lukewarm at best and that the Soviets were mainly concerned with what would benefit their own country. These new insights about Soviet motivations help to explain Kim Il Sung's adoption of the juche *idea of self-reliance after the war, based on North Korea's understanding that it could not necessarily depend on the Soviets and other allies to ensure its survival.*

Kathryn Weathersby, "The Korean War Revisited," *The Wilson Quarterly*, vol. 23, Summer 1999, p. 91. Copyright © 1999 by Kathryn Weathersby. Reproduced by permission.

The end of the Cold War has not done much to reduce the long-simmering hostility between North and South Korea, but it has indirectly shed a great deal of light on the brutal war they fought nearly 50 years ago—and on the behavior of North Korea's leaders during the conflict-ridden years since.

As long as the Soviet Union existed, Moscow and its allies in the war effort, North Korea and China, maintained a united front of secrecy about the conflict, closely adhering to their early declarations about its causes and origins. Over the years, historians learned much about the South Korean–United Nations side of the war, but some of the most basic questions about the conflict remained unanswerable. Now, with the post–Cold War opening of important archives in the former Soviet Union and China, scholars are dramatically rewriting the history of the war.

Civil War or Soviet-Sponsored Aggression?

When Soviet-made tanks led tens of thousands of North Korean soldiers across the 38th parallel early on the morning of Sunday, June 25, 1950, most Western observers swiftly concluded that this was not a border skirmish like those of the previous year but a full-scale offensive. North Korean president Kim Il Sung and his Soviet patrons, however, insisted that the attack was a defensive response to a military provocation by the South—the position North Korea and China maintain to this day. In Washington and elsewhere in the noncommunist world, it also seemed clear that the attack had been planned in Moscow and that it signified a new Soviet aggressiveness. If the West did not resist, there would be similar attacks elsewhere along the Soviet Union's vast periphery, in Europe and perhaps the Near East. Within days of the attack, the United States and 15 other members of the United Nations committed their armed forces to a defense of South Korea, thus escalating the fraternal conflict on the peninsula into a major international war.

The Truman administration, assuming that [Chinese leader] Mao Zedong's new communist regime in Beijing had helped plan the attack, worried that it might also launch an invasion of Chiang Kai-shek's Nationalist stronghold on Taiwan. The U.S. Seventh Fleet was quickly dispatched to the Taiwan Straits, not only committing the United States indefinitely to the defense of Taiwan but helping to goad Beijing four months later into sending its ill-equipped army to rescue North Korea from certain defeat.

Historians began the first substantial revision of the war's history two decades after the 1953 armistice that ended it. Prompted by the Vietnam War to reassess the U.S. role in the world, they began to question many of the assumptions the Truman administration made about the conflict in Korea. The most influential revisionist, Bruce Cumings, argued in his two-volume *Origins of the Korean War* (1981, 1990) that this war, like the one in Vietnam, had begun primarily as a civil conflict, with only marginal involvement by the Soviets. To the extent any great power had influence in [North Korean capital] Pyongyang, Cumings concluded, the Chinese played a more important role. He also suggested that the South Koreans themselves might have provoked the North Korean attack, possibly in collusion with the Chinese Nationalists on Taiwan, in order to ensure U.S. support for their tottering regime. The revisionists viewed America's intervention in Korea, like its involvement in Vietnam, as unjustified and counterproductive.

By the 1980s, most scholars writing on the war also agreed that by pursuing the retreating North Korean army across the 38th parallel after General Douglas MacArthur's stunning landing at Inchon on September 15, 1950, the Americans had needlessly provoked the Chinese into intervening. And in her careful examination of the armistice negotiations, *A Substitute for Victory* (1990), British historian Rosemary Foot also held the United States responsible for prolonging the war by dragging out the Panmunjom talks for two years—an argument many historians found persuasive.

Soviet Archives Show Clear Soviet Offensive

The end of the Cold War has inaugurated a new round of historical inquiry and rethinking. The first major rupture in the wall of secrecy maintained by the communist side came in 1993. Two staff members of the post-Stalin era archive of the Central Committee of the Communist Party of the Soviet Union presented a paper at a Wilson Center conference in Moscow that cited a 1966 survey of Soviet and Chinese involvement in the Korean War prepared by the Soviet Foreign Ministry. Intended as background information for a small group of Soviet officials engaged in negotiations with Beijing and Hanoi during the Vietnam War, this highly classified report baldly contradicted the Soviet position on the Korean War. It explained in straightforward language that Kim Il Sung had repeatedly pressed Joseph Stalin for permission to reunify Korea by military means long before the invasion was launched. Only in early 1950, after nearly a year of entreaties, did the Soviet leader finally approve the plan and send the necessary arms, equipment, and military advisers to North Korea. That May, Kim traveled to Beijing to secure the support of Mao Zedong.

Historians began getting a clearer picture of these high-level dealings in 1992 and '93 with Russia's gradual release of other files. They reveal North Korea's profound dependence on Soviet assistance in the prewar years and the extraordinary degree of control Moscow maintained over its Korean client state. But key questions remained unanswered. Then, in July 1994, Russian president Boris Yeltsin, hoping to improve relations with South Korea, presented President Kim Young Sam with a collection of documents from the Presidential Archive, the still-closed Kremlin repository that holds the Soviet records of greatest sensitivity. Early in 1995, the Wilson Center's Cold War International History Project obtained a larger set of documents from the same archive, many of which I translated and analyzed in the Bulletin of the Cold War International History Project (Spring 1995 and Winter 1995).

The new evidence shows that contemporary observers of the war were much closer to the mark about what was going on than the revisionists were—but that their understanding was still flawed in several important respects. There is now no doubt that the original North Korean attack was a conventional military offensive planned and prepared by the Soviet Union. While Kim Il Sung had pressed Stalin for permission to reunify Korea by force, North Korea was not at that time capable of mounting such a campaign on its own.

Soviet Aggression Was Not a Test of the West

Stalin did not, however, initiate the invasion of South Korea as a test of Western resolve. Indeed, he gave Kim the green light only because he believed the United States would not intervene—something the British spy Donald MacLean had surely communicated to Stalin well before Secretary of State Dean Acheson's infamous speech of January 12, 1950, indicating that the United States would not guarantee South Korea's security. Stalin was so determined to avoid a military confrontation with the United States, fearing that the Soviet Union was not yet strong enough to win, that he would not have approved the invasion if Washington had made it clear that it would respond with force. In May 1950, the Soviet dictator explained to Mao Zedong that it was now possible to agree to the North Koreans' proposal "in light of the changed international situation."

The archival record does not explicitly reveal what changes Stalin was referring to, but it appears that his decision was part of a new approach to security in the Far East adopted at the end of 1949. Moscow decided to abandon cooperation with the Americans and pursue its interests through more aggressive means. Stalin assumed that Japan would eventually rearm and threaten the Soviet Far East. He wanted to gain control over southern Korea in order to ensure that Japan could not again use the peninsula as a staging ground, as it had for invasions of the Soviet Union after the Bolshevik Revolution of 1917 and of China in the 1930s. The fateful decision to attack South Korea was thus part of a regional rather than global strategy, designed to take advantage of the new American policy of avoiding military engagements on the Asian mainland.

While the archives show that Stalin did not conceive of the Korea campaign as a means of gauging the West's will to fight, as many in the West assumed at the time, it was a test nevertheless. Since the Soviet leader based his foreign policy everywhere on calculations of American strength and commitment, he could not have failed to take into account a U.S. failure to come to South Korea's defense.

China Not Part of the Attack

The various archives also show that the Truman administration was wrong to assume Chinese complicity in Stalin's decision to attack. The Russian papers, combined with documents from Beijing analyzed by the Chinese historian Chen Jian in *China's Road to the Korean War* (1994), reveal that while Stalin ordered Kim Il Sung to travel to Beijing in May 1950 to secure Mao Zedong's consent to the invasion, the visit was largely a formality. Having just concluded an alliance with the Soviet Union to secure essential aid for his new state, Mao was in no position to contest Stalin's decision. He would have preferred to defeat his Nationalist foes on Taiwan before risking action on the Korean peninsula. Later, in October 1950, when Stalin pressured the Chinese to enter the war to save North Korea from imminent defeat, Mao complained bitterly about having been excluded from the initial planning for the operation.

Washington's mistaken assumption about China's role in the attack promoted the very action the United States wished to avoid. By challenging Chinese sovereignty over Taiwan, Washington led the leadership in Beijing eventually to conclude that despite the immense hardships an intervention in Korea would entail, Chinese pride and national security required standing up to American "arrogance." The sudden injection of more than two million Chinese "volunteers" in the autumn of 1950 saved the day for Kim Il Sung's communist state. The UN forces were quickly driven south before they were able to regroup and counterattack. By the summer of 1951, the two sides had reached a stalemate that left them arrayed roughly along the 38th parallel.

North Korea's Distrust of the Soviet Union

One more important twist has emerged from the archives. Until the Russian documents were released, it was not known just how far Stalin was willing to go to avoid a direct military confrontation with the United States. The documents reveal that at the end of two weeks of hard bargaining in early October 1950, when it appeared that Beijing would not send its troops to North Korea to stop MacArthur's rapid advance, the Soviet leader ordered the North Korean army to evacuate the country and withdraw to Chinese and Soviet territory. He was not going to pit Soviet forces against the Americans.

Stalin rescinded his order as soon as he received word of Mao's final decision to intervene, but its impact on Kim Il Sung could not be so easily erased. Nor could the effects of Stalin's insistence that North Korea continue to meet its export quotas for minerals and other items to the Soviet Union during the war. The subsequent evolution of Kim Il Sung's aggressively xenophobic worldview was also shaped by Stalin's approach to the armistice negotiations. Once the war became a stalemate, in 1951, the Soviet leader instructed the Chinese and North Koreans to take a hard line in

the negotiations, explaining that the United States had a greater
need to reach a negotiated settlement. As long as the danger of an
American advance toward the Soviet border could be avoided,
Stalin apparently reasoned, the advantages the war brought the Soviet Union—keeping the American military bogged down in Asia
while yielding valuable intelligence about its capabilities—out-
weighed the disadvantages. Even though the North Koreans, en-
during heavy bombing by the U.S. Air Force, were willing in early
1952 to conclude an armistice, and the Chinese were likewise inclined by that fall, Stalin continued until his death in March 1953
to insist on a hard line. As he explained to Chinese foreign minister Zhou Enlai, "the North Koreans have lost nothing, except for
casualties that they suffered during the war."

The Russian archives show that President Dwight D. Eisen-
hower's May 1953 threats to use nuclear weapons in Korea cannot be credited with bringing the communists to a negotiated
settlement. Immediately after Stalin's death, his uncertain successors, concerned about the precariousness of their own rule (before [Soviet leader] Nikita Khrushchev's emergence), decided to
bring the war to an end. When the armistice was signed, on July
27, 1953, more than 33,000 Americans and millions of North
and South Korean soldiers and civilians lay dead.

Since the end of the Korean War, North Korea's leaders have
made much of the devastation their country suffered at the hands
of the South Korean and American "aggressors." But North Korea also suffered at the hands of its closest allies. Indeed, the ma-
lign effects of Stalin's policies toward Pyongyang must be rated
an important legacy of the war. The new information from the
former Soviet archives suggests that Moscow's cynical, high-
handed treatment taught Kim Il Sung and his associates that they
could not count on their fraternal allies to ensure their survival.
Even as Pyongyang grew heavily dependent on Soviet economic
subsidies over the next several decades, it developed a progressively more extreme philosophy of self-reliance, or *juche*. When
the Soviet Union finally collapsed, North Korea was left not only
without an important source of support but without an understanding of normal relations with other states—or even an understanding that such relations can exist. That impossible legacy
is an important reason why North Korea, nearly 50 years after the
end of the Korean War, retains a prominent place near the top of
American security concerns.

The United States Enters the Korean War

By Harry S. Truman

U.S. president Harry S. Truman, in a radio speech given on July 19, 1950, excerpted below, explains to the American people the events leading up to North Korea's invasion of South Korea and the reasons the United States is entering the war. In the address, Truman emphasizes that the United States is entering the war only as part of an effort by the United Nations Security Council to stop the "raw aggression" of the Communists toward South Korea. Fifty-two of the fifty-nine countries that were members of the United Nations supported the decision by the Security Council to repel the attack and restore peace in Korea. The president explains that a unified command has been established and that General Douglas MacArthur has been named the commander of this unified force.

At noon today, I sent a message to the Congress about the situation in Korea. I want to talk to you tonight about that situation, and about what it means to the security of the United States, and to our hopes for world peace.

Korea is a small country, thousands of miles away, but what is happening there is important to every American.

On Sunday, June 25th [1950], communist forces attacked the Republic of Korea.

This attack has made it clear, beyond all doubt, that the international communist movement is willing to use armed invasion to conquer independent nations. An act of aggression such as this creates a very real danger to the security of all free nations.

Harry S. Truman, radio address to the nation, July 19, 1950.

This challenge has been presented squarely. We must meet it squarely.

It is important for all of us to understand the essential facts as to how the situation in Korea came about.

Before and during World War II, Korea was subject to Japanese rule. When the fighting stopped, it was agreed that troops of the Soviet Union would accept the surrender of the Japanese soldiers in the northern part of Korea, and that American forces would accept the surrender of the Japanese in the southern part. For this purpose, the 38th parallel was used as the dividing line.

Later, the United Nations sought to establish Korea as a free and independent nation. A Commission was sent out to supervise a free election in the whole of Korea. However, this election was held only in the southern part of the country, because the Soviet Union refused to permit an election for this purpose to be held in the northern part. Indeed, Soviet authorities even refused to permit the United Nations Commission to visit northern Korea.

Nevertheless, the United Nations decided to go ahead where it could. In August 1948, the Republic of Korea was established as a free and independent nation in that part of Korea south of the 38th parallel.

In December 1948, the Soviet Union stated that it had withdrawn its troops from northern Korea and that a legal government had been established there. However, the communist authorities never have permitted United Nations observers to visit northern Korea to see what was going on behind that part of the iron curtain.

It was from that area, where the communist authorities have been unwilling to let the outside world see what was going on, that the attack was launched against the Republic of Korea on June 25th [1950]. That attack came without provocation and without warning. It was an act of raw aggression, without a shadow of justification.

I repeat—it was an act of raw aggression.

The communist invasion was launched in great force, with planes, tanks, and artillery. The size of the attack, and the speed with which it was followed up, make it perfectly plain that it had been plotted long in advance.

As soon as word of the attack was received, Secretary of State [Dean] Acheson called me at Independence, Missouri, and informed me that, with my approval, he would ask for an immediate meeting of the United Nations Security Council. The Security Council met just twenty-four hours after the communist invasion began.

The Security Council Calls for a Stop to North Korean Aggression

One of the main reasons the Security Council was set up was to act in such cases as this—to stop outbreaks of aggression in a hurry before they develop into general conflicts. In this case, the Council passed a resolution which called for the invaders of Korea to stop fighting, and to withdraw. The Council called on all members to help carry out this resolution. The communist invaders ignored the action of the Security Council and kept right on with their attack.

The Security Council then met again. It recommended that members of the United Nations help the Republic of Korea repel the attack, and help restore peace and security to the area.

Fifty-two of the fifty-nine countries which are members of the United Nations have given their support to the action taken by the Security Council to restore peace in Korea.

These actions by the United Nations and its members are of great importance. The free nations have now made it clear that lawless aggression will be met with force. The free nations have learned the fateful lesson of the 1930s. That lesson is that aggression must be met firmly. Appeasement leads only to further aggression and ultimately to war.

The principal effort to help the Koreans preserve their independence, and to help the United Nations restore peace, has been made by the United States. We have sent land, naval, and air forces to assist in these operations. We have done this because we know that what is at stake here is nothing less than our own national security and the peace of the world.

So far, two other nations—Australia and Great Britain—have sent planes to Korea; and six other nations—Australia, Canada, France, Great Britain, the Netherlands, and New Zealand—have made naval forces available.

Under the flag of the United Nations, a unified command has been established for all forces of the members of the United Nations fighting in Korea. General Douglas MacArthur is the commander of this combined force.

The prompt action of the United Nations to put down lawless aggression, and the prompt response to this action of peoples all over the world, will stand as a landmark in mankind's long search for a rule of law among nations.

The Soviet Union Has Boycotted the Meetings of the United Nations Security Council

Only a few countries have failed to endorse the efforts of the United Nations to stop the fighting in Korea. The most important of these is the Soviet Union. The Soviet Union has boycotted the meetings of the United Nations Security Council, and it has refused to support the actions of the United Nations with respect to Korea.

The United Nations requested the Soviet Government, two days after the fighting started, to use its influence with the North Koreans to have them withdraw. The Soviet Government refused.

The Soviet Government has said many times that it wants peace in the world, but its attitude toward this act of aggression against the Republic of Korea is in direct contradiction of its statements.

The United States Resolves to Restore Peace

For our part, we shall continue to support the United Nations to restore peace.

We know that it will take a hard, tough fight to halt the invasion, and to drive the communists back. The invaders have been provided with enough equipment and supplies for a long campaign. They overwhelmed the lightly armed defense forces of the Korean Republic in the first few days and drove southward.

Now, however, the Korean defenders have reorganized, and an increasing number of American troops have joined them. Our forces have fought a skillful, rearguard delaying action, pending the arrival of reinforcements. Some of these reinforcements are now arriving; others are on the way from the United States. . . .

[Reports] show that our armed forces are acting with close teamwork and efficiency to meet the problems facing us in Korea.

These reports are reassuring but they also show that the job ahead of us in Korea is long and difficult.

Furthermore, the fact that communist forces have invaded Korea is a warning that there may be similar acts of aggression in other parts of the world. The free nations must be on their guard, more than ever before, against this kind of sneak attack.

It is obvious that we must increase our military strength and preparedness immediately. There are three things we need to do.

First, we need to send more men, equipment, and supplies to General MacArthur.

Second, in view of the world situation, we need to build up our own Army, Navy, and Air Force over and above what is needed in Korea.

Third, we need to speed up our work with other countries in strengthening our common defenses.

To help meet these needs, I have already authorized increases in the size of our armed forces. These increases will come in part from volunteers, in part from Selective Service, and in part from the National Guard and the Reserves.

I have also ordered that military supplies and equipment be obtained at a faster rate.

The necessary increases in the size of our armed forces, and the additional equipment they must have, will cost about ten billion dollars, and I am asking the Congress to appropriate the amount required.

These funds will be used to train men and equip them with tanks, planes, guns, and ships, in order to build the strength we need to help assure peace in the world.

When we have worked out with other free countries an increased program for our common defense, I shall recommend to the Congress that additional funds be provided for this purpose. This is of great importance. The free nations face a world-wide threat. It must be met with a world-wide defense. The United States and the other free nations can multiply their strength by joining with one another in a common effort to provide this defense. This is our best hope for peace. . . .

We have the resources to meet our needs. Far more important, the American people are united in their belief in democratic freedom. We are united in detesting communist slavery.

We know that the cost of freedom is high. But we are determined to preserve our freedom—no matter what the cost.

I know that our people are willing to do their part to support our soldiers and sailors and airmen who are fighting in Korea. I know that our fighting men can count on each and every one of you.

Our country stands before the world as an example of how free men, under God, can build a community of neighbors, working together for the good of all.

That is the goal we seek not only for ourselves, but for all people. We believe that freedom and peace are essential if men are to live as our Creator intended us to live. It is this faith that has guided us in the past, and it is this faith that will fortify us in the stern days ahead.

The Effects of the Korean War on the Korean People

By Don Oberdorfer

Don Oberdorfer is a journalist and adjunct professor at the School of Advanced International Studies at Johns Hopkins University in Washington, D.C. This excerpt from his book on the Korean War describes the aftermath of the war for North and South Korea. Although the Korean War was considered a "limited" war because neither the Soviet Union nor the United States used nuclear weapons, the war devastated the Korean peninsula, in both the North and the South, just when it had been beginning to recover from four decades of Japanese occupation. About one-tenth of the population was killed, another 5 million became refugees, and property losses were estimated in the billions of dollars.

Perhaps as serious as the casualties and damage to property, however, was the hostility that developed along ideological lines between North and South Korea, separating not only politicians, but also family members and ordinary citizens. At the end of the war, this ideological separation increased. The leader of North Korea, Kim Il Sung, purged all opposition, created a cult of personality around himself, and learned to manipulate his Communist supporters—the Soviet Union and China. In the South, the Syngman Rhee regime became increasingly dictatorial until he was overthrown in 1960 by a student-led rebellion. Both countries talked about reunification after the war, but little progress was made in that direction.

The Korean conflict was considered the prototype of a limited war in that none of the big powers used the nuclear weapons available to them, and the United States refrained from attacking Soviet or Chinese territory. On the peninsula, however, the war was savage in its destructiveness. Al-

Don Oberdorfer, *The Two Koreas: A Contemporary History*. New York: Basic Books, 2001. Copyright © 1997 by Don Oberdorfer. Reproduced by permission.

though the figures are uncertain, a widely accepted estimate is that 900,000 Chinese and 520,000 North Korean soldiers were killed or wounded, as were about 400,000 UN Command troops, nearly two-thirds of them South Koreans. U.S. casualties were 36,000 dead.

The War's Devastation of Korea

In Korea the war devastated both halves of a country that had only just begun to recover from four decades of Japanese occupation and the sudden shock of division. Around 3 million people, roughly a tenth of the entire population of both sides at the time, were killed, wounded, or missing as a result of the war. Another 5 million became refugees. South Korea's property losses were put at $2 billion, the equivalent of its gross national product for 1949; North Korean losses were estimated at only slightly less.

When the fighting finally stopped in July 1953, the front line

Refugees prepare to evacuate North Korea in December 1950. The Korean War resulted in more than 5 million refugees.

was an irregular tangent slanting across the thirty-eighth parallel very close to where it had all begun. In keeping with the armistice agreement, the forces on each side pulled back two thousand meters from the cease-fire lines to create the demilitarized zone. Although both sides were exhausted by three years of combat, there were fears—which have never died—that the battle might be resumed at any moment.

One of the most important consequences of the war was the hardening of ideological and political lines between North and South. The antipathy that had developed between the opposing regimes was deepened into a blood feud among family members, extending from political leaders to the bulk of the ordinary people who had suffered at the hands of the other side. The thirteen-hundred-year-old unity of the Korean people was shattered.

After the War: Dictators and Hostility

In the aftermath of the war, the Rhee regime in the South became increasingly dictatorial and corrupt until it was forced out of office in 1960 by a student-led revolt. After a year the moderate successor government was ousted by a military junta headed by Major General Park Chung Hee, a Japanese-trained officer who had flirted with communism immediately after the Japanese surrender. Park's background created concern in Washington and initial hope in Pyongyang. Early on, Kim Il Sung dispatched a trusted aide to the South to make secret contact with Park. But instead of exploring a deal, Park had the emissary arrested and executed.

In the North, Kim Il Sung systematically purged his political opponents, creating a highly centralized system that accorded him unlimited power and generated a formidable cult of personality. As the great communist divide between the Soviet Union and China emerged in the mid-1950s, Kim, though profoundly disturbed by it, learned to play off his communist sponsors against each other to his own advantage. In July 1961 he went to Moscow and persuaded Nikita Khrushchev, who was seeking to recruit him as an ally against China, to sign a treaty of "friendship, cooperation and mutual assistance," pledging to come to Pyongyang's aid in case of a new war on the divided peninsula. This done, Kim proceeded to Beijing, where he presented Chinese leaders with his Moscow treaty and asked them to match it, which they did by signing their own nearly identical accord.

While both North and South Korea gave lip service to eventual reunification, there was little but hostility between them in the 1950s and 1960s. In the most notable incident, in January 1968, a thirty-one-man North Korean commando team attempted to assassinate the South Korean president. The team penetrated to within a thousand yards of the Blue House, the South Korean equivalent of the White House, before being repulsed by police and security forces. The prospects for any sort of reconciliation on the divided peninsula appeared slim indeed.

The International Legacy of the Korean War

By Stanley Sandler

In this book excerpt, Stanley Sandler, a military historian with the U.S. Army Special Operations Command, provides an analysis of the Korean War from a geopolitical perspective. The war was a conventional conflict, meaning it did not involve nuclear weapons; indeed, the war resembled World War I with its stalemated trench lines. In addition, nobody won the war, for gains and losses were evenly distributed between the North and the South. Both sides fought for total victory and unification of the peninsula, but in the end neither side won much territory. The human cost of the war was equally shared, and both North and South Korea wound up with brutal dictators.

After the war, the United States adopted a Cold War strategy that threatened massive retaliation in the form of aerial nuclear strikes against the Soviet Union in the event of another war. The United States also provided aid to South Korea, enabling it to develop an impressive modern economy and eventually become a democracy.

In North Korea, Kim Il Sung purged all resistance to his Communist regime, created a militarized cult around himself, and at first made economic strides. Ultimately, however, the North was unable to achieve the same economic success as the South. Sandler concludes that the war was not fought in vain, because it eventually provided South Koreans with a better life and stopped the spread of communism in Asia. In addition, the outcomes of the war have made an invasion of the South far more difficult for North Korea than it was in 1950.

The Korean War itself was primarily a conventional conflict. Nuclear weapons, which featured so dominantly in those late 1940s' "War of Tomorrow" scenarios, both of-

Stanley Sandler, *The Korean War: No Victors, No Vanquished*. Lexington: The University Press of Kentucky, 1999. Copyright © 1999 by Stanley Sandler. Reproduced by permission.

ficial and popular, were, of course, not employed. Few, if any, "push-button" weapons were deployed. In fact, the overwhelming bulk of the weapons employed in Korea were not only conventional on both sides, but most were left-overs from the Second World War. . . .

This war did not just look back to the Second World War. By the summer of 1951 the fighting had hardened into a stalemate with trench lines, night raids, heavy bombardments and limited offensives that won limited terrain. It all was in many ways reminiscent of the Western Front of the First World War. . . .

No Gains, Similar Losses

Few wars in modern history have concluded with such an even distribution of gains and losses as the Korean War. The Republic of [South] Korea [ROK] and the UN side could take satisfaction in having driven the invader from most of the territory of the ROK while the Communists could rejoice that the UNC [UN coalition] forces had been almost completely expelled from the DPRK [Democratic People's Republic of (North) Korea]. The armistice line itself pushed north into the former DPRK in the east, but down into previously ROK territory in the west. Both sides had initially fought for total victory and the actual destruction of their enemy's government; both sides by 1951 had reluctantly come to accept the military fact that total victory would of necessity involve a considerably greater war than either the Chinese or the UN coalition were willing to fight. Significantly, both the governments of the ROK and the DPRK held out the longest for complete victory—and unification of Korea. And both were overruled by their more powerful allies.

The symmetry of both sides in the Korean War holds when it comes to the human cost of the conflict. South Korea's losses of something like one million dead were probably matched by the civilian and military deaths suffered by the North, both on the battlefield and from unrelenting UNC aerial bombardment. The North's figures have remained just an estimate to everyone dealing with the subject outside the archives of Pyongyang itself; the twentieth-century Hermit Kingdom was not about to give out accurate statistics on any matter. The Chinese suffered the most battle and disease deaths, although the ground and air war had halted at China's borders. The war affected the homeland of both China and the USA primarily through higher taxes and the casualty lists.

A major consequence of the Korean War was an increased militarization of both Communist and anti-Communist global camps. By the end of that war much of the world was more divided between the two super-powers than ever before and was considerably more of an armed camp than in June 1950. Large numbers of US troops were dispatched to Europe at the same time that the US forces in Korea were also being built up. In 1950 81,000 troops and one infantry division were stationed in Western Europe and were mostly concerned with occupation duties in Germany. But by the middle 1950s the US military presence there had increased to six divisions and 260,000 men oriented to the "defence of the West", somewhat more than the 238,600 soldiers in Korea. . . .

Later Ramifications of the War

For the first two decades after the armistice it could have been argued that the symmetry of the war extended to both post-war Koreas. Both were dictatorships. The ROK was admittedly more disorderly, with some glimmerings of hope for political freedom. But it was still ruled by a succession of ROK Army generals who employed varying degrees of brutality in putting down pro-democracy demonstrations.

In the meantime, the supposedly monolithic Sino-Soviet axis fissured, and the two great powers eventually came briefly to blows along their border. By contrast, relations between the PRC [People's Republic of China] and the USA, after President Richard Nixon's opening to China, became almost cordial at times. After the decade of the 1960s, the Soviet Union began its long, slow decline towards national collapse, although few of the specialists on the USSR predicted the denouement that today has about it such an air of inevitability.

Through these years the peace held, and the great fear of the 1950s, nuclear Armageddon, never came. Nuclear weapons were never used after the Second World War. In fact nuclear war came closest during the Cuban Missile Crisis of 1962, well after the Korean War. . . .

In line with its global, near-apocalyptic strategic vision of the Cold War, the United States opted for a strategy that came to be known as "massive retaliation", that is, aerial nuclear bombardment of the Soviet Union in case of war. The mere threat of such a response by the United States was deemed sufficient to keep the Communists at bay. The frustrations of the Korean War were considered a "lesson" for future confrontations with the Communists. At the end of the war, Secretary of the US Air Force, Thomas K. Finletter, asserted that "Korea was a unique, never-to-be-repeated diversion from the true course of strategic air power". Strategic air power would keep the peace, and if need be, win the next war. Consideration of anything less than a major confrontation with the Soviet Union was given short shrift. Later, the Kennedy administration's reaction to this nuclear emphasis was to fight "global Communism" and its "wars of national liberation" by means of counter-insurgency. Such a course would supposedly avoid a Korean-type major Asian land war. To the contrary, fashionable counter-insurgency doctrines were a major reason for the US involvement in a second major war on the Asian mainland, this time in Vietnam. Only with the Gulf War of 1991 would the United States, again under UN auspices, fight another conventional, non-nuclear war to victory.

Differing Paths for North and South Korea

The sustained economic expansion of the Western industrialized nations was joined by Japan and the so-called "Asian Tigers" of Singapore, Taiwan, Hong Kong—and The Republic of Korea. By the mid-1960s the ROK was making impressive economic strides and within another decade its booming automobile manufacturing industry would be competing with the Japanese within the United States, a development that would have seemed flatly impossible to any observer of the 1950s. Further, South Korea became a major trading partner with the People's Republic of China and the Soviet Union/Russia. Admittedly, this development in the ROK was aided immensely by large amounts of US economic aid, but the DPRK had also received substantial assistance from the Soviet Union and China.

Political progress took a much longer time in coming, as the ROK government massacre of demonstrators in Kwangju of 1980 showed. But eventually military rule was overthrown, and the ROK emerged into a reasonably free and democratic regime. In fact, the opposition leader, a veteran of South Korea's jails, Kim Dae Jong, was freely elected to the premiership in 1997, with the belated blessings of the former military rulers who had put him there in the first place.

North Korea did not replicate the prosperity and eventual democracy of the ROK. In the immediate post-war years Kim Il Sung purged any potential rivals. Yi Sung Yop, former Minister of Justice, who had engaged in secret talks with ROK leftists, was condemned in 1953 as a "state enemy who colluded with the American imperialists", and was shot. Pak Tu Bong, never having recovered his prestige and power after his disastrous assurances that the exploited masses of South Korea would rise and welcome their liberators from the North, was executed in December 1955. Kim Tu Bong had remained a member of the North Korean Politburo until 1956. But with Kim Il Sung's purge of the Yenan faction in 1957, Kim Tu Bong lost all of his official positions, was expelled from the Korean Workers' Party and was reported to have expired several years later while toiling as a labourer on an agricultural co-operative near Pyongyang. Once again, the revolution had "devoured its own".

For a time after the Korean War the DPRK was one Communist state which "progressive" analysts could point to as having perhaps greater economic development, if not a higher individual standard of living, than its non-Communist counterpart. This progress was undoubtedly brought about more by that nation's hydro-electric complex and its disciplined workers than by the wonders of *juche* ("self-reliance"), Kim Il Sung's mantra for every citizen. Kim ("The Great Leader") himself was deified to an extent that would have made even Josef Stalin envious. According to his publicists/panegyrists, the very trees would bow low as Kim's aircraft passed over the hills. North Korea was officially proclaimed a "paradise" in which all selfishness, all religious feeling had vanished, as all citizens laboured selflessly to achieve *juche* under the perfect guidance of the perfect Kim. "Progressive" visitors to Pyongyang marvelled at the cleanliness, the lack of beggars, the civic dedication, the true devotion to the leader, much as their spiritual brethren had beamed over the joys of Moscow, Beijing, or Jonestown. However, a more perspicacious observer accurately described the Democratic People's Republic of Korea as "more of a cult than a country". . . .

But by the 1970s the DPRK was suffering the same sclerotic leadership and lack of economic development that was concurrently afflicting the Soviet Union. The DPRK leadership lashed out in sheer frustration with bombings, assassinations, and violent border incursions. ROK and US troops were killed in these incidents, and numerous tunnels running from North to South were uncovered, burrowed beneath the "Demilitarized Zone", that scar tissue of the long-past war.

Kim Il Sung died in 1994, a passing which must have surprised the more credulous DPRK citizens who had every reason to believe that "The Great Leader" should have lasted at least "to the end of the sun". But they could take some comfort in the presence of his mummy in its elaborate Lenin-like monument and in its ominous inscription, "The great leader comrade Kim Il Sung will always be with us".

Kim Il Sung was succeeded, at least officially, by his son, Kim Jong Il. Under "The Dear Leader" the economy of the DPRK neared collapse. The nation reached such dire straits that it was actually reduced to appealing for food aid from the traditional enemy, the Japanese, the "puppet" South Koreans, and even from the unspeakable Americans. Pyongyang blamed disastrous floods for food shortages that were causing near-starvation in the countryside. This excuse presented something of a problem for the more thoughtful, in that "The Dear Leader" supposedly could rebuke storms and cause them to cease, and weather in the southern half of the peninsula seemed generally unexceptionable. At any rate, the North Korean Army, something like the world's third largest, appeared well-nourished and possessed enough energy in early 1997 to dispatch a troop of commandos by submarine to the ROK where they proceeded to bludgeon to death three inoffensive South Korean civilians before they were tracked down and killed by security forces.

The DPRK in the late 1990s was the most militarized nation on earth, with a soldier-to-citizen ratio of one soldier for every civilian man, woman, or child. Numerically, North Korea had some 1,128,000 persons in its active forces and could call upon another 115,000 from its security forces and border guards. Its ground forces were divided into 26 infantry divisions, 14 armoured brigades and 23 separate motorized and mechanized infantry brigades. "Special Purpose" corps contained commando, reconnaissance, river crossing, amphibious and airborne units, and 22 separate light infantry battalions, some 100,000 troops that are to fight behind ROK lines. Perhaps even more ominously, since the 1960s the North had concentrated on 13 different strains of bacteria and toxins. On the other hand, most of the equipment of these forces had become obsolete and spare parts would soon run out in any future sustained combat.

The Korean War Was Not Fought in Vain

For all the DPRK militarism, any invasion of the ROK would face much greater obstacles than those in 1950, when Seoul was taken in three days. Highways could be more easily blocked and ROK forces hold substantially more territory north of the 38th Parallel than they did in June 1950. Most importantly, the North could no longer count on Soviet or Chinese sustenance, either in equipment or oil, for any invasion scheme. And US forces are on the peninsula in strength. As one US Marine commander noted of the North, "They remember Inchon" [referring to U.S. general MacArthur's landing of troops at the port of Inchon, which led to the retaking of Seoul from the North Korean invaders].

In the long-range view, the Korean War, for all of its destruction, waste and human cost, was not fought in vain. Whatever the failings of the Rhee regime and its immediate successors, South Korea was spared the worst of the Stalinist regimes and eventually emerged with something far better. Other Asian nations after June 1950 felt that they could count on some tangible US reaction at least to overt aggression. Aside from the collapse of the pro-West regimes of the Vietnam peninsula, the Asian "dominoes" did *not* fall.

Rather, it was the Soviet Union and its Potemkin Village empire that fell in 1991. The beginnings of this denouement, unimaginable in 1950, can be traced to President Harry Truman's decision in July that year, with the support of the United Nations, to dispatch troops to the defence of the Republic of Korea. Yet in that war itself there would be no victors and no vanquished.

THE HISTORY OF NATIONS

Chapter 4

The Uniquely Korean Communist Nation

Kim Il Sung Rebuilds and Consolidates Power

By Geoff Simons

*As the following book excerpt by freelance author Geoff Simons de-
scribes, North Korea faced enormous challenges after the Korean War.
North Korea suffered almost complete destruction during the war because
of the "scorched-earth" tactics used by the United States and other
United Nations countries. By the end of the war, every conceivable target
had been hit, the economy had collapsed, and much of the population
was living in caves.*

*Kim Il Sung, relying on large amounts of Soviet aid, announced his
"Three-Year Plan" for reconstruction and successfully rebuilt North Korea in a remarkably short time. He also consolidated his grip on power by
eliminating all his opponents and created an authoritarian "cult of personality" around himself. With U.S. troops stationed at the southern border, Kim Il Sung also focused on developing North Korea's military and
negotiating mutual defense treaties with China and the Soviet Union.
He continued to view the United States as his greatest threat and declared that North Korea would fight against U.S. imperialism. North
Korea attempted to garner broader international support against the
United States, but this effort failed. North Korea instead became increasingly isolated, as the Soviet Union slowly collapsed and tensions between
the United States and China eased.*

The post–Korean War chronology of North Korea was
largely shaped—as was that in the South—by the impact
of the war; but whereas the South had suffered heavy
damage for less than one year the North was relentlessly pounded
from both air and sea for most of a three-year period. In pro-

Geoff Simons, *Korea: The Search for Sovereignty*. New York: St. Martin's Press, 1995.
Copyright © 1995 by Geoff Simons. Reproduced by permission of Palgrave
Macmillan.

portionate terms the Democratic People's Republic of Korea (DPRK) was more comprehensively devastated than any country (including Germany and the Soviet Union) in the Second World War, and more than North Vietnam would be in the Vietnam War. [As Jon Halliday has stated,] [v]irtually 'every town and village was completely destroyed', bombed or burned down from the air or destroyed in scorched-earth tactics as the US and other 'UN' troops retreated from the Yalu river at the end of 1950. General [Emmett] O'Donnell later testified to the Senate hearings on MacArthur: 'Everything is destroyed. There is nothing standing worthy of the name. Just before the Chinese came in we were grounded. There were no more targets in Korea.' By the end of the first year of conflict the US Air Force had dropped some 7.8 million gallons of napalm and 97,000 tons of bombs on North Korea. In two years, according to the DPRK, North Korea received 15 million napalm bombs, with Pyongyang receiving 1000 bombs per square kilometre. At the end of the bombing, Pyongyang, once a thriving city of nearly half a million people, had only two buildings intact. In late summer 1953 a British navy officer, Lieutenant Dennis Lankford, commented after travelling through the North Korean capital that Pyongyang 'has ceased to exist'.

By the end of the war much of the surviving population of North Korea was living in caves or holes in the ground. Every possible target—factories, power stations, communication facilities, oil refineries, dams—had been hit. With a collapsed economy the DPRK was forced to cope with hundreds of thousands of orphans, the blind and the limbless, with countless thousands of victims disabled or traumatised by napalm. This is the background against which the post-war chronology of the DPRK should be considered.

Kim Il-sung's Plan to Rebuild the North

In 1954 Kim Il-sung launched a Three-Year Plan to organise the people for reconstruction. Here he could rely on the coherent structure of the command economy, and on prodigious Soviet aid. There is a general consensus in the sources that the DPRK made a remarkable recovery. Kim Il-sung also took the opportunity to concentrate power in his own hands, eliminating dissidents and fellow communists seen as a danger to his position, and establishing what many people saw as a 'cult of personality'. In the immediate post-war years Kim moved to crush the communist followers of Pak Hon Yong whom he blamed for the Korean War disasters; and in 1955–6 was criticised by other DPRK activists for economic mismanagement and for creating an authoritarian Kim cult. He responded by denouncing and removing the critics, and by increasing the pressures on activists to follow his political orthodoxy. By the late 1950s Kim Il-sung had removed all the barriers to the development of his own power. Now he alone, so the legend ran, could save a nation struggling for regeneration after receiving a greater tonnage of bombs than everything dropped on Europe during the entire period of World War Two.

In April 1956 the Third Congress of the Workers' Party of Korea (WPK) considered the launching of a new Five-Year Plan for the building of a socialist framework in North Korea. The plan, starting in 1957, was designed to establish agricultural co-operatives and to begin the socialist transformation of private trade and industry. The following year saw the launch of the Chollima Movement, intended to accelerate the social and industrial progress of the Korean people. A principal aim of the Chollima Movement, modelled on China's Great Leap Forward, was to achieve economic self-sufficiency, at the same time developing North Korea's military strength after the withdrawal of the Chinese forces. With substantial American forces remaining in the South, the DPRK entered into a mutual defence treaty with China and the Soviet Union.

North Korea's Foreign Policy: *Juche*

It was inevitable that North Korea continued to regard the United States as the greatest threat to its survival; in some estimates the US had virtually destroyed the DPRK during the horrendous years of the Korean War. Thus a resolution of the WPK Central Committee in 1960 declared:

> The ringleader of the imperialist forces is US imperialism. US imperialism is the greatest international exploiter, the architect of the reactionary forces of the world, an international military police, the citadel of modern-day bourgeois democracy, and the arch-enemy of the peoples of the entire world.

In 1964 the WPK Central Committee adopted the doctrine of

three revolutionary tenets: to build North Korea as a revolutionary base, to support the revolutionary forces in South Korea, and to gain international support. It was hoped that Asian, African and Latin American countries would join the struggle, but the meeting of 29 Asian and African countries at the Bandung Conference (1955) had not been encouraging: it seemed that there was more interest in national independence and peace than in any fight against US imperialism.

With little international support outside China and the Soviet Union, the DPRK emphasised its *juche* (self-reliance) policy as both a domestic scheme and an independent foreign policy opposed to any kind of imperialism. At the same time Kim Il-sung continued to stress the importance of the international struggle against US hegemony: 'The Korean people support the peoples of all countries fighting against US imperialists. I regard their anti-US struggle as the support of my struggle for liberation of the Korean people.' He also attacked both China and the Soviet Union for giving too little material support to the struggle against US imperialism throughout the world. In the late 1960s, in an effort to garner more international support, North Korea launched various diplomatic initiatives, inviting cultural missions from other countries and establishing 'friendship associations' (in seven countries, only one of which had diplomatic relations with the DPRK). During this period North Korea also began giving aid to Third World countries, developing its trade links, and expanding its contacts with Asian and African countries. At the DPRK's Independence Day celebrations in 1968, 71 delegations (34 from Africa) represented governments, parties, front organisations, social organisations and liberation movements. But various international developments were working against North Korea's attempts to build a global anti-US consensus. Through the 1970s, despite the Vietnam War (by 1973 in its final phase), there were growing signs of *détente* between the Soviet Union and China on the one hand and the United States on the other. Moreover the Soviet invasion of Czechoslovakia in 1968 had led many Third World leaders to believe that there were few differences between Soviet aggression and American imperialism. By the 1980s, with the Soviet Union witnessing the progressive collapse of the East European political/military alliance, there was little international appetite for an anti-US crusade. Increasingly the DPRK was forced to rely on its policy of *juche* self-reliance, a posture that would come under mounting pressure in the so-called New World Order of the 1990s.

The Succession of Kim Jong Il

Throughout this entire period Kim Il-sung had managed to out-manoeuvre every faction that had emerged to challenge his authority. His position seemed secure. He had founded the Korean People's Revolutionary Army in 1932 and proclaimed the DPRK in 1948, serving as effective head of state thereafter. Kim Il-sung became the President of North Korea in 1972 under the terms of his new 'socialist constitution', a position he held until his death (July 1994). Through the 1970s he gave increasing thought to the question of the succession, and was re-elected President in 1982, having named his son Jong Il as his eventual political successor.

In October 1980 the Sixth Congress of the Korean Workers' Party officially confirmed that Kim Jong Il would succeed his father, Kim Il-sung, the supreme leader who had dominated North Korea for three and a half decades. Opposition to the decision continued until 1983 when more than 1000 political and military leaders were reported to have been purged, but by 1984, heavily exploiting the authority of his father, Kim Jong Il had emerged as the established heir apparent and effective ruler of the DPRK. The rationale behind Kim Il-sung's decision has been discussed at length. It was obvious that the choice of Kim Jong Il would raise many questions; in particular, how could a great revolutionary leader contemplate creating what would obviously be seen as a feudalistic dynasty? One possible answer is that Kim Il-sung was struggling to confront the problem that Mao Tse-tung had also faced: how could a new generation, untried in revolution and war, be trusted to maintain the impetus of continuous revolution? . . . Kim Il-sung's answer seems to have been that the dynamic of the revolution could best be maintained by a leader from a great revolutionary family. Thus in 1945, immediately after liberation, the Korean communists created the Mangyongdae School to train the heirs of revolutionaries as future leaders of the country.

Kim Il Sung's *Juche* Philosophy

By Han S. Park

Han S. Park, a scholar on North Korea, professor of political science, and director of the Center for the Study of Global Affairs at the University of Georgia, discusses in this selection Kim Il Sung's unique political philosophy of juche. *Although* juche *can be translated simply as self-reliance, Park examines the different stages of evolution of the concept and shows how its meaning has changed depending on different domestic and international political contexts facing North Korea.*

For example, Park explains that Kim Il Sung began using the term as early as the 1920s to express the idea that Koreans must fight for their nation against the much stronger Japanese military. Later, juche *evolved into a resistance to Soviet hegemony, or domination. Eventually, it became a type of national ideology whose objectives included political sovereignty, economic self-sufficiency, and military self-defense. Ultimately, Park maintains that promoting the ideology of* juche *became a way for Kim Il Sung to legitimize his leadership and role as the Confucian "father" and divine ruler whose decisions cannot be questioned.*

Finally, Park argues the philosophy has developed into a legitimate ideological worldview that can be described as a type of Korean socialism. The ideology is founded upon the development of certain elements of human nature, such as the supremacy of human beings over nature, and the ability of humans to make conscious choices. Because of this basis in human self-determination, juche *promotes national self-determination and self-sufficiency. For example, North Korea opposes the modern global economy because it makes nations with raw materials and labor dependent on nations with capital and technology.*

To trace the origin of *Juche* is difficult because it depends largely on which of the various stages of the ideological evolution can be legitimately called a form of ideology

Han S. Park, *North Korea: The Politics of Unconventional Wisdom.* Boulder, CO: Lynne Rienner Publishers, 2002. Copyright © 2002 by Lynne Rienner Publishers, Inc. Reproduced by permission.

as opposed to a slogan. The Korean word *Juche* is a common word that has been in use as long as the language itself. The word simply means self-reliance or self-support, which can be applied to individuals as well as groups in all situations. The term *Juche*, or *Jaju*, was commonly used during the Japanese occupation by all the nationalist leaders who lamented the incapability of the Korean people themselves to govern an independent sovereign state and attributed the colonial humiliation to this lack of self-governance. It is not surprising that Kim Il Sung allegedly used the concept as early as the 1920s because he was involved at various times in anti-Japanese campaigns. However, the use of the term *Juche* does not coincide with the birth of an ideology. There were five distinct stages in the evolution of the ideology. . . .

Juche as Anti-Japanism

Kim Il Sung, as the "creator" of *Juche*, used the concept extensively from the mid-1920s to the early 1950s to express his deeply felt sentiments against Japanese colonial rule and especially against those political leaders who were incapable of preserving national independence and political sovereignty. He advocated, as did many others, that Koreans must fight to win back their nation by promoting combat capability and spiritual solidarity against the militarily stronger Japanese soldiers. In fact, the formation of Kim Il Sung's charisma began with the theme that he sacrificed his personal well-being for the noble cause of saving the country from Japanese colonialism. Even when he was a little boy at the age of twelve, he was said to be preoccupied with the aspiration for national independence. As the liberation of the country from Japanese control was the most important policy goal, the country naturally advanced the popular theme of anticolonialism. At this stage, the term *Juche* meant little more than antagonist sentiment against a specific target. In this sense, *Juche* was not established even as a rudimentary form of ideology.

Juche as Antihegemonism

In the decade following the Korean War, North Korea found a new enemy that helped South Korea and destroyed much of the northern half of the country with massive air strikes; the new enemy was the United States of America. In the war, the city of Pyongyang was practically leveled to the ground, leaving no physical structures untouched and millions of people killed or wounded. Ever since the war, there has been a genuine fear among North Korean residents that U.S. forces might renew hostilities. The fact that U.S. forces have been stationed continuously in the South and have performed routine military exercises jointly with South Korean armed forces has always made North Korea uneasy and apprehensive. Since the adoption of the armistice agreement in 1953, Pyongyang has persistently demanded the withdrawal of U.S. troops from the Korean peninsula. North Koreans were particularly resentful of the hegemonic expansion of U.S. military influence.

Coupled with the presence of the United States in Korea, the growing Sino-Soviet dispute in 1960, which drove the two communist giants to the brink of war, and Soviet involvement in Eastern Europe and Vietnam were instrumental in the growth of antihegemonism in the North Korean political and diplomatic orientation. Pyongyang was put in a precarious position between the two superpowers of the communist bloc; it did not wish to antagonize either of them by maintaining intimate relations with one at the expense of the other. This situation forced the Pyongyang government to declare a path of equidistance and thus self-reliance. But it was the Soviet Union that became a more convenient target of North Korean criticism because of Moscow's expansionist policy. By contrast, China provided a role model of sorts by indulging in the massive indigenization of Marxism-Leninism during the fanatical phase of the Great Proletariat Cultural Revolution in the late 1960s. Although North Korea did not express great enthusiasm for the Cultural Revolution, it restrained itself from publicly denouncing the Chinese campaign for creating a personality cult for [Chinese leader] Mao Zedong. In fact, North Korea followed in the footsteps of Mao in instigating concerted efforts to develop an indigenous ideology and in creating a charismatic leadership for Kim Il Sung. Just as Mao criticized Moscow for its hegemonic policies, Kim expressed displeasure with the Soviet Union's interventionist policies. As pointed out in the preceding discussion, this doctrine of antihegemonism was further reinforced by Pyongyang's interest in denouncing U.S. influence in South Korea. In short, the ideological insistence of political sovereignty under *Juche* became reinforced by the political reality surrounding the peninsula.

Antihegemonism was also used by Kim Il Sung to consolidate his power and to integrate the country politically. By 1958, contenders for power challenging Kim's leadership and factions within the Workers' Party of Korea had been harshly purged under the pretension that they were leaning toward and siding with the Soviets or the Chinese.

Juche as Nationalist Ideology

By the end of the 1960s, North Korea had become a stable regime devoid of any immediate source of opposition to Kim's authority. His leadership could not be challenged, for it was steadily gaining a charismatic quality. By this time, as pointed out above, almost all political enemies had been eliminated from leadership circles. Furthermore, the economy had fully recovered from the shambles of the Korean War. It may sound unbelievable, but until 1970, the North Korean gross national product per capita was higher than that of South Korea.

What Pyongyang needed at this historical juncture was a persuasive ideology with which to legitimize Kim's charismatic leadership and to demonstrate ideological superiority to the South. It may be generalized that once a regime is established and stability is secured, the next step taken by the regime is to expand its legitimacy through political education. During this stage of development, which may be termed political integration, the ruling elite attempts to further the basis of regime legitimacy through the introduction of an official political ideology. Many newly independent countries have consistently promoted nationalism as their official ideology. North Korea was not an exception.

Nationalism began to be accentuated as the cornerstone of *Juche*. The fact that South Korea was led by Rhee Syngman, who was educated in and had been a long-term resident of the United States, indicated a strong U.S. influence on the Rhee regime and provided Kim Il Sung with the necessary ammunition to condemn the South for being shamelessly antinationalistic and pathetically subjected to foreign domination. In contrast to the South, the North was in a position to declare a policy of equidistance to its communist allies and join the nonaligned movement. Pyongyang managed to establish *Juche* institutes in nonaligned countries such as India. This political climate proved to be an ideal situation for Pyongyang to adopt ultranationalism as the foundation of *Juche* ideology.

In the mid-1960s, nationalism was still primarily antiforeignism without a coherent philosophical structure. But as the ideology was further refined in the late 1960s and much of the 1970s, goals and strategies to implement nationalism were identified. Specifically, *Juche* was defined in terms of three analytically distinct objectives: political sovereignty, economic subsistence, and military self-defense. Political sovereignty forced the regime to limit its political and diplomatic ties to those countries Pyongyang found ideologically compatible, thus limiting foreign relations to only a handful of socialist countries. It is in this period that North Korea campaigned against the South for superiority in legitimacy. Overwhelmed by nationalist sentiment, Pyongyang believed that the Seoul regime could be overthrown by its own masses on the grounds that the South lacked nationalist solidarity and thus political legitimacy. The North Korean government believed that the people in the South could be induced to participate in an antiregime mass movement only if their precarious stability was disturbed. The infiltration of the Blue House, the

THE JUCHE IDEA

Kim Il Sung's concept of juche *(pronounced "choocheh") refers to his particular brand of Marxism-Leninism as applied to North Korea, emphasizing Korean self-reliance and independence. In this excerpt from a speech to party workers on December 28, 1955, shortly after the end of the Korean War, Kim Il Sung claims that the country's ideological work suffers from dogmatism and formalism and introduces* juche *as the remedy.*

Today I want to address a few remarks to you on the shortcomings in our Party's ideological work and on how to eliminate them in the future. . . .

It is to be regretted that it suffers in many respects from dogmatism and formalism.

The principal shortcomings in ideological work are the failure to delve deeply into all matters and the lack of Juche. It may not be correct to say Juche is lacking, but, in fact, it has not yet been firmly established. This is a serious matter. We must thoroughly rectify this shortcoming. Unless this presidential residence in Seoul, by a North Korean commando unit in 1968 could be interpreted as the expression of Pyongyang's determination to disturb political stability in hopes of inciting mass uprisings against the Park Chung Hee regime.

Juche as Economic Self-Reliance

The policy of economic self-reliance deterred economic growth, and North Korea fell further behind its neighboring countries through the 1970s and beyond, especially South Korea. This period happened to coincide with the high-growth years for the newly industrializing countries (NICs) and the "Asian tigers," of which South Korea was one. All these countries employed the export-led strategy toward economic growth. Instead of promoting balanced growth, as was the case in North Korea, the NICs concentrated their efforts on the production of export goods that could be competitive in the international market. But

---

problem is solved, we cannot hope for good results in ideological work.

Why does our ideological work suffer from dogmatism and formalism? Why do our propaganda and agitation workers only embellish the facade and fail to go deeply into matters, and why do they merely copy and memorize things foreign, instead of working creatively? This offers us food for serious reflection.

What is Juche in our Party's ideological work? What are we doing? We are not engaged in any other country's revolution, but solely in the Korean revolution. Devotion to the Korean revolution is Juche in the ideological work of our Party. Therefore, all ideological work must be subordinated to the interests of the Korean revolution. When we study the history of the Communist Party of the Soviet Union, the history of the Chinese revolution, or the universal truth of Marxism-Leninism, it is entirely for the purpose of correctly carrying out our own revolution.

Kim Il Sung, *On Juche in Our Revolution*. New York: Weekly Guardian Associates, Inc., 1977, pp. 135–57.

North Korea alienated itself from world economic activities in order to establish a *Juche* economy. One should not forget that at this time there was growing support among Third World countries for the *dependencia* movement, which proclaimed that economic and cultural independence was the only way of avoiding certain subjugation to the industrialized countries.

What has been most economically detrimental is the principle of military self-reliance. Kim Il Sung's opinion on the importance of military power was unambiguously demonstrated in his early years when he was campaigning for national independence. In his Manchuria days, his group was known for its employment of militant means for which weapons had been secured at all costs. He criticized Kim Koo, Yo Woon Yong, and Ahn Chang Ho, who had a broad base of support for their patriotism and reliance on the nonmilitary/nonviolence principle. According to Kim, a nonviolent revolution would not work in the fight against colonialism and expansionism. In fact, military self-reliance was viewed as a necessary condition for political sovereignty. No amount of resources devoted to building military strength was considered too large; North Korea has consistently invested an inordinate proportion of its national wealth in the weapons industry. Kim also witnessed the dramatic event when the formidable Japanese imperial forces, which had invaded East and Southeast Asia and Russia and eventually bombed the Hawaiian Islands, had to unconditionally surrender to the power of U.S. atomic bombs. Thus it is not surprising for Kim to be engulfed by his own obsessive desire for weapons, specifically atomic bombs.

Although the military principle may have deterred economic growth in general, North Korea's primary source of foreign currency earnings has been the export of everything from conventional weapons to sophisticated missiles. There seems to be no shortage of demand for North Korean weapons in the international market, especially in the Arab world. . . .

In short, the policies designed to adhere to the principles of political, economic, and military self-reliance may not be designed to attain maximal material payoff. In fact, they have been largely counterproductive for the development of industry and often detrimental to the welfare of the society as a whole. Nevertheless, the principles were intended to promote nationalism among the masses and to demonstrate a position of superiority for regime legitimacy over the South.

As the ideology became intimately tied to the regime as an instrument of legitimatization of power, the leadership articulated a new theoretical dimension in which the leadership itself was sanctified as the generator and embodiment of the ideology. This process not only coincided with a quantum leap in the charisma of the Great Leader but also with the regime's need for the official promotion of Kim Jong Il's leadership caliber, which began in conjunction with the Sixth Party Congress in 1980. After observing the succession process in the Soviet Union, Vietnam, and China, Kim Il Sung decided that the great flaw of socialist systems was the almost universal inability of the ruling elite to solve the succession issue. It was not accidental that North Korea selected the hereditary approach as the succession mechanism. The North Korean people had never seen a popularly elected leadership in their entire history. The dynastic systems of early modern Korea were replaced abruptly by Japanese colonial power. Kim Il Sung was quickly and naturally seen as a royal leader of sorts. Thus, deification of the leader's family was not a deviation from the age-old Oriental despotic cultural perspective. Civic education textbooks were written or rewritten with the clear ideological objective of political socialization of the masses into the belief that not only the Great Leader himself was superhuman but also his entire family line. At Mankyongdae [a shrine to Kim Il Sung], exhibits were designed to promote the charisma of the leader and his family. In North Korea, everyone, regardless of age, education level, geographical origin, or sex, has visited this shrine at least several times. . . .

By the late 1980s, Kim's charisma had developed to the level of a "charismatic giant," whereby his leadership was believed to be predestined. He became a natural leader, much like the father of a family. At this point, his actual leadership defied the contractual foundation of leadership. A leader who has solidified his leadership on the grounds of paternalism is not subject to impeachment of any kind because such a leadership is perceived as a matter of natural order. In the context of Confucianism, respecting the father is an obligation that constitutes the utmost virtue. This fact, regardless of the father's conduct or contribution to the family, bears profound implications. Most of all, the leadership of the "father" is not to be judged by what it does but instead by what it is. Under such a system, the basis of regime legitimacy has nothing to do with the theory of social contract, thus giving Kim Il Sung the natural right to rule. Another significant implication of paternalism is that not only the "father" himself but the whole family is destined to rule. This idea will naturally sanctify the hereditary succession of power by the son. Thus, it was not coincidental that Kim Jong Il was officially designated as the heir apparent at the Sixth Party Congress in 1980. It is intriguing to note that the young Kim's ascension to power was initially promoted on the basis of his abilities rather than on his family ties. In fact, one scholar at the Kim Il Sung University unequivocally told me in the summer of 1981 that the legitimization of Kim Jong Il's leadership would have been easier if he had not been the son of Kim Il Sung; he explained that the son's ability and achievements tended to be discredited because of his relationship to the Great Leader. His superb qualifications, according to this scholar, stand on their own merit. However, as the charismatization process advanced more quickly, the young Kim benefited from the family relationship. As his father attained charisma as the paternalistic leader, the son was naturally expected to partake of the charisma of the family. At Mankyongdae, a family museum was erected in the early 1980s in which the Kim clan is heralded as the center of the independence movement. The historical documentation ends with the young Kim having demonstrated unusual leadership quality and unparalleled patriotism.

Juche as a Worldview

Unlike the earlier stages of ideological evolution, Juche soon evolved into a legitimate Weltanschauung [worldview] with a philosophical structure. The articulation of the structure of human nature and the theory of the political-social life are relatively recent developments. I do not suggest that Juche represents a unique and complete worldview, but it is a worldview with some coherent structure, as opposed to a mere political slogan.

The idea that man is the center of the universe is by no means a new perspective; nor is the doctrine of political sovereignty or self-determination. Furthermore, nothing is new about Juche's emphasis on human consciousness as the determinant of human behavior. What is original, however, is the theory that coherently integrated yet distinctly different components of human faculty perform unique and diverse functions.

As will be discussed more fully later, human nature inherently

longs to be in "the center of the universe," where man's relationship with nature and society is clearly prescribed. Nature exists solely for the sake of human beings; thus man is fully entitled
to explore natural resources. Yet man also has the obligation to
manage and "control" the global physical environment. According to *Juche*, science is a tool designed to utilize as well as reha-
bilitate nature for the advancement of human well-being for
both the present and future. According to this perspective, no
person should be subjected to another person's capricious control, nor should he be submitted to institutional manipulation.
Institutions, as in the case of science, are designed to serve human beings rather than be served by them. Even ideologies themselves are regarded as institutional means to human well-being.
Another component of human nature is faculty, which makes
value judgment possible. Humans are endowed with the natural
right and capability to make behavioral choices through free consciousness. Yet another component of human nature allows
people to keep themselves from enslavement by material resources and social institutions.

These elements of human nature are to be cultivated and developed through socialization and political education. For this
reason, ideological education becomes an integral part of human
development, and such an education should be continuous
throughout one's life. The practice of "education through work"
in the form of a factory college should be seen in this vein. A
factory college refers to the practice whereby college-level classes
that would fulfill degree and certification programs in a variety
of specialized fields are offered at factories. College professors
from regular institutions of higher education, such as Kim Il Sung
University and Kim Chaek University, are brought in as instructors. Classes routinely begin with rituals that are intended to glorify the two Kims' works and their legacy.

In 1973, North Korea introduced an eleven-year public school
education in conjunction with the expansion of *Juche*, for the
regime felt it necessary to provide ideological education. The
eleven years of compulsory education are followed by "education through work" in all walks of life. Practically all workplaces
and schools in North Korea are required to set aside at least one
full day each week for study-learning (*haksop*) in which every citizen participates. A typical *haksop* day begins with the announcement of directives and instructions from the Party, fol-

lowed by self-criticism by each member. In this session, workers confess wrongdoing that may have been committed during the preceding week, followed by vows to redeem themselves through deepened loyalty to the Party and the country. After this, discussion centers on *Juche.*

Juche as a Weltanschauung becomes more obvious in its exposition of the properties of the human mind.... The human faculty is viewed as having a series of concomitant properties. They are consciousness (*Uisiksong*), creativity (*Changuisong*), and self-determination (*Jajusong*)....

Jajusong ... prescribes the principle of self-rule at the individual, group, and national levels. This idea is extensively used in rationalizing national self-determination and self-sufficiency. According to this theory, the international division of labor is counterproductive because it perpetuates the dependence of nations with raw materials and labor upon nations with capital and technology.... Here, *Juche* is faced with the formidable task of discrediting the achievements of the newly industrializing countries, especially South Korea, because the NICs have shown that countries participating in the international division of labor and developing export-led economies could be prosperous....

The very need for dissociation from other socialist countries has been instrumental to the rapid transition of *Juche* into a unique ideological system under the banner of "socialism in our style" (*urisik sahoejuii*). This ideological position may sound similar to other forms of nationalized socialism, such as China under Deng Xiaoping and Yugoslavia under Josip Broz Tito. But what is radically unique about North Korea is that *Juche* in its advanced version is a completely different breed of ideology, as opposed to a variation of socialism.

North Korea's Continuing Attacks on South Korea

By Andrea Matles Savada

This selection is excerpted from a Library of Congress publication on North Korea's history. It describes North Korea's continuing pattern of infiltration, sabotage, and terror attacks on South Korea since the time of the division of the Korean peninsula. Shortly after the end of the Korean War in 1953, North Korea began sending military infiltrators into the South to obtain intelligence information and foment revolution, as part of its strategy to reunite the two Koreas. In the 1960s, North Korea shifted to a more violent strategy, seeking to destabilize the South through commando raids and terrorist attacks. In addition to military altercations along the demilitarized zone, the North has attempted on several occasions to assassinate South Korean presidents and has conducted terrorist attacks against South Korean targets.

Since the division of the peninsula, North Korea has used subversion and sabotage against South Korea as part of its effort at reunification. Historically, the military part of this effort has centered on military infiltration, border incidents designed to raise tensions, and psychological warfare operations aimed at the South Korean armed forces. Infiltration by North Korean military agents was commonplace in South Korea after the armistice in 1953. Over time, however, there were clear shifts in emphasis, method, and apparent goals. P'yongyang initially sent agents to gather intelligence and to build a revolutionary base in South Korea.

The 1960s saw a dramatic shift to violent attempts to destabilize South Korea, including commando raids and incidents along

Andrea Matles Savada, "Incidents and Infiltrations: Target South Korea," *North Korea: A Country Study*. Washington, DC: Library of Congress, 1994.

the DMZ [demilitarized zone] that occasionally escalated into firefights involving artillery. The raids peaked in 1968, when more than 600 infiltrations were reported, including an unsuccessful commando attack on the South Korean presidential mansion by thirty-one members of North Korea's 124th Army Unit. The unit came within 500 meters of the president's residence before being stopped. During this incident, twenty-eight infiltra-

NORTH KOREA'S CONTINUING HOSTILITIES TOWARD THE SOUTH

After the Korean War, the hostilities between North and South Korea continued. Although both countries sent spies to infiltrate the other side, North Korea conducted a more aggressive infiltration and destabilization campaign, aimed at fomenting revolution in the South. Especially beginning in the 1960s, the North shifted from infiltrations to violent attempts to destabilize South Korea, including commando raids and incidents along the demilitarized zone (the "neutral" zone between the North and the South) that occasionally escalated into artillery exchanges. Below is a listing of some of North Korea's terrorist activity following the war.

North Korea's Terrorism, 1953–1974

Date	Terrorist Occurrence
February 16, 1958	Hijacking of a KNA airplane with 34 passengers
December 6, 1958	Kidnapping of 7 fishing boats including 42 crewmen
July 22, 1960	Firing at a vessel heading to Inchon, killing one crewman
December 15, 1960	Attempted kidnapping of the passenger vessel *Kyongju*
March 20, 1964	Kidnapping of 2 fishing boats including 26 crewmen

tors and thirty-seven South Koreans were killed. That same year, 120 commandos infiltrated two east coast provinces in an unsuccessful attempt to organize a Vietnamese-type guerrilla war. In 1969 over 150 infiltrations were attempted, involving almost 400 agents. Thereafter, P'yongyang's infiltration efforts abated somewhat, and the emphasis reverted to intelligence gathering, covert networks, and terrorism.

October 29, 1965	Kidnapping of 109 fishermen who were picking clams
November 19, 1966	Kidnapping of a fishing boat
November 3, 1967	Kidnapping of 10 fishing boats including 81 crew
December 25, 1967	Kidnapping of 4 fishing boats including 34 crew
January 6, 1968	Kidnapping of 3 fishing boats including 31 crew
January 21, 1968	Armed raid almost reaching the ROK president's office
June 17, 1968	Kidnapping of 5 fishing boats
October 30, 1968	Armed guerrilla killing of civilians in Ulchin and Samch'ok
December 9, 1968	Killing of student Lee Seung-bok and his family
December 11, 1969	Hijacking of a South Korean airliner with 51 passengers
June 22, 1970	Assassination attempt on ROK president, National Cemetery
January 23, 1971	Attempted hijacking of a Korean Air airliner
February 4, 1972	Kidnapping of 5 fishing boats after wrecking one
August 15, 1974	Attempted assassination of ROK president (killing the first lady)

Yongho Kim, "North Korea's Use of Terror and Coercive Diplomacy: Looking for Their Circumstantial Variants," *Korean Journal of Defense Analysis*, Spring 2002, vol. XIV, no. 1, pp. 49–50.

Subsequent incidents of North Korean terrorism focused on the assassination of the South Korean president or other high officials. In . . . 1970, an infiltrator was killed while planting a bomb intended to kill South Korean president Park Chung Hee at the Seoul National Cemetery. In 1974 a Korean resident of Japan visiting Seoul killed Park's wife in another unsuccessful presidential assassination attempt.

From the mid-1970s to the early 1980s, most North Korean infiltration was conducted by heavily armed reconnaissance teams. These were increasingly intercepted and neutralized by South Korean security forces.

Terrorism in the 1980s

After shifting to sea infiltration for a brief period in the 1980s, P'yongyang apparently discarded military reconnaissance in favor of inserting agents into third countries. For example, on October 9, 1983, a three-man team from North Korea's intelligence services attempted to assassinate South Korean president Chun Doo Hwan while he was on a state visit to Rangoon, Burma. The remote-controlled bomb exploded prematurely. Chun was unharmed, but eighteen South Korean officials, including four cabinet ministers, were killed and fourteen other persons were injured. One of the North Korean agents was killed, two were captured, and one confessed to the incident. On November 29, 1987, a bomb exploded aboard a Korean Air jetliner returning from the Middle East, killing 135 passengers on board. The bomb was placed by two North Korean agents. The male agent committed suicide after being apprehended. The female agent was turned over to South Korean authorities; she confessed to being a North Korean intelligence agent and revealed that the mission was directed by Kim Jong Il as part of a campaign to discredit South Korea before the 1988 Seoul Olympics. In the airliner bombing, North Korea broke from its pattern of chiefly targeting South Korean government officials, particularly the president, and targeted ordinary citizens.

The Succession of Kim Jong Il

By Don Oberdorfer

*Kim Il Sung, North Korea's "Great Leader," died in 1994. At the time
of his death, his son, Kim Jong Il, had already been given the title of
"Dear Leader" and named as his successor. Indeed, as Don Oberdorfer
describes in the following excerpt from his book on Korea, the succession
process had begun years before. After years behind the scenes, Kim Jong Il
was introduced to the Korean public in 1980, when he was given senior
posts in the government and proclaimed as Kim Il Sung's successor.
Thereafter, Kim Jong Il was rarely seen by foreigners, although rumors
spread concerning his lifestyle. He is said to love drinking, womanizing,
and spending money. He also is credited with the kidnapping of a prominent South Korean actress and with terrorist attacks on South Korea in
the 1980s. On the other hand, Kim Jong Il is credited with intelligence,
confidence, and an interest in modernizing North Korea.*

*Don Oberdorfer is a journalist and adjunct professor at the School of
Advanced International Studies at Johns Hopkins University in Washington, D.C.*

T he plump, bespectacled, moon-faced man who stood
apart and ahead of all others at the state funeral and the
memorial service in Kim Il Sung Square was the most
important mourner. Despite some expectations to the contrary,
however, the eldest son and political heir of the Great Leader said
nothing about his father, his loss, or his priorities for the country. Rather, he looked on enigmatically as others spoke in praise
of the Great Leader, and of the ordained succession process that
had been established more than a decade earlier.

In many respects, father and son were a study in contrasts. Kim
Il Sung was a guerrilla fighter, the founder of the state, and a
charismatic, outgoing, outspoken figure until the day he died.

Don Oberdorfer, *The Two Koreas: A Contemporary History*. New York: Basic Books,
2001. Copyright © 1997 by Don Oberdorfer. Reproduced by permission.

Kim Jong Il grew up in privilege from his teenage years, had never served a day in the military until he was named supreme commander of the People's Army in December 1991, wore his hair in an artsy pompadour, and was notably uncomfortable amid the roar of the crowd. Even when important pronouncements were made in his name, they were read by an announcer while he remained out of sight. As this is written [in 1997], the only time the North Korean public has heard the voice of Kim Jong Il was in April 1992, when he uttered a single sentence during a ceremony marking the army's sixtieth anniversary: "Glory to the people's heroic military!"

A great deal about North Korea and its unique and inward-oriented system is mysterious; whatever pertains to Kim Jong Il is typically the most mysterious of all. His rise to power and selection as his father's successor were unacknowledged for many years, and his activities were masked under the vague euphemism "the party center." Since emerging from anonymity in 1980, he has rarely seen foreigners and is known to have traveled outside the country only twice: in 1983, when he toured Beijing and other Chinese cities for ten days; and in 1984, when he turned up briefly and unannounced in his father's entourage in Berlin. On the latter occasion, East German officials confirmed his presence only by studying photographs taken aboard Kim Il Sung's special train.

According to North Korean propagandists, Kim Jong Il was born in a log cabin on Mount Paekdu, the legendary birthplace of Tangun, the mythic father of the Korean people. More objective sources say the younger Kim was born on February 16, 1942, in a Russian military camp in the Far East, where his father's guerrilla band had taken refuge from the Japanese. After the Japanese surrender, at age three Kim Jong Il moved to Korea with his father but was evacuated to China at age eight during the Korean War. In his early years, a younger brother accidentally drowned, and his mother died while giving birth to a stillborn child, leaving Jong Il and a younger sister. Kim Il Sung remarried in the early 1960s and had two sons and two daughters by his second wife, Kim Song Ae.

A Family State

North Korea has been aptly described by historian Bruce Cumings as "a corporate state and a family state." Kim Jong Il's sister,

Kim Kyong Hui, is director of light industry in the Workers Party; her husband, Chang Song Taek, has become Kim Jong Il's right-hand man and one of the most powerful figures in the country. Kim Jong Il's half-brother, Kim Pyong Il, is ambassador to Finland after an earlier posting in Hungary. The husband of one of his half-sisters is a four-star general, and the other's husband is an ambassador. Family members and in-laws hold a very large number of the top leadership posts in the country.

Although passage of power from father to eldest son was traditional in Korean dynasties and Confucian families, it was heretical in a nominal "people's democracy." As recently as 1970, the official *Dictionary of Political Terminologies* published in Pyongyang defined hereditary succession as "a reactionary custom of exploitive societies." This entry was dropped in the early 1970s, when Kim Il Sung decided to make his son his closest aide and successor.

Kim Jong Il graduated from Kim Il Sung University in 1964 and went to work in the Central Committee of the Workers Party, with special responsibility for films, theater, and art, which became his lifelong passion. He is credited with the production of six major films and musicals in the early 1970s. Kim became a secretary of the Central Committee of the Workers Party in September 1973 and a member of its Politburo the following year. By then, songs were being sung about him among party cadres, who carried special notebooks to record his instructions.

Despite his prominence in the Workers Party, little was said about him publicly, which suggests that his father felt the need to fully prepare the domestic and external public for the first family succession of the communist world. North Korean media referred instead to a mysterious "party center" who was given credit for wise guidance and great deeds. The veil was lifted at the Sixth Workers Party Congress in October 1980, when the younger Kim was simultaneously awarded senior posts in the Politburo, the Military Commission, and the Party Secretariat and was openly proclaimed to be Kim Il Sung's designated successor. He was given the title of Dear Leader, close to that of the Great Leader. Both father and son were addressed and referred to in special honorific terms that were not used for anyone else.

Kim Jong Il's Hedonistic Lifestyle
Stories of Kim Jong Il's high living, hard drinking, and womanizing are legion. Kim was married to his college sweetheart in

1966, but they divorced in 1971. He married his present wife, another Kim Il Sung University graduate who was a typist at Workers Party headquarters, in 1973. He is widely reported to have had other liaisons, including a long-term affair in the early 1970s with a prominent actress who was eventually sent off to live in a villa in Moscow.

For many years the most extensive glimpses of Kim Jong Il in action came from a prominent South Korean actress, Choi Eun Hee, and her former husband, film director Shin Sang Ok, who were kidnapped separately to North Korea from Hong Kong in 1978 on the younger Kim's orders. Without embarrassment, he baldly told the movie couple in a meeting that they surreptitiously tape-recorded that he had ordered their forcible abduction because "I absolutely needed you" to improve Pyongyang's unprofessional film industry. Speaking in matter-of-fact fashion about this bizarre kidnapping, Kim told them, "I just said, 'I need

KIM JONG IL AND WAR

In 1997 two prominent North Koreans defected to South Korea. Hwang Jang Yop, former secretary of North Korea's Workers' Party, and Kim Tok Hong, former general president of North Korea's Yogwang Trading Combined General Company, held a news conference on July 10, 1997, to answer reporters' questions about North Korea. Hwang Jang Yop emphasized North Korea's militaristic goals, stating:

North Korea's basic strategy toward South Korea which it has espoused for almost 50-odd years is to make South Korea collapse from within and to achieve reunification by force. North Korea's Workers' Party has many offices that carry out anti–South Korea activities. These include the United Front Department, the Social and Cultural Department, departments that carry out overt activities, departments that handle underground organizations in South Korea, the operation department which infiltrates into South Korea, and a department that carries out intelligence work. . . .

these two people, so bring them here,' so my comrades just carried out the operation."

Director Shin spent more than four years in North Korean prisons for trying to escape. After he was released and he and his wife were reunited, they made motion pictures for Kim Jong Il for almost three years. Kim Jong Il treated them as important artists and members of his social circle until their escape in Vienna in 1986. During this period they had extensive personal contact with him and his friends and entourage.

The country was struggling economically and was unable to pay its debts, but the filmmakers reported that Kim Jong Il spent money lavishly. He housed Choi and eventually Shin in luxurious surroundings, including a house where he himself had previously lived. He gave each of them a new Mercedes 280 sedan with a license plate number beginning with 216, a reference to his February 16 birthday that is celebrated as a national holiday

---

It is common sense and a firm policy to believe the North will wage war without fail, whenever that may be. Whether the war will be general or local, I am not certain since I am not the supreme commander. However, I believe that if it breaks out, it will be full-scale, although the North may be able to touch off a provocation.

As for when North Korea will provoke a war, it will take into consideration both the international situation and the domestic one.

The most appropriate time will be when its operations to make South Korea collapse from within and its strategy to launch an armed aggression will work well in combination. I think North Korea will provoke a war when the South Korean situation is complicated and when chaos prevails there.

In terms of the international political situation, the time will come when allies cannot afford to assist in a Korean war because they will need to dispatch their troops to other fronts. This is only my guess.

Hwang Jang Yop Press Conference, July 10, 1997, Korea Web Weekly, www.kimsoft.com.

in North Korea, and that designates the automobile as that of a very important person. He built a new motion picture studio costing more than $40 million for their productions and put $2.3 million for their film company's use in a foreign bank account. An aide told Shin that the Dear Leader had use of the proceeds from a gold mine, which provided nearly unlimited funds for his gifts, motion picture hobby, and other activities.

In interviews shortly after their escape, Choi and Shin depicted Kim Jong Il as confident, bright, temperamental, quirky, and very much in charge of governmental as well as theatrical affairs. To his kidnapped "special guests," he could be privately self-deprecating, as when he said to actress Choi in their first dinner meeting, "What do you think of my physique? Small as a midget's turd, aren't I?" Or audacious, as when he summoned Choi at five A.M. to the final hours of an all-night party with his friends, a band, and lots of whiskey, of which he had imbibed too much.

Kim Jong Il's Links to Terrorism

While the kidnapping of Choi and Shin is the best documented of the many violent acts associated with the name of the younger Kim, it is not the only one. The terrorist bombing that killed South Korean cabinet members at Rangoon in 1983 was attributed to a clandestine agency reporting to him. Kim Hyon Hui, the female agent in the bombing of Korean Air Lines flight 858, in which 115 people were killed in 1987, was told that her orders came directly from Kim Jong Il in his own handwriting, although she did not see them. Various unconfirmed accounts suggest that the younger Kim had direct supervision of the North Korean nuclear weapons program.

At the same time, Kim Jong Il is believed to be more interested in modernizing than most others in the ruling circles. In a diplomatic dispatch to Berlin in 1982, the East German embassy remarked on the younger Kim's "modern" outlook and credited him with a loosening up of popular lifestyles, including the approval of more fashionable women's clothing, the reintroduction of dice, card, and board games, and the increased consumption of alcoholic beverages, especially beer.

In a tape recording brought out by the filmmakers, Kim Jong Il said in 1984, "After having experienced about thirty years of socialism, I feel we need to expand to the Western world to feed the people. The reality is that we are behind the West." At the same meeting, however, he said that North Korea could not open up, as even the Chinese were urging. "We have been stuck strategically" because opening up in his militarily embattled country, even for tourism, "would be naturally tantamount to disarmament." This could only be done after unification, he said.

The Korean Views on Kim Jong Il

In preparation for his succession, North Korean authorities went to extraordinary lengths to glorify Kim Jong Il: his portrait, along with that of his father, was placed in every home, office, and workplace. A fascinating example of the indoctrination was recounted to me by a Russian correspondent whose wife gave birth in the late 1980s at Pyongyang's maternity hospital during his assignment in the DPRK. The hospital is one of dozens around the country sponsored by Kim Jong Il in honor of his mother, who died in childbirth. After the correspondent's baby was born, the head nurse presented the newborn child to his father, declaring, "Congratulations from Comrade Kim Jong Il!" A few minutes later, several nurses paraded in military style into the birthing room with a large jar and a long-handled spoon. They ceremoniously placed a spoonful of honey into the mouth of the astonished new mother, chanting, "This is a gift from Comrade Kim Jong Il!" Sugar and honey were in such short supply among ordinary North Koreans that a spoonful of honey was a great delicacy. Despite such gestures, defectors and outside experts say that affection for Kim Jong Il in North Korea is much more limited than it was for his father. . . .

In July 1994, wearing a dark cadre suit with a black mourning armband, Kim Jong Il kept his own counsel at the ceremonies for his father. Pyongyang radio referred to him as "the Dear Leader, the sole successor to the Great Leader," and Korea experts speculated about how quickly he would assume his father's titles of general secretary of the Workers Party and president of the DPRK. Initial predictions were that he would claim the posts and titles of supreme leadership after a hundred days of mourning, then after one year of mourning, then after two years, and so on. His failure to take the two top posts stirred speculation that Kim Jong Il faced important opposition within the hierarchy. [In 1997, however, Kim Jong Il was named secretary of the Korean Workers Party and he consolidated his power with the title of National Defense Commission Chairman in 1998.]

Modern Challenges for North Korea

North Korea's Economic Problems

BY DANIEL GOODKIND AND LORAINE WEST

The selection below, published in a periodical called Population and Development Review, *provides a description of the background and status of North Korea's economic problems. Its authors are Daniel Goodkind, a demographer, and Loraine West, an economist, who are both with the International Programs Center, part of the U.S. Census Bureau. As described in the article, North Korea suffered from a lack of food throughout the 1990s. An inefficient economic model, the collapse of the Soviet Union, and droughts and floods in the mid-1990s have left the country unable to recover without massive food aid from the United Nations and other countries. The famine has caused deaths, starvation, and severe malnutrition. Some have speculated that deaths have been in the millions, but the authors of this article believe the number to be between 600,000 and 1 million. Yet the famine is only one part of a larger economic collapse. Domestic power shortages and an inability to import raw materials and replacement parts have exacerbated the declines in industrial and agricultural production. Another problem has been the regime's diverting of food aid away from hungry citizens to the military and government officials. How North Korea will solve its economic problems remains to be seen.*

Among the world's famines during the twentieth century, one of the longest and most severe began in the Democratic People's Republic of Korea (North Korea) in the mid-1990s. The origins and duration of the North Korean famine can be attributed to a series of natural calamities, human and organizational deficiencies in responding to them, and the general economic decline the country experienced after the collapse of the Soviet Union. In addition to the obvious human suffering the famine wrought, some observers worried that it might destabilize an unpredictable regime with a growing military capability to attack its neighbors, including the Republic of Korea (South Korea). . . .

The Number of Deaths

Although the situation remains precarious, the worst effects of the famine have apparently subsided. Yet the actual demographic toll of the famine remains uncertain owing to a lack of reliable data. Despite recent overtures to the international community, North Korea is still ruled by one of the few remaining Stalinist regimes, one that continues to sequester information about basic social and economic conditions in the country. Several media reports based on officially released crude death rates for 1995 and 1998 (to be analyzed further herein) inferred about 220,000 excess deaths from 1995 to 1998. Figures based on other evidence, however, are far higher. A bipartisan team of US Congressional staff members visiting North Korea in August 1998 concluded that famine-related deaths amounted to 300,000–800,000 annually. The Agence France-Presse cites a wide array of figures ranging up to 3.5 million excess deaths. The figure of 3 million or more was denounced by the North Korean government as a vicious rumor spread by the South Korean intelligence agency.

More recently, the figure we have heard most often is "up to two million" excess deaths over the course of the famine. Such a phrase points to an upper limit but does not rule out any figure below it. At its upper limit, 2 million excess deaths would constitute almost 10 percent of North Korea's 1993 population of 21 million. That would be an astonishing loss, especially for a country with a life expectancy at birth of 68 years for males and females combined in 1993, just two years prior to the famine. To our knowledge, among sustained famines since World War II, North Korea's was unique for having occurred in a country with longevity approaching that of developed countries.

Yet, given the shaky foundations and enormous range of the aforementioned figures of excess deaths, they are best viewed as conjectures rather than reliable estimates. . . . Although some uncertainty remains, we conclude that famine-related deaths in North Korea from 1995 to 2000 most likely numbered between 600,000 and 1 million.

The Collapse of the Soviet Union

As in other socialist command economies throughout the world, the lack of market incentives in North Korea had likely begun to hinder the economy by the early 1980s, if not before. We say "likely" because of the difficulties in gleaning reliable trends from the limited, nonstandard, and otherwise questionable statistics released by the government, and because of the seclusion of its people from international discourse. By the early 1990s, in any event, there was clear evidence of a severe economic decline, one that occurred well before the summer floods of 1995 that formally precipitated the famine. With the collapse of the Soviet Union in 1991, North Korea lost both its major trading partner and a generous provider of agricultural and other subsidies. The value of Soviet exports to North Korea plummeted from US$1.97 billion in 1990 to US$0.58 billion in 1991. By 1993 Russia's exports to North Korea were only 10 percent of what had been received from the Soviet Union prior to 1991.

China thereafter became North Korea's major trading partner. China, however, sought to limit its role in propping up the North Korean economy and filled only a small portion of the gap left by the Soviet Union. The value of China's exports to North Korea (primarily coal, petroleum products, and grain) rose from $0.39 billion in 1990 to $0.58 billion in 1991 and $0.66 billion in 1993, but thereafter declined to $0.47 billion in 1994. North Korea's weapons exports, which had been a substantial source of revenue in the 1980s, did not offset the lost trade. In fact, the value of its annual arms exports declined from $423 million in 1987–90 to only $160 million in 1991–94 and only $80 million in 1995–97. Hampered by a longstanding US trade embargo, unable or unwilling to allocate resources to purchase grain in the international market, and lacking a partner willing to provide extensive concessionary aid, North Korea could not meet the basic needs of its people.

Even under ordinary climatic conditions, North Korea has been barely able to feed itself. Its geography and climate permit only one season for growing food, lasting from about June to October. Given typical caloric needs, the natural fertility of the land, and the size of North Korea's population (about 21 million prior to the famine), a 12 percent shortfall of grain might be expected in any given year. Thus, the loss of agricultural subsidies from the Soviet Union in 1991 had an almost immediate impact. One can infer tightening food supplies from the launching of a "let's eat only two meals a day" campaign in 1991. That campaign was followed in 1993 by reports of food shortages and in 1994 by North Korean radio broadcasts admitting to the existence of hunger.

Floods and Drought

A series of natural disasters that began in the summer of 1995 seriously compounded these underlying problems. In July and August of 1995 floods damaged over 400,000 hectares of arable land, displaced some 500,000 people, and reduced grain production by about 1.9 million tons. The summer's loss of grain represented about 30 percent of the 6.5 million tons needed annually to feed the country's people. The floods in 1995 were especially bad in North Pyongan and Chagang provinces in the mountainous northwestern part of the country, two of the four northern provinces sharing a border with China. Nearly a year after the floods, a delegation from the Carter Center visited Huichon city in Chagang province in June 1996. There was no visible evidence of famine or malnutrition, but clear evidence of the 1995 flooding still existed. For 1995, North Korea reported a grain harvest of just 3.49 million tons. Early in the summer of 1995, with few alternatives available, the North Korean government began to ask the United Nations, as well as the governments of several countries, for food assistance.

The floods in July of 1996, while not as severe as the 1995 floods, caused the most damage in provinces across the southern part of the country (North Hwanghae, South Hwanghae, and Kangwon, as well as Kaesong municipality). This area is North Korea's breadbasket, producing about 60 percent of the country's food grain (primarily rice). One estimate placed the reduction in grain output at about 300,000 tons.

Early prospects for the 1997 crop appeared favorable, following an early winter thaw in March and good rains in May. However, June and July brought above-average temperatures and below-average rainfall. North Korea's official Central News Agency reported on 25 July that, owing to the two-month drought, water levels in large reservoirs were 10 to 20 percent below normal and more than 620 small reservoirs were nearly empty. The provinces most seriously affected by the drought were North Pyongan, South Pyongan, North Hwanghae, and Kangwon, many of the same provinces that had been affected by sudden floods in the preceding years. Estimates of grain losses ranged from 700,000 tons to 1.9 million tons. The prolonged drought in 1997 and light snowfall in winter 1997–98 left the 1998 grain crop facing very limited water resources.

The flooding in 1995 and 1996 affected mortality both through a reduction in the availability of food and through the destruction of health infrastructure. In all, 298 health facilities were severely damaged, including the only factory able to produce oral rehydration solution. The combination of natural disasters and the general economic decline resulted in a 60 percent drop in pharmaceutical output between 1995 and 1998.

Domestic power shortages and an inability to import raw materials and replacement parts exacerbated the declines in industrial and agricultural production. Experts from the United Nations Development Programme (UNDP) identified fertilizer as

SECRET WITNESS TO STARVATION

Ahn Chol, a twenty-eight-year-old North Korean refugee living in China, snuck back into North Korea in 1998 to secretly film conditions there. In the following interview with Hideko Takayama of Newsweek *magazine, published September 27, 1999, he describes what he saw and what he thinks of North Korea's leader, Kim Jong Il.*

In North Korea, people suffer, starve, struggle and roam around looking for food. . . .

[Kim Jong Il] is a villain. History rarely witnessed such a devil. People in North Korea can never say anything against him because it means death. That's why they say it is the fault of Kim's subordinates that they have to starve and die. Living in North Korea is like a life in jail. There is no freedom, no human rights, they cannot even go to places as they wish, and the distribution system had collapsed.

"Secret Witness to Starvation (North Korean refugee Ahn Chol) (Interview)," *Newsweek International*, September 27, 1999, p. 58.

the most important constraint on food production, citing a shortage of energy to run fertilizer plants and a lack of raw materials. UNDP has estimated that about 350,000 tons of urea equivalent are needed annually; however, since raw materials, which must be imported, were lacking, domestic nitrogen fertilizer production fell to 217,000 tons in 1995 and to only 81,000 tons in 1997.

Population Affected by the Famine

Ironically, the presumed strong suit of North Korea's socialist system—its control over the distribution of food and other resources—might have provided a buffer against the impending famine. Since the 1950s, food has been allocated through a public distribution system whereby, in keeping with socialist principles, agricultural areas producing a food surplus subsidized urban areas and other regions with a food deficit. Collective farmers were required to turn over all grain to the government, receiving in return a certain allotment of grain along with industrial and other goods as payment in kind. Historically, the public distribution system allocated food to about 62 percent of North Koreans, roughly equal to the country's urban population. Among those outside the system were the wage workers on state farms, who typically received half rations, as well as those on cooperative farms, who relied on what they themselves produced.

Those covered under the public distribution system were ostensibly guaranteed a certain amount of food. Prior to the famine, official daily quotas of grain for urban dwellers were typically about 600–700 grams per person. Larger quotas of 700–800 grams per day were established for high officials, the military, public security personnel, and heavy laborers. Yet the actual amount of grain available through the distribution system often dipped below these quotas and was falling sharply even before the summer floods of 1995, probably because of low productivity. Although special subsidies were allocated to residents of the capital of Pyongyang, famine refugees traveling to China in search of food reported that their rations had fallen to 150 grams per day in 1994. In an attempt to increase the amount of grain flowing into the public distribution system, in 1995 the government reduced the allotment that farm families were allowed to keep from 167 kilograms of grain per person annually to 107. Yet this policy backfired badly, encouraging farmers to defy "corn police" by hiding large stockpiles of grain and focusing their efforts ever more intently on small plots of private land, practices that further siphoned off the grain available to the distribution system. Through such circumventions, these farmers were more likely than other North Koreans to survive the food shortages.

In contrast, the two groups of citizens suffering the most were farmers living in communities that had little or no grain owing to the floods or other circumstances and all those served by the public distribution system who lacked political connections to obtain food through other channels. Among the latter disadvantaged group were miners, factory and transport workers, and even some members of the ruling party. Indeed, the aforementioned survey of North Korean famine refugees in China indicated some diversity in their government-designated "class backgrounds." Three-quarters of respondents belonged to what North Korea calls the "wavering" class, while the remaining quarter were evenly split between "loyalist" and "hostile" classes. Among all of these famine refugees, public distribution rations amounted to a mere 30 grams per day by 1997, less than 5 percent of the official quota. These citizens tried to compensate for the shortfall in rations through food purchases, bartering, foraging, and other means. Yet food from all sources in 1996 was only one-third to two-thirds of what was required.

International Aid

The World Food Programme played an increasingly important role in responding to the unfolding crisis. World Food Programme food shipments to North Korea rose from 5,000 tons in 1995 (the first year of shipments) to 387,000 tons in 1998. The share of World Food Programme aid among all sources of international aid also increased over the same period from less than 1 percent to almost half. The United States also emerged as a major bilateral donor. Regrettably, however, the North Korean government has limited or prevented monitoring of the distribution of this aid, so there is little assurance that it is reaching those most in need of it. Some officials reportedly profiteer by rerouting food aid to open markets where it sells at elevated prices. Such aid has also been diverted to the military. For instance, a North Korean submarine that ran aground in 1997 in South Korean waters was found stocked with food packages bearing the labels of international donors. According to one well-placed source, of all food aid received by North Korea only 10 percent goes directly to hungry civilians, while 10 percent is diverted to the military and 80 percent ends up in the hands of government officials. Such irregularities in the distribution and monitoring of food and medical assistance led several international relief organizations to cease operating in North Korea. In June 2000, Care International was the latest to withdraw, joining Oxfam, Action Against Hunger, Doctors Without Borders, and Doctors of the World.

The Struggle for Unification Between North and South Korea

BY TAE-HWAN KWAK AND SEUNG-HO JOO

As the following selection describes, North and South Korea in recent years have pursued reconciliation and cooperation policies aimed at eventual reunification. The authors are Tae-Hwan Kwak, former president of the Korea Institute for National Unification in Seoul and professor emeritus at Eastern Kentucky University, and Seung-Ho Joo, an assistant professor of political science at the University of Minnesota–Morris. Although concluding that the two Koreas are still engaged in a kind of cold war, the authors view the historic June 2000 summit between North Korean leader Kim Jong Il and South Korea's president Kim Dae Jung as a hopeful beginning for a peaceful relationship between the two countries.

In the first year after the summit, the two Koreas held additional talks and made progress on many issues, but these talks have been largely suspended since March 2001. The two sides finally met in October 2002 and again in January 2003, but these talks were overwhelmed by news of the developing nuclear weapons program in North Korea. In addition, four-party international talks among North and South Korea, China, and the United States faltered and have been deadlocked since August 1999. North Korea refused to participate after rejection of its repeated demands for U.S. troop withdrawal and a U.S.–North Korea peace treaty. Adding to these difficulties are other political realities: the end of South Korean president Kim Dae Jung's term in office and U.S. president George Bush's new, tough policy stance toward North Korea's nuclear weapons program. The authors conclude that North and South

Tae-Hwan Kwak and Seung-Ho Joo, "The Korean Peace Process: Problems and Prospects After the Summit," *World Affairs*, vol. 165, Fall 2002, p. 79. Copyright © 2002 by Heldref Publications. Reproduced by permission.

Korea can achieve a peaceful coexistence through a gradual process supported by the United States, Russia, Japan, and China.

Although more than half a century has passed since the two Korean governments were established in 1948, the Korean peninsula is still divided between the Republic of Korea (ROK, or South Korea) and the Democratic People's Republic of Korea (DPRK, or North Korea). Inter-Korean relations are still characterized by mutual distrust, animosity, a lack of mutual cooperation, and conflicting ideologies. The cold war continues on the Korean peninsula.

The first-ever inter-Korean summit meeting between President Kim Dae-jung and Chairman Kim Jong-il, held in Pyongyang on 13–15 June 2000, was indeed historic. The summit produced an inter-Korean joint declaration of 15 June 2000, which provided a framework for institutionalizing a peaceful coexistence between the two Korean states. Chairman Kim Jong-il's decision to attend the June summit meeting symbolized his strategic policy change toward the South. The new inter-Korean peace process continues to build mutual trust and understanding on which a durable peace on the Korean peninsula can be firmly established. . . .

A Soft Landing for North Korea Is Best

North Korea is suffering from multiple crises. Despite its numerous problems, most believe that North Korea under Kim Jong-il is likely to survive in the short and intermediate terms but is bound either to change or to fall in the long term. The question is how to manage the inter-Korean peace process by inducing Pyongyang's transformation and controlling its downfall. Seoul can pursue one of two endings for Pyongyang: "crash landing" or "soft landing." North Korea's crash landing, or sudden collapse from within, is not desirable for a number of reasons. Seoul does not have the economic capability to absorb North Korea's collapse. Considering Seoul's economic setbacks in recent years (even after significant recovery), Korean unification after the German model would be a heavy blow to Seoul's economy, and it might lose its competitive edge for many years to come. The South Korean people cannot afford to lose their hard-earned economic prosperity for immediate national unification.

If North Korea's economic situation deteriorates, its famine spreads, and its international isolation deepens, Kim Jong-il may attempt to hold on to power by causing a military crisis on the Korean peninsula. Under those circumstances, tensions in Korea and Northeast Asia will increase. Seoul's hard-line policy toward Pyongyang will strengthen the position of hardliners in Pyongyang, and there will be great danger of war. North Korea's political instability, poverty, and social unrest may lead to an implosion of the country. It is, therefore, in Seoul's interest to help Pyongyang improve its economic situation and join the international community as a full-fledged member.

North Korea's soft landing, or gradual adoption of a market economy and liberal democracy, is desirable and feasible. North Korea is trying to implement calculated economic reforms and an open-door policy, following China's model, to cure its chronic economic illness and end its diplomatic isolation. Economic reforms and an open-door policy, no matter how limited they may be, will set in motion the transformation of the Stalinist regime. As its economic structure begins to change under the impact of market-oriented economic policies and increased contacts with the outside world, its political and social structure is bound to change. We, therefore, argue that a shortcut to the peaceful unification of Korea is through inter-Korean reconciliation and economic cooperation.

Kim Dae-jung's "Sunshine Policy"

The question, then, is how to bring about North Korea's soft landing. The best way is for South Korea to increase its economic activities with North Korea and help the North become a full member of the international community. Pyongyang will engage in a meaningful dialogue with Seoul if its status in the international community improves and its economic situation stabilizes. An isolated and insecure North Korea will retrench, but a self-confident and stable North Korea will reach out and seek dialogue with Seoul.

To help North Korea achieve a soft landing, in 1998 the Kim Dae-jung government adopted the "sunshine policy" toward North Korea. The objective of the new policy is to improve inter-Korean relations by promoting reconciliation, cooperation, and peace. The policy also assumes that, at the present stage, it is more important to establish peaceful coexistence between the two Koreas than to push for immediate unification. Two specific

SUNSHINE AND PEACE ON THE KOREAN PENINSULA

Following the historic June 2000 summit meeting between the leaders of North and South Korea, South Korean president Kim Dae Jung was awarded the Nobel Peace Prize in December 2000 for his "sunshine policy" of reconciliation with North Korea and his efforts to achieve peace on the Korean peninsula. The following is an excerpt of Kim Dae Jung's Nobel acceptance speech, given on December 10, 2000.

In mid-June, I traveled to Pyongyang for the historic meeting with Chairman Kim Jong-il of the North Korean National Defense Commission. I went with a heavy heart not knowing what to expect, but convinced that I must go for the reconciliation of my people and peace on the Korean peninsula. There was no guarantee that the summit meeting would go well. Divided for half-a-century after a three-year war, South and North Korea have lived in mutual distrust and enmity across the barbed-wire fence of the demilitarized zone.

To replace the dangerous stand-off with peace and cooperation, I proclaimed my sunshine policy upon becoming President in February 1998, and have consistently promoted its message of reconciliation with the North: first, we will never accept unification through communization; second, nor would we attempt to achieve unification by absorbing the North; and third, South and North Korea should seek peaceful coexistence and cooperation. Unification, I believe, can wait until such a time when both sides feel comfortable enough in becoming one again, no matter how long it takes. At first, North Korea resisted, suspecting that the sunshine policy was a deceitful plot to bring it down. But our genuine intent and consistency, together with the broad support for the sunshine policy from around the world, including its moral leaders such as Norway, convinced North Korea that it should respond in kind. Thus, the South-North summit could be held.

I had expected the talks with the North Korean leader to be extremely tough, and they were. However, starting from the shared desire to promote the safety, reconciliation and cooperation of our people, the Chairman and I were able to obtain some important agreements.

First, we agreed that unification must be achieved independently and peacefully, that unification should not be hurried along and for now the two sides should work together to expand peaceful exchanges and cooperation and build peaceful coexistence.

Second, we succeeded in bridging the unification formulas of the two sides, which had remained widely divergent. By proposing a "loose form of federation" this time, North Korea has come closer to our call for a confederation of "one people, two systems, two independent governments" as the pre-unification stage. . . .

Third, the two sides concurred that the US military presence on the Korean peninsula should continue for stability on the peninsula and Northeast Asia. . . .

We also agreed that the humanitarian issue of the separated families should be promptly addressed. Thus, since the summit, the two sides have been taking steps to alleviate their pain. The Chairman and I also agreed to promote economic cooperation. . . .

Furthermore, for tension reduction and the establishment of durable peace, the defense ministers of the two sides have met, pledging never to wage another war against each other. They also agreed to the needed military cooperation in the work to relink the severed railway and road between South and North Korea. . . .

I am confident that these developments will have a decisive influence in the advancement of peace on the Korean peninsula.

Kim Dae Jung, 2000 Nobel Peace Prize Laureate, Oslo, Norway, December 10, 2000.

goals of the sunshine policy are (a) peaceful management of the national division and (b) promotion of a favorable environment for North Korea to change and open itself without fear. The ROK government wants to reduce tensions and negotiate arms control with the DPRK, with a view to deterring another war on the peninsula, as well as encourage the North to transform its economy by adopting a market-oriented system.

The policy is based on three principles: First, South Korea will not tolerate any armed provocation by North Korea. The ROK will maintain a strong security posture toward the North and will make it clear that it will respond to any provocation. At the same time, South Korea will continue to make efforts to reduce tensions and build mutual confidence.

Second, South Korea will not attempt to take over or absorb North Korea. Rather than promoting the collapse of North Korea, South Korea intends to work toward peaceful coexistence and a favorable environment for the creation of a South-North national community, gradually leading to peaceful unification.

Third, inter-Korean reconciliation and cooperation will be expanded. The South Korean government will do its best to resolve hostility that has accumulated between the two Koreas since the division of the peninsula. The South wants to implement the 1991 inter-Korean Basic Agreement on Reconciliation, Nonaggression, and Exchanges and Cooperation between the South and the North.

Using those three principles, the Seoul government has adopted six guidelines for implementing the ROK's new North Korea policy: (a) strong national security and inter-Korean cooperation will be promoted in parallel; (b) the promotion of peaceful coexistence and inter-Korean cooperation will be a top priority; (c) an environment conducive to the opening and system transformation of North Korea needs to be created; (d) common interests need to be promoted; (e) the principles of self-determination and winning support from the international community should be adhered to; and (f) the implementation of a North Korea policy needs to be based on national consensus.

President Kim's government put forward six ways to implement the new policy guidelines. They are reactivation of the 1991 basic agreement through inter-Korean dialogue; separation of business from politics; reunion of separated families; flexibility in providing food aid to North Korea; continued commitment to the light-water reactor project; and creation of a peaceful environment on the Korean peninsula.

The Kim Dae-jung government has consistently implemented its engagement policy toward North Korea since February 1998. As a result, the policy has been successful. First, the engagement policy has prevented a war on the Korean peninsula and has contributed to an international environment in which the cold war system on the peninsula could be dismantled. Further, it has also contributed to the stable management of problems relating to North Korea's nuclear freeze and long-range missile testing.

Second, the engagement policy has contributed to reducing tension and creating a favorable environment for improving inter-Korean relations. Inter-Korean economic cooperation and exchanges on a nongovernmental level have been substantially expanded. The Mt. Gumgang sightseeing project constitutes a milestone in the history of inter-Korean cooperation. More than four hundred thousand tourists visited Mt. Gumgang, in North Korea, between 18 November 1998, when the first cruise ship bound for Mt. Gumgang left, and the end of May 2001. Inter-Korean trade began in 1989 with a meager turnover of approximately $18 million, and its volume reached $330 million in 1999.

Third, the ROK government policy encouraged inter-Korean sports games, exchanges of separated family members, and cultural exchanges between Seoul and Pyongyang, contributing to more understanding between South and North Koreans. The ROK's policy of engagement contributed to Chairman Kim Jong-il's decision to agree to the landmark inter-Korean summit meeting.

The Significance of the Inter-Korean Summit Talks

President Kim Dae-jung and Chairman Kim Jong-il held summit meetings in Pyongyang on 13–15 June 2000. The inter-Korean summit, the first in the fifty-five years since the division of the country, produced a South-North joint declaration of 15 June 2000, which included the following:

1. The South and the North agreed to resolve the question of reunification independently and through the joint efforts of the Korean people.

2. Both sides recognized that there is a common element in the South's proposal for a confederation and the North's proposal

for a low level of federation as the formulae for achieving reunification, and the South and the North agreed to promote reunification in that direction.

3. The South and the North agreed to promptly resolve humanitarian issues such as exchange visits for separated family members and the question of unswerving communists who have been given long prison sentences in the South.

4. The South and the North agreed to consolidate mutual trust by promoting balanced development of the national economy through economic cooperation and by stimulating cooperation and exchanges in the civic, cultural, sports, public health, environmental, and other fields.

5. The South and the North agreed to hold a dialogue among relevant authorities in the near future to implement the agreement expeditiously.

President Kim Dae-jung and Chairman Kim Jong-il had frank, heart-to-heart talks for more than eleven hours. President Kim Dae-jung cordially invited Chairman Kim Jong-il to visit Seoul, and Chairman Kim agreed to visit South Korea in the near future.

Let us look at the significance of this first agreement by the leaders of South and North Korea. The declaration confirmed the principle of independence: Koreans themselves can solve the Korean issue through dialogue and negotiation. South and North agreed that they would first lay a foundation for unification through peaceful coexistence, reconciliation, and cooperation, working out their unification formulae through talks.

Both leaders agreed that reuniting separated family members is a humanitarian issue that must be resolved as a top priority. The South and North agreed that the issue should be worked out gradually and institutionalized so that ultimately all separated families will be reunited. As the first step, the two sides agreed to allow separated family members to meet on the occasion of the fifty-fifth anniversary of the National Liberation.

Inter-Korean economic cooperation is beneficial to both sides. Initial cooperative projects include the reconnection of the Seoul-Shinuiju railroad line and the anti-flood project on the Imjin-gang River. The two sides will discuss inter-Korean agreements on financial settlement, investment guarantees, avoidance of double taxation, and arbitration of disputes. And there was agreement on the return visit to Seoul by Chairman Kim Jong-il. The exact date for Chairman Kim's visit to Seoul will be determined in upcoming meetings. Clearly, the declaration contributes to the stability of Northeast Asia and thus to world peace.

The two leaders have confirmed that they will refrain from any acts threatening the other side. President Kim urged Chairman Kim to settle pending international disputes, including that of the North's missiles, at an early date, so that Pyongyang's relations with neighboring countries would improve. According to President Kim, Chairman Kim said that "it is desirable that the American troops continue to stay on the Korean peninsula and that he sent a high-level envoy to the United States to deliver this position to the American side." In short, the landmark declaration provided a framework for building a peace regime on the Korean peninsula.

Developments After the Summit

Let us now take a brief look at inter-Korean efforts since the summit to develop a peace process to build mutual confidence and cooperation between the Korean states.

Reunion of Separated Family Members. Resolution of the separated-family issue is a top priority for the Seoul government because it is an issue of fundamental human rights. It also has a symbolic importance for inter-Korean reconciliation and cooperation. Family reunions resumed after a fifteen-year break following the first exchange in 1985. According to the inter-Korean agreement on reunion of separated family members, by August 2001 three rounds of reunions of separated family members took place, with one hundred persons from each side participating in each group. As a result, a total of 3,600 persons were able to meet with at least one of their separated family members or relatives. . . .

Reconnection of the Seoul-Sinuiju Railway. The South and the North agreed on 1 September 2000 to reconnect the railway between Seoul and Sinuiju and to open a highway between Munsan and Gaeseong. A groundbreaking ceremony was held on 18 September 2000 to begin the reconnection of the Seoul-Sinuiju railway. South Korea began to clear landmines buried in the demilitarized zone to prepare for the reconnection of the railway. The segment requiring reconnection is a twenty-four-kilometer-long stretch of railway running between Munsan station in the South and Gaeseong station in the North. The highway to be built is 17.1 kilometers long and runs between the southern end of Unification Bridge and Gaeseong city in the North. Since the road construction will be completed in the demilitarized zone and across the military demarcation line, North Korea has not yet signed a "military guarantee agreement."

FAMILY REUNIONS AND HOPES FOR A UNITED KOREA

Following the peace summit between South Korea's President Kim Dae Jung and North Korea's Chairman Kim Jong Il in June 2000, the two countries have permitted family reunions between North and South Koreans separated since the end of the Korean War in 1953. The reunions are a small step taken to ease the tensions between North and South, and a small step toward the dream of most Koreans—the eventual reunification of the Korean peninsula. The following excerpt from Current Events *describes the reactions of a few of the families.*

Consoling his weeping girls at the reunion, Lee Kyoo Yom . . . said, "Stop crying. We shall meet again when the nation is reunified."

When South Korean Kim Hae-on, 93, touched the wrinkled hands of his wife for the first time in 50 years, he said, "Can you recognize me? You're alive. Thank you. I've waited for this day." His wife wept.

South Korean sisters Lee Jin-ock and Lee Jin-geum broke down when they saw their 82-year-old father. For years, the sisters held memorial services for their father, assuming he had died when he went out shopping during the war and never returned. . . .

"I will probably die before I see you again," cried 78-year-old Sohn Kap-soon as she clasped her North Korean brother's hands.

"Homecoming: Family Reunions Spark Hopes for a United Korea," *Current Events*, October 11, 2002, vol. 102, no. 6, p. 1(5).

Reconnection of the inter-Korean rail and road links will ensure a direct South-North trading route. Land transportation via this route to Eastern Europe would save considerable cost and time in comparison with sea transportation. The reconnection of the railway would also contribute to the peaceful use of the demilitarized zone and reduce tensions between the two sides.

Development of the Gaeseong Industrial Complex. The Hyundai Group and the Korea Land Corporation conducted a field study in August 2000 in the Gaeseong area for the planned development of an industrial complex in North Korea. Subsequently, an agreement was concluded between Hyundai and North Korea's Asia-Pacific Peace Committee to develop an industrial complex in Gaeseong. In November 2000, Hyundai and the Korea Land Corporation conducted a survey and geological testing on a 3.3-million-square-meter lot in Gaeseong and adjoining Panmun County. South Korea requested that the North enact laws related to wages, employment, leases, taxes, and remittances at an early date so that free economic activity and international competitiveness could be guaranteed at the Gaeseong industrial complex. The project has not made any significant progress, primarily because of stalemated inter-Korean relations since March 2001.

Joint Imjin River Flood Prevention Project. Though there has been recurring extensive flood damage along the Imjin River basin for the past several years, damage control efforts by either side have been hampered by the fact that the river flows across and along the border between the two Koreas. The North agreed on a joint flood prevention project for the Imjin River. Working-level flood prevention consultations took place in Pyongyang in February 2001. A consensus emerged from this meeting to set up an inter-Korean investigation team to look into possible joint flood prevention projects. The Imjin River flood control project will also contribute to the peaceful use of the demilitarized zone and symbolizes a joint effort by South and North Korea to promote mutual trust and benefits. The project did not make any further progress because the inter-Korean dialogue deadlocked.

Adoption of Four Economic Cooperation Agreements. At the inter-Korean working-level economic cooperation talks on 11 November 2000, South and North Korea adopted four agreements. The Agreement on Investment Protection stipulates the protection of invested assets and guarantees free investment activities, including remittances, free entry and exit, as well as the right to travel in the investment zone. The Agreement on Clearing Settlement stipulates the items that are subject to accounts clearance credit limits and designates a clearance of accounts bank. For items not subject to accounts clearance, international practice shall apply. The Agreement on Prevention of Double Taxation stipulates the prevention of double taxation by defining the scope of tax rights by income categories such as business income, interest, dividends, and royalties. It also provides for the exchange of tax information and methods of solving tax-related disputes. Finally, the Agreement on Procedure for Resolution of Commercial Disputes stipulates the formation of the South-North Arbitration Committee, a joint troubleshooting organization, as well as its functions and procedures for dispute settlement. The four agreements were sent to the South Korean National Assembly for approval.

People Exchanges Between the North and the South. During the one-year period (June 2000–May 2001) after the inter-Korean summit, there was an increase in exchanges of people between the two Koreas. Not including the South Korean tourists (more than four hundred thousand) who visited Mt. Gumgang on cruises, a total of 7,318 South Koreans visited the North and 647 North Koreans visited the South, increases of 1,698 and 381 persons, respectively, from the year before. Since exchanges began in 1989, the total number of individuals who have participated in these programs amounts to 21,909, 36 percent of them traveling across the border during the past year [2001] alone.

Social, Cultural, and Sports Exchanges. After the agreement to promote cooperation and exchanges in the civic, cultural, sports, public health, and environmental fields, a group of South Korean media executives visited the North in August 2000 and concluded a media exchange protocol. KBS and SBS televised live from Mt. Baekdu and Pyongyang, respectively, in September and October of last year [2001]. The newspaper *Hankyoreh* and MBC visited North Korea.

On the cultural front, the symphony orchestras of the two Koreas gave a joint performance in Seoul in August 2000, and a South Korean film entitled *JSA* (Joint Security Area) was shown in the North three months later. Other cultural exchanges include a South Korean classical opera troupe's performance of the musical *Chunhyangjeon* in Pyongyang in February 2001 and pop singer Kim Yeon-ja's solo performance in Hamheung two months later. A group of 109 South Korean tourists visited Mt. Baekdu in the North in September 2000, and a group of North Korean tourists were scheduled to visit Mt. Halla on Jeju Island in 2001.

A number of goodwill table tennis matches were held in Pyongyang to highlight the cause of unification, and an international motor rally was held at Mt. Gumgang, both in July 2000. In September 2000, the two Korean Olympic teams marched together during the opening ceremony of the Sydney Olympics, under a flag emblazoned with an undivided map of the Korean peninsula.

In religion, an Easter service was held in Seoul that was attended by Christians from the South and the North, two Buddhist services were held simultaneously in both capitals to celebrate the 15 August Liberation Day, and another joint service in commemoration of Buddha's birthday was held in 2001.

Meanwhile, the South proposed an exchange of groups of professors, college students, and literary figures, to which the North agreed in principle. . . .

Peace Process Stalled

In the year after the first inter-Korean summit, South–North Korean relations were transformed from hostility and confrontation to reconciliation and cooperation. Since the summit, through various channels, including four rounds of inter-Korean ministerial talks, the two Koreas have worked together to resolve thirty-one pending issues. . . .

[However,] the inter-Korean peace process has been discontinued since March 2001, when official talks were unproductive. The inter-Korean railway project has halted. The humanitarian project to promote the reunions of separated families has ended, with no more scheduled. The inter-Korean economic talks concerning the supply of electricity to the North have been put on hold. Hopes of fielding joint sports teams have dissolved. All inter-Korean government talks have been deadlocked. President Kim Dae-jung has made more than eight calls for Chairman Kim to visit Seoul as promised, but Chairman Kim has not given his itinerary yet. Furthermore, President Kim now faces domestic economic problems, the major opposition party's political criticism, and erosion of public support for his sunshine policy.

After reviewing U.S. policy toward North Korea, the Bush administration proposed negotiations on nuclear and conventional weapons issues, as well as North Korea's military presence at the demilitarized zone. As expected, North Korea rejected those terms, stating that it would not respond to the proposed talks before the United States withdraws those agenda items. North Korea has sent hostile signals to the U.S. government by including U.S. troop pullout from South Korea as a demand in the Moscow declaration on 4 August 2001. Unless the United States softens its hard-line policy toward North Korea, the inter-Korean peace process will likely fall apart. Chairman Kim Jong-il has made no move to visit Seoul for a second summit meeting as he promised [in 2001], but Kim's return visit to Seoul will be certain if the United States changes its hard-line policy toward North Korea. . . .

The Four-Party Peace Talks Stall

On 16 April 1996, the ROK and U.S. governments jointly proposed a four-party peace conference among the two Koreas, China, and the United States to initiate a process aimed at achieving a permanent peace treaty to replace the 1953 Korean armistice agreement. After sixteen months of negotiations, the first round of preliminary peace talks was convened on 5–7 August 1997 in New York to decide on the date, venue, and agenda for substantive negotiations. The United States, China, and the two Koreas agreed to meet in Geneva and also agreed on a format for the peace talks, which envisaged a general conference and subcommittee meetings on separate agenda items. . . .

Although six plenary sessions were held, the four parties have yet to set agenda items to be discussed at the talks. Whereas South Korea has kept its stand that it wanted to discuss issues that are easily resolved, North Korea has tenaciously maintained its position that the issues of the withdrawal of U. S. troops and a Washington-Pyongyang peace treaty should be resolved before anything else. . . .

Future Prospects for Peace

The Korean peace process depends largely on three major factors: (a) the political will of the two Korean leaders, (b) the South Korean domestic political process and its economic conditions, and (c) international factors, especially President Bush's new hard-line policy toward North Korea. . . .

The divided Korean peninsula issue should be solved peacefully by South and North Koreans themselves with the support of the four major powers surrounding the Korean peninsula. Since normalization of inter-Korean relations will take time, the two Korean states should patiently work together to create a stable peace system on the peninsula, and the four major powers— the United States, China, Japan, and Russia—should play supporting roles in building a stable peace between the two Koreas.

Human Rights and North Korean Repression

By the Bureau of Democracy, Human Rights, and Labor, U.S. Department of State

North Korea's human rights abuses are documented in the following selection, excerpted from a U.S. State Department report published in 2002. The report describes in detail the types of abuses carried out by the Kim Jong Il regime in North Korea, including reports from defectors that the government executes political prisoners, opponents of the regime, repatriated defectors, and others. The regime also is reported to be responsible for disappearances, in which individuals suspected of political crimes are taken from their homes by state security officials, and South Koreans and other foreigners are kidnapped abroad. Other human rights abuses described in the report are the torture and mistreatment of prisoners, many of whom have died from disease, starvation, or exposure, arbitrary arrests and detentions, and the denial of civil liberties such as the right to a fair trial, workers' rights, the right of privacy, and freedom of press, religion, and association. Finally, North Korea severely restricts travel, intensely indoctrinates children with political propaganda, and prohibits citizens from pursuing any change in their government—common characteristics of a highly repressive, totalitarian regime.

T he Democratic People's Republic of Korea (DPRK) is a dictatorship under the absolute rule of the Korean Workers' Party (KWP). Kim Il Sung led the DPRK from its inception until his death in 1994. Since then his son Kim Jong Il has exercised unchallenged authority. Kim Jong Il was named General Secretary of the KWP in October 1997. In September 1998, the Supreme People's Assembly reconfirmed Kim Jong Il

Bureau of Democracy, Human Rights, and Labor, *Korea, Democratic People's Republic of: Country Reports on Human Rights Practices—2001.* Washington, DC: Bureau of Democracy, Human Rights, and Labor, U.S. Department of State, March 4, 2002.

as Chairman of the National Defense Commission and declared that position the "highest office of state." The presidency was abolished leaving the late Kim Il Sung as the DPRK's only president. The titular head of state is Kim Yong Nam, the President of the Presidium of the Supreme People's Assembly. Both Kim Il Sung and Kim Jong Il continue to be the objects of intense personality cults. The regime emphasizes "juche," a national ideology of self-reliance. The judiciary is not independent.

The Korean People's Army is the primary organization responsible for external security. It is assisted by a large military reserve force and several quasi-military organizations, including the Worker-Peasant Red Guards and the People's Security Force. These organizations assist the Ministry of Public Security and the KWP in maintaining internal security. Members of the security forces committed serious human rights abuses.

The State directs all significant economic activity, and only government-controlled labor unions are permitted in this country of 22 million persons. Industry continued to operate at significantly reduced capacity, reflecting antiquated plants and equipment and severe shortages of inputs. This decline is due in part to the collapse of the former Soviet Union and East European communist governments and the subsequent sharp decline in trade and aid. Efforts at recovery have been hampered by heavy military spending—which amounted to perhaps one-quarter of gross domestic product before the economy went into decline and is probably now larger as a share of national output. The economy also has been held back by a lack of access to commercial lending stemming from the DPRK's default on its foreign debt, and its inability to obtain loans from international financial institutions. Never food self-sufficient, the country relies on international aid and trade to supplement domestic production, which has been hobbled by disastrous agricultural policies. This is true even when crop production is relatively good, as it was during the year [2002]. Since 1995, nearly annual droughts and floods have destroyed crops and ruined agricultural land, and hunger and malnutrition have been widespread. Famine has caused internal dislocation and widespread malnutrition, and an estimated several hundreds of thousands to two million persons died from starvation and related diseases. Economic and political conditions have caused thousands of persons to flee their homes. The Government continued to seek international food aid, produce "alternative foods," and take other steps to boost production. It has permitted the spread of farmers' markets to make up for the contraction of food supplied through the public distribution system. Food, clothing, and energy are rationed throughout the country. The U.N.'s World Food Program provides assistance to children and mothers, the elderly, and persons employed in flood damage recovery efforts. The gross national product (GNP) may have grown slightly in 2000 due largely to international aid and limited South Korean investment, but this followed nearly a decade of steady decline in which GNP is estimated to have shrunk by half since 1993. Most foreign observers note improved food and other economic conditions over the last year.

The Government's human rights record remained poor, and it continued to commit numerous serious abuses. Citizens do not have the right peacefully to change their government. There continued to be reports of extrajudicial killings and disappearances. Citizens are detained arbitrarily, and many are held as political prisoners; prison conditions are harsh. The constitutional provisions for an independent judiciary and fair trials are not implemented in practice. The regime subjects its citizens to rigid controls. The leadership perceives most international norms of human rights, especially individual rights, as illegitimate, alien, and subversive to the goals of the State and party. During the year, the Government entered into a human rights dialogue with the European Union; two meetings were held, but no significant results were reported. The Penal Code is Draconian, stipulating capital punishment and confiscation of assets for a wide variety of "crimes against the revolution," including defection, attempted defection, slander of the policies of the party or State, listening to foreign broadcasts, writing "reactionary" letters, and possessing reactionary printed matter. The Government prohibits freedom of speech, the press, assembly, and association, and all forms of cultural and media activities are under the tight control of the party. Radios sold in North Korea receive North Korean radio broadcasts only; radios obtained abroad by the general public must be altered to work in a similar manner. Cable News Network (CNN) television is available in one Pyongyang hotel frequented by foreigners. Under these circumstances, little outside information reaches the public except that approved and disseminated by the Government. The Government restricts freedom of religion, citizens' movements, and worker rights. There were reports of trafficking in women and young girls among refugees and workers crossing the border into China. . . .

Arbitrary and Unlawful Deprivation of Life

Defectors and refugees report that the regime executes political prisoners, opponents of the regime, some repatriated defectors, and others (reportedly including military officers suspected of espionage or of plotting against Kim Jong Il). Criminal law makes the death penalty mandatory for activities "in collusion with imperialists" aimed at "suppressing the national liberation struggle." Some prisoners are sentenced to death for such ill-defined "crimes" as "ideological divergence," "opposing socialism," and other "counterrevolutionary crimes." In some cases, executions reportedly were carried out at public meetings attended by workers, students, and school children. Executions also have been carried out before assembled inmates at places of detention. Border guards reportedly have orders to shoot–to–kill potential defectors. . . .

Disappearances

The Government reportedly is responsible for cases of disappearance. According to defector reports, individuals suspected of political crimes often are taken from their homes by state security officials late at night and sent directly, without trial, to camps for political prisoners. There also have been reports of past government involvement in the kidnapping abroad of South Koreans, Japanese, and other foreign nationals. As many as 20 Japanese may have been kidnapped and detained in North Korea. According to Japanese government officials, these abductions took place between 1977 and 1983.

Following a December 1999 meeting between officials from the Red Cross societies of North Korea and Japan, the Government agreed to conduct an investigation into the fate of the missing Japanese nationals. However, on December 17, the Government announced it was suspending the investigation. In addition several suspected cases of kidnapping, hostage-taking, and other acts of violence apparently intended to intimidate ethnic Koreans living in China and Russia have been reported. There were unconfirmed reports that North Korean agents kidnapped a South Korean citizen, Reverend Dongshik Kim, in China and took him to North Korea in January 2000. There is credible evidence that North Korea may have been involved in the July 1995 abduction of a South Korean citizen working in China as a missionary. This missionary subsequently appeared publicly in North Korea and was portrayed as a defector. The DPRK denies that it has been involved in kidnappings. . . .

Torture and Other Cruel, Inhuman, or Degrading Treatment or Punishment

While information on recent practices is sparse, credible reports indicate that prisoners are mistreated and that many have died from disease, starvation, or exposure. . . .

[For example,] in 1998 a Polish newspaper reported the experiences of a woman who spent 10 years in a North Korean concentration camp before fleeing first to China and then to South Korea. The approximately 1,800 inmates in this particular camp typically worked 16 to 17 hours a day. The woman reported severe beatings, torture involving water forced into a victim's stomach with a rubber hose and pumped out by guards jumping on a board placed across the victim's abdomen, and chemical and biological warfare experiments allegedly conducted on inmates by the army. South Korean media reported that the DPRK State Security Agency manages the camps through use of forced labor, beatings, torture, and public executions.

Arbitrary Arrest, Detention, or Exile

There are no restrictions on the ability of the Government to detain and imprison persons at will and to hold them incommunicado.

Little information is available on criminal justice procedures and practices, and outside observation of the legal system has been limited to "show trials" for traffic violations and other minor offenses.

According to an NGO [nongovernmental organization], family members and other concerned persons find it virtually impossible to obtain information on charges against or the length of sentences of detained persons. Judicial review of detentions does not exist in law or in practice.

Defectors claim that the Government detains between 150,000 to 200,000 persons for political reasons, sometimes along with their family members, in maximum security camps in remote areas. The Government denies the existence of such prison camps but admits that there are "education centers" for persons who "commit crimes by mistake.". . .

The Government is not known to use forced exile. However, the Government routinely uses forced resettlement and has relocated many tens of thousands of persons from Pyongyang to the countryside. Although disabled veterans are treated extremely well, there also are reports that other persons with physical disabilities and those judged to be politically unreliable have been sent to internal exile. Often those relocated are selected on the basis of family background. Nonetheless, there is some evidence that class background is less important than in the past because of the regime's emphasis on the solidarity of the "popular masses," and united front efforts with overseas Koreans. According to unconfirmed September 1997 foreign press reports, some 500 senior officials were sent into internal exile.

Denial of Fair Public Trial

The Constitution states that courts are independent and that judicial proceedings are to be carried out in strict accordance with the law; however, an independent judiciary and individual rights do not exist. The Public Security Ministry dispenses with trials in political cases and refers prisoners to the Ministry of State Security for punishment.

The Constitution contains elaborate procedural protections, and it states that cases should be heard in public and that the accused has the right to a defense; under some circumstances hearings may be closed to the public as stipulated by law. When trials are held, the Government apparently assigns lawyers. Reports indicate that defense lawyers are not considered representatives of the accused; rather, they are expected to help the court by persuading the accused to confess guilt. Some reports note a distinction between those accused of political crimes and common criminals and state that the Government affords trials or lawyers only to the latter. The Government considers critics of the regime to be "political criminals.". . .

Arbitrary Interference with Privacy, Family, Home, or Correspondence

The Constitution provides for the inviolability of person and residence and the privacy of correspondence; however, the Government does not respect these provisions in practice. The regime subjects its citizens to rigid controls. The state leadership perceives most international norms of human rights, and especially individual rights, as alien social concepts subversive to the goals of the State and party. The Government relies upon an extensive, multilevel system of informers to identify critics and potential troublemakers. Whole communities sometimes are subjected to massive security checks. The possession of "reactionary material" and listening to foreign broadcasts are both considered crimes that may subject the transgressor to harsh punishments. In some cases, entire families are punished for alleged political offenses committed by one member of the family. For example, defectors have reported families being punished because children had accidentally defaced photographs of one of the two Kims. Families must display pictures of the two Kims in their homes, and must keep them clean. Local party officials have conducted unannounced inspections once per month, and if the inspectors find a family has neglected its photos, the punishment is to write self-criticism throughout an entire year.

The Government monitors correspondence and telephones. Telephones essentially are restricted to domestic operation although some international service is available on a very restricted basis.

The Constitution provides for the right to petition. However, when an anonymous petition or complaint about state administration is submitted, the Ministries of State Security and Public Safety seek to identify the author through handwriting analysis. The suspected individual may be subjected to a thorough investigation and punishment.

The regime justifies its dictatorship with arguments derived from concepts of collective consciousness and the superiority of the collective over the individual, appeals to nationalism, and citations of "the juche idea." The authorities emphasize that the core concept of juche is "the ability to act independently without regard to outside interference." Originally described as "a creative application of Marxism-Leninism" in the national context, juche is a malleable philosophy reinterpreted from time to time by the regime as its ideological needs change and is used by the regime as a "spiritual" underpinning for its rule. . . .

The authorities subject citizens of all age groups and occupations to intensive political and ideological indoctrination. Even after Kim Il Sung's death, his cult of personality and the glorification of his family and the official juche ideology remained omnipresent. The cult approaches the level of a state religion. . . .

Freedom of Speech and Press

Although the Constitution provides for freedom of speech and the press, the Government prohibits the exercise of these rights in practice. Articles of the Constitution that require citizens to follow "socialist norms of life" and to obey a "collective spirit" take precedence over individual political or civil liberties. The regime only permits activities that support its objectives.

The Government strictly curtails freedom of speech. The authorities may punish persons for criticizing the regime or its policies by imprisonment or "corrective labor.". . .

The Government attempts to control all information. Claiming that the country is under continuing threat of armed aggression, the Government carefully manages the visits of foreign journalists. . . . Although more foreign journalists have been allowed into the country, the Government still maintains strict control over the movements of foreign visitors. For example, journalists accompanying the U.S. Secretary of State were not allowed to visit a department store or a train station; they were not allowed to talk to officials or to persons on the street. Those who arrived with cellular or satellite phones had them confiscated for the duration of their stay. Domestic media censorship is enforced strictly, and no deviation from the official government line is tolerated.

The regime prohibits listening to foreign media broadcasts except by the political elite, and violators are subject to severe punishment. Radios and television sets receive only domestic programming; radios obtained from abroad must be submitted for alteration to operate in a similar manner. CNN television broadcasts are available in a Pyongyang hotel frequented by foreigners. Private telephone lines operate on an internal system that prevents making and receiving calls from outside the country. International phone lines are available under very restricted circumstances. According to a press report, there may be very limited Internet access in the country for government officials; an Internet service provider based in China has begun e-mail service that may link to an Intranet used by senior officials. . . .

Freedom of Peaceful Assembly and Association

Although the Constitution provides for freedom of assembly, the Government does not respect this provision in practice. The Government prohibits any public meetings without authorization.

Although the Constitution provides for freedom of association, the Government does not respect this provision in practice. There are no known organizations other than those created by the Government. Professional associations exist primarily as a means of government monitoring and control over the members of these organizations.

Freedom of Religion

The Constitution provides for "freedom of religious belief"; however, in practice the Government discourages organized religious activity except that which is supervised by officially recognized groups. Genuine religious freedom does not exist. The Constitution also stipulates that religion "should not be used for purposes of dragging in foreign powers or endangering public security.". . .

Freedom of Movement Within the Country, Foreign Travel, Emigration, and Repatriation

Although the Constitution provides for the "freedom to reside in or travel to any place," the Government does not respect these rights in practice. In the past, the regime has controlled strictly internal travel, requiring a travel pass for any movement outside one's home village. These passes were granted only for official travel or attendance at a relative's wedding or funeral. Long delays in obtaining the necessary permit often resulted in denial of the right to travel even for these limited purposes. In recent years, it appears that the internal controls on travel have eased significantly. Due to the worsening food conditions in the country, the Government at times has taken a benign approach to those who violate internal travel rules, allowing citizens to leave their villages to search for food, and there are reports of large-scale movement of persons across the country in search of food. Only members of a very small elite have vehicles for personal use. The regime tightly controls access to civilian aircraft, trains, buses, food, and fuel. . . .

The Right of Citizens to Change Their Government

Citizens have no right or mechanisms to change their leadership or government peacefully. The political system is dominated completely by the KWP, with Kim Il Sung's heir Kim Jong Il in full control. Very little reliable information is available on intraregime politics following Kim Il Sung's death. The legislature, the Supreme People's Assembly (SPA), which meets only a few days per year, serves only to rubber-stamp resolutions presented to it by the party leadership. In 1997 Kim Jong Il acceded to the position of General Secretary of the KWP. In 1998 the SPA reconfirmed Kim as the Chairman of the National Defense Commission and declared that position the "highest office of State." The presidency was abolished, leaving the late Kim Il Sung as the country's only President. The titular head of state is Kim Yong Nam, the President of the Presidium of the SPA.

In an effort to give the appearance of democracy, the Government has created several "minority parties." Lacking grassroots organizations, they exist only as rosters of officials with token representation in the SPA. Their primary purpose appears to be promoting government objectives abroad as touring parliamentarians. Free elections do not exist, and the regime has criticized the concept of free elections and competition among political parties as an artifact of capitalist decay. . . .

Investigation of Alleged Violations of Human Rights

The Government does not permit any independent domestic organizations to monitor human rights conditions or to comment on violations of such rights. Although a North Korean Human Rights Committee was established in 1992, it denied the existence of any human rights violations in the country. However, by offering international human rights organizations an identifiable official interlocutor, the Committee helped increase the ability of international human rights organizations to enter into two-way communication with the regime. . . .

In April 1998, during the 54th meeting of the U.N. Commission on Human Rights, the North Korean delegation accused the international community of slandering the Government's human rights record, adding that the DPRK Government would not tolerate "any attempt to hurt the sovereignty and dignity of the country under the pretext of human rights." In July a North Korean delegate reporting to the U.N. Human Rights Committee dismissed reports of human rights violations in the country as the propaganda of "egoistic" and "hostile forces" seeking to undermine the sovereignty of the country. . . .

Discrimination Based on Race, Sex, Religion, Disability, Language, or Social Status

The Constitution grants equal rights to all citizens. However, in practice the Government denies its citizens most fundamental human rights. There was pervasive discrimination on the basis of social status.

Women . . . The Constitution states that "women hold equal social status and rights with men." However, although women are represented proportionally in the labor force, few women have reached high levels of the party or the Government. In many small factories, the work force is predominantly female. Like men, working-age women must work. They are thus required to leave their preschool children in the care of elderly relatives or in state nurseries. However, according to the Constitution, women with large families are to work shorter hours. There were reports of trafficking in women and young girls among North Koreans crossing the border into China.

Children Social norms reflect traditional, family-centered values in which children are cherished. The State provides compulsory education for all children until the age of 15. However, some children are denied educational opportunities and subjected to other punishments and disadvantages as a result of the loyalty classification system and the principle of "collective retribution" for the transgressions of their parents.

Like others in society, children are the objects of intense political indoctrination; even mathematics textbooks propound party dogma. In addition, foreign visitors and academic sources report that children from an early age are subjected to several hours a week of mandatory military training and indoctrination at their schools. School children sometimes are sent to work in factories or in the fields for short periods to assist in completing special projects or in meeting production goals.

According to the WFP, the international community is feeding nearly every child under the age of 7 years. In some remote provinces, many persons over the age of 6 years reportedly appear to be suffering from long-term malnutrition. A nutrition survey carried out by UNICEF and the WFP in the aftermath of flood disasters found that 16 percent of children under 7 years of age suffered from acute malnutrition and that 62 percent suffered from stunted growth. In 1997 a senior UNICEF official said that approximately 80,000 children in North Korea were in immediate danger of dying from hunger and disease; 800,000 more were suffering from malnutrition to a serious but lesser degree. . . .

In the fall of 1998, the NGO's Doctors Without Borders (DWB) and Doctors of the World closed their offices in the country because the Government reportedly denied them access to a large population of sick and malnourished children. DWB officials stated that they had evidence that orphaned and homeless children had been gathered into so-called "9-27 camps." These camps reportedly were established under a September 27, 1995 order from Kim Jong Il to "normalize" the country. Refugees who have escaped from the 9-27 camps into China have reported inhuman conditions. . . .

Persons with Disabilities Traditional social norms condone discrimination against persons with physical disabilities. Apart from veterans with disabilities, persons with disabilities almost never are seen within the city limits of Pyongyang, and several defectors and other former residents report that persons with disabilities are assigned to the rural areas routinely. According to one report, authorities check every 2 to 3 years in the capital for persons with deformities and relocate them to special facilities in the countryside. There are no legally mandated provisions for accessibility to buildings or government services for persons with disabilities. In a 1998 statement, the UNCRC criticized "de facto discrimination" in the country against children with disabilities.

Worker Rights Nongovernmental labor unions do not exist. The KWP purports to represent the interests of all labor. There is a single labor organization, the General Federation of Trade Unions of Korea, which is affiliated with the formerly Soviet-controlled World Federation of Trade Unions. Operating under this umbrella, unions function on the classic "Stalinist model," with responsibility for mobilizing workers behind production goals and for providing health, education, cultural, and welfare facilities. Unions do not have the right to strike. . . .

Workers have no right to organize or to bargain collectively. Government ministries set wages. The State assigns all jobs. Ideological purity is as important as professional competence in deciding who receives a particular job, and foreign companies that have established joint ventures report that all their employees must be hired from lists submitted by the KWP. Factory and farm workers are organized into councils, which do have an impact on management decisions. . . .

In its 2000 and 2001 reports to the U.N. Human Rights Committee, the Government claimed that its laws prohibit forced or compulsory labor. However, the Government frequently mobilizes the population for construction projects. Military conscripts routinely are used for this purpose as well. "Reformatory labor" and "reeducation through labor" are common punishments for political offenses. Amnesty International reports that forced labor, such as logging and tending crops, is common among prisoners. School children are assigned to factories or farms for short periods to help meet production goals.

North Korea's Struggle for Regime Legitimacy and Security

By Han S. Park

North Korea is viewed by many political analysts as a "rogue" nation that pursues erratic and irrational foreign policies of brinkmanship and nuclear threats. In the following selection, Han S. Park, a political science professor and director of the Center for the Study of Global Affairs at the University of Georgia, analyzes the reasons for North Korea's policies from the perspective of that country's leadership. He explains that North Korea sees itself as the only legitimate Korean government, surrounded by hostile forces that seek its overthrow by force or by other means. For example, the North not only fears military invasion, it also views attempts by South Korea and the United States to open up the North Korean economy as threatening and subversive because they may undermine the legitimacy and control of the North Korean regime. Above all, Park states, North Korea seeks to ensure regime stability. To do this, it pursues unconventional policies that other countries view negatively. These policies include information control to protect its citizens from "undesirable" capitalist influences; acquisition of food and economic aid to alleviate famine and economic hardships; adoption of a nationalist ideology; and pursuit of militarism combined with pragmatic diplomatic overtures to advance its security goals. North Korea's development of nuclear weapons and long-range missiles, viewed in this light, provides critical bargaining leverage for the small country, and will not be abandoned lightly.

Han S. Park, *North Korea: The Politics of Unconventional Wisdom.* Boulder, CO: Lynne Rienner Publishers, 2002. Copyright © 2002 by Lynne Rienner Publishers, Inc. Reproduced by permission.

The Korean peninsula is the most heavily armed area in the world in terms of both manpower and weaponry. One need only to travel to the DMZ [demilitarized zone] to view the massive forces confronting each other. What is not visible to the casual observer is the pervasive mistrust that exists between the two systems, mistrust that makes the security system all the more precarious. North Korea is often vilified as irrational, unpredictable, and lacking in civility. Such criticisms are made of North Korea with little knowledge about the thought processes, policy motivations, and behavioral traits of this alienated system. Simple labels such as reclusive system, Stalinist state, irrational actor, and rogue regime have not been very helpful in explaining its policies. . . .

North Korea's Fears

Pyongyang [North Korea] sees itself surrounded by hostile and evil forces that are undermining its legitimacy. It further believes that these forces are constantly preparing to overthrow the system by force or other means. During the Cold War era, Pyongyang's primary concern was to prepare itself against possible military provocation by the United States and South Korea. But in the post–Cold War world order, Pyongyang also feels its existence to be threatened by subversive means of inducing changes and reforms that are designed to destroy the very fabric of the political system, thus causing system collapse. In addition to the traditionally adversarial systems of the United States and its "puppet" South Korea, Japan has joined the ranks of Pyongyang's primary enemies.

Pyongyang has never forgotten the stark reality that the Korean War has never ended. It is in a state of temporary truce. The continuing presence of U.S. forces in South Korea, including some 36,000 ground troops, is keenly felt in North Korea as a formidable and direct threat to the security of the region. The annual military exercises by the joint forces of the United States and South Korea, termed Team Spirit, cause the utmost alarm throughout the country. . . .

The explosive economic expansion of South Korea, which coincided with difficulties in the North, has been no source of comfort for Pyongyang. After German reunification, in which the socialist east was absorbed by the capitalist west, the Seoul government acted as though the collapse of the Pyongyang regime was imminent. The Seoul government even contended that the fate of North Korea was in its hands. Furthermore, Seoul has changed its longstanding position by publicly maintaining that the collapse of the Pyongyang government would not be in the interest of South Korea. Seoul is open about its reluctance in assuming what it terms as the "burden" of reunification. Since the beginning of Kim Young Sam's government in 1992, it has been Seoul's official position to induce reform and changes in the North Korean system, as opposed to a sudden collapse. The much-orchestrated "soft landing" policy of the Kim Young Sam administration resulted from this consideration. This policy was designed to force North Korea to terminate the journey of socialism by inducing an economic soft-landing through gradual reforms rather than crashing into a sudden collapse. It was little more than an insult to and humiliation of the North Korean system. As expected, this policy did not generate any sympathy from Pyongyang. It was indeed a policy of gradual absorption rather than a peacefully negotiated integration. It is not surprising that the sunshine policy of the Kim Dae-jung [South Korean] government is also seen in this light.

The North's Legitimacy War with the South

The mythical notion of saving humanity from consumerism and the decadent culture of capitalism is seldom taken seriously by North Koreans. This visionary concept is only for rhetoric and propaganda, except for a small number of blind believers. But North Koreans are deadly serious about the ongoing legitimacy war with the South. . . . The survival of the system is directly linked to the regime's legitimacy competition with the South. The nature of this competition is "unconventional" in the sense that economic prosperity is of little relevance. It is the support for the system (the citizens' state of mind) that determines whether it is legitimate or illegitimate. In this sense, what matters is the subjective basis on which regime legitimacy is established rather than such objective factors as economic output or material life conditions. Although prolonged deprivation of basic needs such as food may lead to criticism of the government and diminishing support for the leadership, material life conditions do not determine system legitimacy directly or immediately. Viewed in this context, we can see that North Koreans may well be persuaded that the spiritual and ideological solidarity of the North might generate a broad basis of support, not only in the North but in the South as well.

To the South Korean journalists who visited following the historic summit in June 2000, Kim Jong Il reportedly said that "we can make a great unified country when South Korea's economic and technological assets become empowered with North Korea's spiritual and ideological achievement." This comment was clearly meant to indicate that North Korea is the ideologically fit Korean nation because of its strong nationalism and spiritual integrity. Kim Jong Il's apparent concession that South Korea is economically and technologically more advanced in no way undermines Pyongyang's position in its age-old legitimacy war with the South. On the contrary, the comment was an open affirmation to the South Korean audience of North Korea's longstanding insistence that nationalist ideology provides legitimacy to the Korean nation and that the Pyongyang regime is, therefore, a more legitimate system. North Korea is encouraged by the apparent acceptance of Kim Jong Il himself among South Koreans as an able and sophisticated leader and the rising popularity of northern entertainers, artists, and sportsmen who have visited the South following the summit.

To Pyongyang, the rapidly changing public opinion among the South Korean people in the second half of the year 2000 was encouraging indeed. . . . The terms of the summit agreement seem to be consistent with the long-held North Korean policies of national self-determination and confederacy, which gives Pyongyang sound grounds for claiming a victory in the legitimacy competition. This "victory" was publicly and tangibly demonstrated by the return of sixty-eight prisoners of war who had been held in South Korea since the Korean War. None of them denounced their loyalty to the North Korean regime for some fifty years. . . .

North Korea's Goals

The national goals of the North Korean system have been remarkably salient and consistent. The decisionmakers seem to have a clear sense of goals, strategies, and tactics. People from all walks of life share their perceptions. Once the center (meaning the Party) makes a decision, it will be efficiently transferred to the rank and file through the most effective channels of Party cells, community residential units, workplaces, and all the aforementioned agents of socialization.

The goals of North Korea are not fundamentally different from those of any other system, in that it pursues first and foremost system survival and a stable leadership. Like any other system, North Korea seeks prosperity as much as possible but not at the expense of system survival. Furthermore, North Korea's desire to establish a system identity is by no means unique to that country. In other words, North Korea has a set of goals shared by any system: survival, prosperity, and identity.

With respect to the goal of system survival, what is unique about North Korea is the nature of the system itself. The goal is not just keeping the leadership in power or maintaining the political entity without being swallowed up by another system. It means the perpetuation of the system characteristics that tend to be unique and peculiar. Once these characteristics are compromised, the system faces the danger of being absorbed into the South. The system simply cannot stay alive by being similar to the South; it would only be poorer, inferior, and less popular among the people. Pyongyang has been vigorously waging the legitimacy war against South Korea since the inception of its system. One must realize that North Koreans believe for good reason that system change means system collapse. Therefore, their resistance to change is in fact their resistance to collapse. Viewed from this perspective, it is not hard to understand why the North Korean leadership has refused to compromise its stance on the question of reforms and opening to the outside. It is a huge dilemma for North Korea that it cannot participate in the global market to make best use of its high-quality labor force, rich mineral resources, and strategically placed geographical location, which may well bring the necessary comparative advantage in market competition. This fixation on survival constrains the choice of acceptable strategies and tactics for the goal of system identity. The identity of the system cannot be easily altered from an ideological (*Juche*) system to a pragmatic system without losing the legitimacy war with the South, thereby risking system survival.

Information Control

The imperative of system survival in the peculiar context of North Korea at this historical juncture requires a specific set of conditions. Among the central conditions are the defense of the country from military provocation, the preservation of system legitimacy vis-à-vis South Korea, and the protection of the population from disruptive, capitalist, decadent culture. These conditions have led to the development of a series of policy strategies and tactical maneuverings.

First and foremost, information control is an indispensable strategy. To criticize North Korea for maintaining a closed system whereby the population is protected from external forces without considering the aforementioned adversarial conditions is irresponsible. No government will allow its system to drift into a course of feared demise. Pyongyang has every reason to shield the population from the same forces that swallowed up the former socialist systems in Eastern Europe. It is true that Pyongyang does not allow undesirable information and materials to be smuggled in. It is true that tourists coming into the country as part of the Hyundai project at Mt. Kumkang are carefully monitored and guarded so that the population will not come into contact with the tourists and their consumerist lifesyle. It is true that the border is not open. It is true that there is no diversity in the content of mass media outputs, which are strictly controlled by the government. These seemingly "undemocratic" practices may be a source of displeasure to the outside observers, but one can hardly characterize the strategic policy postures as being irrational or abnormal. Considering Pyongyang's perception of the demise of the Soviet Union and the socialist systems in Europe, it is only natural for the leadership to protect the population and system from the same adversarial forces that induced their collapse in the first place.

For Pyongyang, it is also imperative to view the reforms and "democratization" in those countries as mistakes that only worsened the situation. Therefore, it is not unusual for Pyongyang to claim that the "former Soviet Union and Eastern European countries are grieving and repenting today . . . countries where capitalism is restored presented a serious lesson to the people . . . if one defends socialism, it is victorious and if one discards socialism it is death" [from the newspaper *Rodong Shinmun*].

Economic Aid

Second, North Korea's strategic move at this time has to do with alleviating grim economic realities. The country has been suffering from extremely severe economic hardships. Although no accurate account of the number of deaths resulting from starvation is available, it is generally assumed that "since 1995, two million people of a population of 24 million have died of hunger and disease" [*Washington Post*]. Malnutrition and inadequate health care are so pervasive that the government places the highest emphasis on alleviating these problems, and all policy efforts are geared in this direction. Western observers tend to attribute the food shortage problem to the failure of the socialist system, a generalization that has routinely been made with respect to the European socialist experience. But the North Korean case is far more complicated. There are multiple reasons for the food shortage and accompanying economic difficulties. The first and most obvious reason was indeed the disruptive weather. Heavy rainfall and floods swept away as much as 40 percent of the arable land in 1996. Since then, the weather conditions have never been favorable. Also true is the fact that much of the hillside farming areas are no longer arable because of erosion that may have been exacerbated by the practice of removing trees and natural vegetation in an effort to expand much-needed arable plots. Another major cause of general economic difficulty is the cessation or reduction of trade relations with North Korea's traditional partners, including China. The vacuum created by the drastic and abrupt change in the political spectrum of the socialist bloc has never been filled with alternative economic ties with the international market.

In seeking humanitarian aid, Pyongyang has restrained itself from making overtures that would be excessively embarrassing to the dignity of the people. Furthermore, the leadership has been constrained by the imperative of protecting the population from contact with capitalist consumerism. In fact, Pyongyang often points to Western relief efforts as nothing more than an excuse for the capitalists to infiltrate North Korea and seize upon the misfortune of a people to achieve political and economic objectives. The government's determination to solve the food shortage problem has steered efforts in boosting agricultural productivity. Pyongyang does not enjoy the status of being a "bread basket." It has tried to develop agricultural and livestock industries by allowing its scientists to go abroad to learn about transferable technology, more productive seeds, and improved animal husbandry. The current mass campaign to increase the use and productivity of potatoes should be seen as an attempt to add options to the people's diet beyond rice. Pyongyang's desire for increased agricultural productivity has forced it to agree to "invite" U.S. inspectors to the Kumchangri underground site, which was suspected to be a hidden site for the nuclear weapons program. At first, North Koreans refused to open the site to foreign inspectors on the grounds of protecting national sovereignty. But in the end, they agreed and allowed inspection. The agreement called for a bilateral "agricultural pilot project" that included the farming of potatoes.

One of the policy strategies aimed at increasing agricultural productivity without relying on external intervention is found in "localization" efforts. In fact, Jagang Province, under the governorship of former prime minister Yeon Hyong Muk, has been singled out as a model case of regional economic self-help. Small power plants by the thousands have been constructed to promote self-reliance in electricity at the local level. The popularity enjoyed by the windmill project provided by a California-based organization, Nautilus Institute, can be seen in this same light. In short, Pyongyang has been responding to the challenge of food shortage concertedly and concretely.

Nationalism

Third, the new leadership under Kim Jong Il has adopted a policy strategy that placed a premium on ultranationalism. The only rational course of action on the part of the new leadership was nationalism. Pyongyang had to be alarmed by the massive tide of market forces and reformist ideology that had swept the socialist world. Especially alarming in this regard was the absorption of East Germany by West Germany. After German unification in 1989, most observers predicted that the North Korean system would inevitably follow in the footsteps of East Germany, giving it a limited lifespan ranging from a few months to no more than three years. These observers predicted that the North Korean system might survive under the charismatic leadership of Kim Il Sung but that it could never survive the death of the revered leader. Pyongyang could not simply disregard these observations and do nothing to cope with the new political dynamism in the region and the world. The nationalism of Kim Il Sung had helped solidify power and consolidate the diverse and competing factions in the formative stage of the republic. After his death, that same nationalism was used by the current leadership to protect regime stability and integrate the political system.

Militarism

A fourth policy strategy involves the military. Following the death of Kim in 1994, the junior Kim's efforts were devoted to the promotion of the military in the belief that defense preparedness precedes any other national goal, including even the people's livelihood. The principle of militarism is not new in North Korea. It has always been sustained since the Korean War. What is relatively new is the supremacy of the military leadership in the political system itself. At no time in the past was the military given the ultimate authority in policymaking that it has today. The new constitution, adopted in September 1998, clearly endorses the centrality of the military, as evidenced by the ascendance of the chairman of the Military Commission as the supreme commander and the ultimate reservoir of state authority. The doctrine of military supremacy, however, does not advocate control by physical force alone. In fact, the ideology of *Juche* has been undergoing a transformation from being an abstract worldview to a concrete nationalist doctrine that employs the principle of militarism as the policy yardstick.

Coincidental with this development was the defection of Hwang Jang Yop, who was believed to be the leading architect of *Juche* ideology. His defection reinforced criticism among intellectuals in North Korea of *Juche* for having been little more than a useless armchair philosophy, as typified by the works of Hwang. Thus, one of the challenges Pyongyang faced was to redirect *Juche* as a practical ideology. This challenge led the leadership to reinstate the centrality of pragmatic socialism, as opposed to the abstract notion of humanism.

Subversive Engagement Policies

Another area of strategic and tactical change can be seen in Pyongyang's approach toward Seoul and Washington. Both South Korea and the United States have lately shown more conciliatory gestures toward Pyongyang, using recently coined terms such as "sunshine policy" and "engagement policy." Yet, Pyongyang is not in a position to welcome them. To Pyongyang, the sunshine policy is even more subversive and conspiratorial than the previous policy of a soft landing. Pyongyang objects to the assumption inherent in this policy that North Korea will voluntarily take off the socialist jacket when the "sunshine" makes it unbearably hot. Both policies advanced by South Korean administrations have relied on the same political strategy of opening up the North Korean economy and providing its citizens with the opportunity to interact with their counterparts from the South and to witness the "superior lifestyle" across the border. Pyongyang views this strategy as subversive and vicious in its intention. . . .

As for the U.S. engagement policy, Pyongyang has never shown any degree of enthusiasm for it. Pyongyang views engagement as a unilateral concept whereby only North Korea is to be engaged with the United States and the West. Pyongyang observes that the engagement policy does not call for U.S. engagement with North Korea, as evidenced by the fact that the lifting of the U.S. economic embargo against it has never been implemented. This U.S. policy is also predicated upon the expectation that North Korea will have to reform if it is to engage with the outside world, especially the global market system. Also, North Korea has not failed to point out that the notion of "engagement" is essentially imperialist. Pyongyang contends that the policy implies that North Korea is the "subject" that is to adjust its behavior in order to conform itself to foreign norms and practices, rather than the United States searching actively for means and ways in which it can engage itself with North Korea. . . .

Protecting Bargaining Leverage

The North Korean leadership is well aware that its bargaining leverage is limited and should be treasured. Two such forms of leverage stand out. First and foremost, Pyongyang is mindful that its greatest bargaining leverage is its military capability, especially the ability to produce long-range missiles, nuclear bombs, and other chemical and biological weapons. North Korea would not be what it is today without the suspected nuclear weapons program in the early 1990s. North Korea would not have attracted Japanese attention as much as it has without the launching of a long-range missile over its territory in 1998. Should North Korea exhaust this leverage, it will become merely a less developed country, and the Pyongyang leadership is more keenly aware of this than anyone. Related to this weapons leverage is the mystery or uncertainty surrounding the weapons program and intentions of the leadership. To this day, no one knows for sure whether North Korea has produced nuclear bombs. The suspicion and mystery help Pyongyang in maintaining leverage, and it will not be inclined to relinquish it. This fact suggests that continuously maintaining a system closed to outsiders and thereby protecting the leverage itself in the mind of the leadership is a rational course of action.

Interestingly, the very closed nature of North Korean society can act as important leverage. It is not easy for a foreigner to enter North Korea. For a South Korean to enter is even more difficult. Each entry visa is issued after rigorous assessment of the merit of the visit. Every visit is by invitation only. There is no tourism industry. No tourist agency, foreign or domestic, is commissioned to bring in tourists. Furthermore, there is no physical infrastructure to handle large numbers of visitors or unexpected requests. As a result, the demand for foreigners, South Koreans, and overseas Koreans to visit Pyongyang is extremely high. Even businesses aspiring to enter North Korea are competing with one other, giving Pyongyang a bargaining edge. . . .

North Korea has earned a reputation as a tough bargainer. The toughness is largely due to the simple fact that Pyongyang tends to see its course of action not as an alternative but as an imperative. The notorious label of "brinkmanship diplomacy" that North Korea has been given is a relatively new concept in diplomacy studies. It simply suggests that once a country is pushed into a corner, leaving little room for maneuver, the country does not tend to retreat because space has run out. It is not difficult for an empathetic observer to see this limitation on North Korea's behavior and to understand, but not necessarily agree with, the behavioral pattern exhibited by Pyongyang. . . .

As discussed earlier, as long as North Korea feels its national security is threatened, Pyongyang will not ease its military preparedness. Furthermore, as long as the leadership feels the political system is threatened, the ruling elite will do everything possible to prevent its demise. These premises are not unusual, nor are they only relevant to North Korea. Since the fall of the Soviet Union and much of that support system, North Korea's security requirements have become multifaceted and include both external and internal sources of destabilization.

North Korea and Missile Proliferation

By Gaurav Kampani, Evan Medeiros, Greg J. Gerardi, and James A. Plotts

The following selection was written by Gaurav Kampani, Evan Medeiros, Greg J. Gerardi, and James A. Plotts, staff members of the Center for Nonproliferation Studies, a nongovernmental organization devoted to research and training on nonproliferation issues located at the Monterey Institute of International Studies in California. The report describes North Korea's role in international missile proliferation, an activity that has serious implications for instability in Asia as well as the Middle East. As the report describes, North Korea began to develop missiles in the early 1980s to compensate for the lack of a long-range strike capability in its air force. Full-scale production of the Scud-C ballistic missile began in 1991. The North then tested a short-range Nodong-1 ballistic missile in May 1993; this missile has a range of about 500 km. Longer-range Nodong missiles have since been produced, with a range of approximately 1,500 km. In August 1998, however, the North stunned the world by testing the intermediate-range Taepodong-1 ballistic missile, launching it over the main Japanese island of Honshu. The 1998 missile test confirmed that North Korea possesses missiles that can reach not only South Korea, China, and Russia, but also Japan. The launch also showed that North Korea possesses a high degree of technical ability and suggested that it could develop even longer-range missile systems in the future, including missiles with an intercontinental range that could reach the United States.

North Korea relies on the missiles for more than security. For more than a decade, North Korea has sold missiles and missile technology to countries such as Iran, Syria, Egypt, and Pakistan. These exports have provided the North with much-needed hard currency as North Korea no

longer can rely upon Soviet aid as a result of the collapse of the Soviet Union in 1991. The missiles also have given the North bargaining leverage with the United States. North Korea, for example, has offered to halt missile exports if the United States were to lift the economic embargo and compensate North Korea $500 million annually for the loss of missile sales.

North Korea's proliferation of missiles and technology has already created instability in both Asia and the Middle East, as missile sales give countries in those areas the ability to threaten their neighbors and contribute to the risk of regional arms races.

North Korea's ballistic missile program remains a source of significant concern to countries in Northeast Asia. For the past decade, North Korea has been both an active producer and seller of Scud-type ballistic missiles. North Korea's missile programs have raised the specter of conflict in Northeast Asia. North Korea now has the capability to strike targets in South Korea and Japan, including US military bases in both countries. Further, by selling complete missile systems, components, and missile technologies to Iran, Syria, Egypt, and Pakistan, North Korea has undermined regional stability in the Middle East and South Asia.

The 1998 Missile Test

On 31 August 1998, North Korea test fired a multi-stage rocket. The prototype rocket was launched from the Hwadaegun Missile Test Facility. US intelligence agencies tracked the rocket's flight path over the Pacific. The first stage of the rocket fell into international waters roughly 300km east of the launch site. The rocket flew over the main Japanese island of Honshu and the second stage fell roughly 330km away from the Japanese port city of Hachinohe after flying for approximately 1,320km.

Initial media reports described the test as that of a two-stage intermediate-range Taepodong-1 ballistic missile. However, on 4 September 1998, the *Korean Central News Agency* clarified that North Korea had not tested a ballistic missile. Instead, it had launched a satellite into orbit via a multi-stage rocket. Later, the United States confirmed that North Korea had tried and failed to place a satellite in orbit. Apparently, the satellite broke into pieces seconds before reaching orbit. What was initially thought to be a two-stage Taepodong-1 missile with a range of 1,600km, is now believed to have had a solid fuel third stage with a potential range between 3,800km to 5,900km.

North Korea last tested its Nodong-1 ballistic missile in May 1993; then the missile was tested to a range of 500km only. While precise technical details on the Taepodong-1 launch are still unavailable, few analysts previously believed that North Korea could achieve a multi-staging capability in so short a period of time. More significantly, the technical breakthroughs achieved in the latest rocket launch, opens the possibility for North Korea to develop even longer-range missile systems, including missiles with an intercontinental range. North Korea's latest test can be explained in several ways. It could be an attempt by the North to gain international attention as a means to secure further economic assistance for its faltering economy. In June 1998, North Korea admitted to developing ballistic missiles as a means to safeguard its security and generate hard currency. It also declared that missile exports would be halted only if the United States lifted the economic embargo and compensated North Korea ($500 million annually) for the loss of missile sales. Thus North Korea may have wanted to use the test as a bargaining point in its negotiations with the United States.

Furthermore, the rocket test came within weeks of reports that North Korea was excavating a huge underground cavern at a site 25km north of its nuclear facilities at Yongbyon. US intelligence sources allege that the underground cavern is designed to house a nuclear reactor or a nuclear-fuel reprocessing plant. Other analysts believe, however, that the excavation effort like the latest rocket launch may be intended to focus international attention on the troubled 1994 Agreed Framework. Under the agreement, North Korea agreed to halt its nuclear weapons program in return for two light-water reactors and 500,000 tons of heavy-fuel oil annually until the reactors came on-line. The 1994 agreement ... [was] in trouble due to financing problems [in the late 1990s].

North Korea's Missile Production

North Korea, in common with many developing countries, originally turned to missile forces to compensate for its air force's lack of a long-range strike capability. While this was originally the case, the demand for short- and medium-range missiles during the 1980–1988 Iran-Iraq war demonstrated the profit potential of selling such systems. With North Korea becoming increasingly isolated with the worldwide collapse of communism, missile sales have become a valuable means of acquiring hard currency and desperately needed commodities such as oil.

After a period of limited production, full-scale production of the Scud-C ballistic missile began in 1991. There are conflicting reports on whether North Korea has deployed the 1,500km-range Nodong-1 ballistic missile. In September 1997, it did seem that North Korea had begun deploying military units with equipment designed to transport the Nodong. At that time, however, no missiles were sighted. . . . US intelligence reports suggest that North Korea has operationalized its Nodong missiles. However, since North Korea has exported some Nodong missiles to Iran and Pakistan, it may not have enough missiles to field a full brigade.

A number of factors indicate that North Korea's ballistic missiles are under air force, rather than army, command and control. The original purpose for missile development was to add a long-range strike capability to the Korean People's Army (KPA) to compensate for its weak and obsolescent air force. As the missiles were essentially assuming an air force mission, they may have been placed under the air force's command. In this regard, it is significant that General Cho Myong-rok, commander of the North Korean Air Force, led the North Korean delegation sent to Iran in February 1994 to discuss, among other things, testing of the Nodong-2 in Iran. It should also be noted that Iranian ballistic missiles fall under the command and control of the air wing of the Iranian Revolutionary Guard Corps (IRGC). As Iran and North Korea have maintained close relations, especially concerning issues such as ballistic missiles, and have exchanged data on wartime missile use and deployment, it would not be surprising if North Korea mirrored the Iranian ballistic missile command-and-control structure.

North Korea purchased its first Scud-B from Egypt, reverse-engineered the missile, and then developed subsequent versions, which allowed it to gain expertise in the production and testing of missiles. North Korea has developed several longer-range versions by significantly modifying the basic Scud-B designs. Subsequent versions of the Scud-B had their ranges progressively extended. Also, the development time, from conception to testing, seems to be diminishing with each successive system. According to David Wright of the Union of Concerned Scientists, North Korea's development of the 1,500km Nodong marks the developmental limits of Scud technology.

All significant North Korean missile development successes have been achieved with outside financing and/or technological assistance. Iran is a good example of the former, while Russia is an example of the latter. Pakistan may have also been a funding source for the Nodong and Taepodong programs; Pakistan's Ghauri is suspected to be a Nodong purchased from Pyongyang.

The Iranian Factor

Several analysts believe that in the past, Iran was the primary financial supporter of North Korea's missile development program. The Iran–North Korea relationship dates from 1983 when Iran agreed to fund the reverse-engineering of the Scud-B missile in exchange for the option to purchase production models. There are two interesting aspects of the Iran–North Korea relationship: Iran's use of oil to purchase missiles, and the potential use of Iranian test-sites for North Korean missiles. North Korea has been in perpetual need for oil since the end of favorable pricing with China and the former Soviet Union. The restructuring of North Korea's debt to Iran in 1987 allowed it to pay in goods rather than cash. The May 1991 test-launch of the Scud-C missile in . . . Iran opened a new phase in North Korea's relationship with Iran. In late 1993, North Korea appeared ready to use Iran's Lut Desert test-site for the Nodong-1. However, the test was cancelled, probably under international pressure. More recently, Iran may have shared test data from its 23 July 1998 launch of the Shahab-3 with North Korea. Russian assistance to Iran's missile program in areas of guidance and metallurgy may also indirectly benefit Pyongyang's own missile programs.

The Russian Factor

There is some evidence of a concerted North Korean effort to recruit Russian experts for their missile programs. The new technologies that North Korea will have to master in order to operationalize the Taepodong and subsequent series of missiles will increase the development time considerably. However, North Korea may be able to reduce development time with outside assistance. Although many Russian missile specialists have been stopped in transit on their way to North Korea, Russian authorities acknowledge that, given the number of people with missile development expertise, it is almost impossible to control their movements. The knowledge and experience of these Russian experts could reduce the time needed to develop the staging and re-entry technologies required for longer-range missile systems such as the Taepodong.

Missile Sales

Initial deliveries of North Korean missiles to customers in the Middle East in the 1980s consisted of complete missile systems. More recently, deliveries have been in the form of "knockdown" kits and associated production or assembly equipment. For example, North Korea may currently be transferring equipment, which will allow countries such as Iran and Pakistan to become indigenous producers of intermediate- and medium-range ballistic missiles.

Deliveries to Iran, Pakistan, and Syria have changed in two ways. First, as Western resistance to the deliveries has increased, shipments have begun to be made by air rather than by sea. In some instances, this has been accomplished with private-sector Russian assistance, thereby calling into question the Russian government's ability and/or willingness to control North Korea's missile proliferation. Second, instead of transferring complete missile systems, North Korea has resorted to selling missile components and missile production equipment to clients. These changes will allow more rapid shipping deliveries and interception of such shipments will become more difficult.

The International Implications of Missile Proliferation

North Korea's Scud-C inventory gives it the capability of striking South Korea's rear areas and US staging areas around Pusan. This is a capability that North Korea did not have during the 1950–1953 Korean War, and which could substantially influence the course of future conflicts on the Korean Peninsula. With its Nodong missiles, North Korea could also threaten Japan, as well as China and the Russian Far East. North Korea's Taepodong has the range but not the accuracy to strike all parts of Japan and the US military bases there. Other long-range missiles now in the design stage, such as the Taepodong-2, could potentially allow North Korea to threaten the entire western Pacific region. If such missiles were transferred to Iran, Syria, Pakistan, or Libya, it could trigger off a regional missile race in the Middle East and South Asia.

North Korea's continued development of long-range missiles could also lead to a strategic arms race in Northeast Asia. South Korea is already seeking to develop a 300km-range missile. Indeed, both South Korea and Japan could respond to this impetus by seeking to build a missile defense system. Given the unreliability of current missile defense systems, South Korea and Japan may also find it necessary to develop their own delivery systems to carry out deep strikes within North Korea. Furthermore, in the event of the collapse of the 1994 Agreed Framework and the emergence of a North Korean nuclear capability, South Korea, which had a nuclear weapons program in the 1970s, may go nuclear as well.

Despite the advances made by North Korea, it still has to cross several technical hurdles before it can field long-range ballistic missiles. The developmental leaps to successful multiple-stage systems using large rocket motors cannot be achieved without external technological assistance. Some of this assistance is probably being provided by Russian specialists, both in North Korea and Russia. Russia may be able to stem the "brain-drain," but it is unable to completely halt the leakage of information. Despite concerns in the US Congress, a 1995 US National Intelligence Estimate concluded that North Korea was at least 15 years away from fielding ballistic missiles capable of striking the continental United States.

Even if the threat posed by North Korea itself is controlled, the export of missile production equipment and the establishment of production facilities in Syria, Iran and Pakistan have already occurred. Thus, the effects of North Korea's production and proliferation of missiles and missile technology promise to extend well into the future.

The Nuclear Weapons Issue and U.S. Relations

By Paul Kerr

The following article by Paul Kerr, a reporter for Arms Control Today *magazine, reports that North Korea admitted in October 2002 that it is once again developing nuclear weapons. The United States claims this action violates the 1994 Framework Agreement negotiated by then– U.S. president Bill Clinton, in which North Korea agreed to halt its nuclear weapons production in exchange for fuel oil and light water reactors for the production of electricity. The revelation puts the United States in a difficult position. On the one hand, it does not want to give in to North Korean demands in order to halt their new nuclear weapons program. Such a step would, in essence, reward the North's failure to abide by its agreements. On the other hand, the United States is reluctant to attack North Korea, given its large military force within close proximity to South Korea. In a sense North Korea is continuing a foreign policy that it has used for many years: The nation quickly moves between aggressive and diplomatic postures, and threatens with weapons of mass destruction to achieve its strategic goals of aid or security.*

The U.S. Bush administration hopes that a strategy of political and diplomatic pressure on the North and the assistance of surrounding countries such as China, Russia, and Japan will convince North Korea to disarm.

North Korea revealed that it has a clandestine nuclear weapons program during an early October [2002] meeting with a high-ranking U.S. official. The admission, which the United States made public October 16 [2002], indicates that Pyongyang [North Korea's capital] has violated several key nonproliferation agreements, raising concern worldwide.

The New Uranium Enrichment Program

North Korean First Vice Foreign Minister Kang Suk Ju admitted that Pyongyang has a uranium-enrichment program during October 3–5 meetings with a U.S. delegation after Assistant Secretary of State James Kelly confronted him with intelligence data proving the program's existence, Kelly stated during an October 19 press conference in Seoul [South Korea].

The intelligence included evidence that Pyongyang was purchasing material for use in a gas centrifuge program that could enrich uranium for use in nuclear weapons, according to Bush administration officials. Various press reports have cited Russia, China, and Pakistan as potential suppliers. All three governments have denied any role.

The status of the program is unclear. Kelly said during the Seoul press conference that the enrichment program is "several years old," but Bush administration officials have reported to Congress and allies that North Korea's program still appears to be in its "early stages" and would take a relatively long time to produce enough weapons-grade material for a nuclear device. It is unclear how much time that is.

North Korea's Nuclear Program Violates Agreements

Kelly stated that North Korea's nuclear program violates "its commitments" under several international agreements: the Agreed Framework, the nuclear Nonproliferation Treaty (NPT), Pyongyang's safeguards agreement with the International Atomic Energy Agency (IAEA), and the Joint North-South Declaration on the Denuclearization of the Korean Peninsula.

The United States and North Korea concluded the Agreed Framework in October 1994, ending a standoff resulting from the IAEA's discovery that Pyongyang was diverting plutonium from its graphite-moderated nuclear reactors for use in nuclear weapons. The Agreed Framework requires North Korea to "freeze its graphite-moderated reactors and related facilities," thereby ending its plutonium-based nuclear weapons program.

In exchange for shutting down its reactors, the United States agreed to provide North Korea with two proliferation-resistant light-water reactors (LWR), to create an international consortium called the Korean Peninsula Energy Development Organization (KEDO) to build them, and to provide shipments of heavy fuel oil in the interim. The first reactor was originally scheduled to be completed by 2003, but construction has fallen behind schedule, and the reactor is not expected to be finished before 2008, barring further delays.

The Agreed Framework requires North Korea to accept full IAEA safeguards when "a significant portion of the LWR project is completed.". . . Under those safeguards, Pyongyang must declare the existence of any nuclear facilities and allow the IAEA to inspect them.

The Agreed Framework does not specifically mention uranium enrichment, a different method of obtaining fissile material for nuclear weapons, but it does require North Korea to remain a party to the NPT, under which non-nuclear-weapon states agree "not to manufacture or otherwise acquire nuclear weapons or other nuclear explosive devices." The framework also says that North Korea "will consistently take steps to implement" the 1992 Joint Declaration, which states that "South and North Korea shall not possess nuclear reprocessing and uranium enrichment facilities."

The Agreed Framework has been controversial, with some Republicans, including President George W. Bush, questioning whether the United States can trust North Korea. The Bush administration refused last March [2001] to certify that North Korea was fully complying with the agreement, a congressionally mandated condition for KEDO to receive U.S. funding. Bush waived the certification requirement, however, allowing funding to continue. Then, in August the United States asked North Korea to allow immediate IAEA inspections of its nuclear facilities, although they are not required by the Agreed Framework at this time.

Status of the 1994 Agreed Framework

Meanwhile, IAEA Director-General Mohamed ElBaradei said in September [2002] that the agency has not been able to verify that Pyongyang "has declared all the nuclear material that is subject to Agency safeguards." U.S. intelligence estimates that North Korea separated enough plutonium for at least one, and possibly two, nuclear weapons before signing the Agreed Framework. Other spent fuel produced before the Agreed Framework is under IAEA safeguards, but if North Korea decided to reprocess it, the country could recover enough plutonium in six months for approximately six nuclear devices.

The current and future status of the Agreed Framework is unclear. Kelly said during the October 19 [2002] press conference that North Korean officials "declared that they considered the Agreed Framework to be nullified" when he met with them.

THE 1994 U.S.–NORTH KOREA FRAMEWORK AGREEMENT

On October 21, 1994, following months of negotiations, the United States and North Korea signed the Agreed Framework, excerpted below. Under the terms of this agreement, North Korea agreed to freeze its nuclear activities and eventually dismantle its nuclear facilities in exchange for two light water reactors designed to produce electricity and five hundred thousand metric tons of heavy oil as an interim energy source.

Delegations of the Governments of the United States of America (U.S.) and the Democratic People's Republic of Korea (DPRK) held talks in Geneva from September 23 to October 17, 1994, to negotiate an overall resolution of the nuclear issue on the Korean Peninsula. . . .

The U.S. and the DPRK decided to take the following actions for the resolution of the nuclear issue:

I. Both sides will cooperate to replace the DPRK's graphite-moderated reactors and related facilities with light-water reactor (LWR) power plants.

1) In accordance with the October 20, 1994 letter of assurance from the U.S. President, the U.S. will undertake to make arrangements for the provision to the DPRK of a LWR project with a total generating capacity of approximately 2,000 MW (e) by a target date of 2003. . . .

2) In accordance with the October 20, 1994 letter of assurance from the U.S. President, the U.S., representing the consortium, will make arrangements to offset the energy foregone due to the freeze of the DPRK's graphite-moderated

Regarding the agreement, he added that "we haven't made any decisions since we were informed it was nullified." In an October 20 interview on ABC's "This Week," Secretary of State Colin Powell repeated that Pyongyang had declared the agree-

reactors and related facilities, pending completion of the first LWR unit.

—Alternative energy will be provided in the form of heavy oil for heating and electricity production.

—Deliveries of heavy oil will begin within three months of the date of this document and will reach a rate of 500,000 tons annually, in accordance with an agreed schedule of deliveries.

3) Upon receipt of U.S. assurances for the provision of LWR's and for arrangement for interim energy alternatives, the DPRK will freeze its graphite-moderated reactors and related facilities and will eventually dismantle these reactors and related facilities. . . .

4) As soon as possible after the date of this document, U.S. and DPRK experts will hold two sets of expert talks. . . .

II. The two sides will move toward full normalization of political and economic relations. . . .

III. Both sides will work together for peace and security on a nuclear-free Korean peninsula.

1) The U.S. will provide formal assurances to the DPRK, against the threat or use of nuclear weapons by the U.S.

2) The DPRK will consistently take steps to implement the North-South Joint Declaration on the Denuclearization of the Korean peninsula.

3) The DPRK will engage in North-South dialogue, as this Agreed Framework will help create an atmosphere that promotes such dialogue.

IV. Both sides will work together to strengthen the international nuclear nonproliferation regime.

"Agreed Framework Between the United States and the Democratic People's Republic of Korea, Appendix I," *Rogue Countries: Background and Current Issues*, Alexandra Kura, ed. Huntingdon, NY: Nova Science Publishers, 2001, pp. 159–61.

ment "nullified," but he would not say that it was "dead." Powell explained that Washington had to consult with its allies before deciding on the framework's future.

A North Korean Foreign Ministry spokesman said October 25 [2002] that past U.S. actions had already invalidated the Agreed Framework, citing reactor construction delays, U.S. economic sanctions, and U.S. threats of pre-emptive attack against North Korea, according to the state-run Korean Central News Agency (KCNA).

The Agreed Framework requires the United States to "provide formal assurances to the DPRK [North Korea], against the threat or use of nuclear weapons." Recent U.S. reports and statements have reportedly raised concerns in North Korea that the United States might consider a nuclear preemptive strike on the country, although the United States has not directly threatened North Korea. For example, a leaked version of the Bush administration's January 2002 classified Nuclear Posture Review lists North Korea as a country against which the United States should be prepared to use nuclear weapons if necessary.

KEDO's work continues despite North Korea's admission, according to a KEDO spokesman, but it is unclear what decisions the United States, South Korea, Japan, and the European Atomic Energy Community—KEDO's executive board members—will make in the near future. KEDO's most recent shipment of fuel oil arrived in North Korea October 18 [2002], according to a State Department official interviewed October 30.

International Response

President Bush, Japanese Prime Minister Junichiro Koizumi, and South Korean President Kim Dae-jung issued a joint statement October 26 [2002] during the Asia-Pacific Economic Cooperation (APEC) forum meeting in Los Cabos, Mexico, saying that the uranium-enrichment program violates Pyongyang's nuclear agreements. The statement also calls upon Pyongyang to "dismantle" the program "in a prompt and verifiable manner and to come into full compliance with all its international commitments."

The declaration stresses the three countries' desires for a peaceful resolution to the nuclear issue. The declaration also indicates that both Japan and South Korea intend to continue their bilateral engagement efforts with Pyongyang but that "North Korea's relations with the international community . . . rest on . . . prompt and visible" dismantlement of its uranium-enrichment program.

On October 29 and 30, [2002] Japan and North Korea held normalization talks in Kuala Lumpur that covered a variety of issues, including North Korea's nuclear and missile programs, according to a Japanese Foreign Ministry statement. In the October 26 joint statement, Koizumi indicated that relations could not be normalized without resolution of Pyongyang's missile and nuclear programs, but the talks ended without an agreement on the programs, according to an October 30 BBC report.

South Korea has also continued its engagement efforts with the North. The two governments held interministerial talks October 19–22 [2002] in Pyongyang. According to a KCNA October 23 statement, the two sides agreed to "make joint efforts to ensure peace and security on the Korean Peninsula" and "to seek negotiated settlement of . . . the nuclear issue.". . .

Meanwhile, Chinese President Jiang Zemin stated after an October 25 [2002] meeting with Bush in Texas that Beijing and Washington would "work together to ensure a peaceful resolution" to the North Korea nuclear problem, adding that China is a "supporter of a nuclear-free Korean Peninsula."

Russia called for talks between Washington and Pyongyang and for both sides "to renounce the policy of mutual threats and military pressure," emphasizing the importance of adherence to the NPT and "implementation" of the Agreed Framework "by all concerned parties," according to an October 25 [2002] statement from the Russian Foreign Ministry.

The U.S. Strategy

Pyongyang has proposed that the United States conclude a nonaggression treaty with North Korea in order to resolve the dispute. An October 27 [2002] KCNA statement says that Washington should negotiate such a treaty, which would include a guarantee that the United States will not use nuclear weapons against North Korea, "if the U.S. truly wants the settlement of the nuclear issue on the Korean Peninsula." North Korea "will be ready to clear the U.S. of its security concerns" if the United States does so, according to the statement.

North Korea also proposed further engagement with the United States to discuss its nuclear program during the October 3–5 meeting. When asked during the Seoul press conference if, in exchange for discussions about ending the enrichment program, Pyongyang had requested U.S. diplomatic recognition and guarantees that the United States would not attack North Korea, Kelly stated that North Korea had suggested "measures . . . generally along those lines" but that North Korea must dismantle the program before any discussions could take place.

Powell stated at an October 26 press conference during the APEC meeting that Washington has "no plans . . . for a meeting" with North Korea and that the United States would not negotiate for the dismantlement of the uranium-enrichment program. He added that the "international community" agreed that applying "political" and "diplomatic" pressure on Pyongyang was the best course of action, but he did not elaborate.

Powell also stated that "we have no intention of invading North Korea or taking hostile action against North Korea"—a promise Bush made earlier this year in Seoul. Powell also restated Washington's policy of requiring discussions about missile development and proliferation, nuclear issues, human rights abuses, and North Korea's conventional forces in order for negotiations to begin. Kelly also articulated this position during the meeting in Pyongyang, Powell said.

Pyongyang's admission occurred against a backdrop of what appeared to be increased engagement between North Korea and the United States. Kelly is the highest-level U.S. official to visit Pyongyang since Secretary of State Madeleine Albright did so in October 2000. The United States had also sent Jack Pritchard, State Department special envoy for negotiations with North Korea, to the August 7, [2002] KEDO ceremony in North Korea marking the pouring of the concrete foundation for the first LWR that the United States agreed to provide under the Agreed Framework. And North Korea had pledged to indefinitely extend its moratorium on testing long-range missiles—a top U. S. security concern.

The Bush administration's decision to seek a peaceful resolution with North Korea contrasts with its position on Iraq, where it has threatened to use military force to overthrow the government in Baghdad because of its weapons of mass destruction programs.

Chronology

2000 B.C.
A culture develops in the area of Korea that emphasizes agriculture and a clan social structure, but it is not clear that Koreans are descended from these people.

1100–109 B.C.
The state of Ancient Choson rules on the Korean peninsula.

108 B.C.–A.D. 313
The Han Chinese rule the Korean peninsula.

37 B.C.–A.D. 936
The Three Kingdoms develop on the Korean peninsula (Paekche, Koguryo, and Silla).

668
After years of conflict among the Three Kingdoms, the kingdom of Silla emerges victorious, defeating the other kingdoms. This begins a thirteen-hundred-year period of unification on the Korean peninsula.

936–1392
The Koryo dynasty rules Korea.

1392–1910
The Choson or Yi dynasty rules Korea.

1895
In the Sino-Japanese Treaty of Shimonoseki, China recognizes the independence of Korea, giving Japan greater influence over the area.

1905
Japan wins the Russo-Japanese War, and Russia acknowledges Japan's rights to Korea, opening the way for Japanese annexation.

1910

Japan officially annexes Korea, beginning a period of four decades of brutality and repression for Koreans as Japanese colonists.

1919

Mass protests of Japan's colonization of Korea occur throughout Korea (March First Movement).

1931–1941

Japan is successful in a series of military conquests that eventually lead Japan into World War II, aligned with Germany and Italy.

1941

The Japanese attack Pearl Harbor, Hawaii, bringing the United States into World War II.

1945

Japan surrenders to the Allies, ending World War II. Korea is freed from Japanese colonialism but occupied by Russia in the north and the United States in the south. Russia and the United States propose a five-year trusteeship for Korea.

1945–1947

Russia and the United States attempt but fail to negotiate the terms of the trusteeship and provisional government.

1947

The United Nations votes to sponsor elections in Korea, over Russian objections.

1948

Russia prohibits the United Nations representatives from entering the north, so the United Nations holds elections in the south. In August the Republic of Korea (ROK) is created in the south, and Syngman Rhee is elected as its first president.

On September 9, the Democratic People's Republic of Korea (DPRK) is proclaimed in North Korea and Kim Il Sung, backed by the Soviet Union, is chosen to become its leader. North Korea begins to make guerrilla raids on South Korea. At the end of the year, the Soviets withdraw their troops from North Korea.

1950

The Korean War begins when North Korean troops invade South Korea on June 25, with backing from the Communist Soviet Union. U.S. president Harry S. Truman sends American troops to defend South Korea. The United Nations adopts a resolution demanding that North Korea retreat and asking member states to help South Korea.

In September, U.S. general Douglas MacArthur leads allied troops in a military campaign that lands in the port of Inch'on, pushes North Korean troops northward, and retakes South Korea. MacArthur then captures P'yongyang in North Korea and pushes northward toward the Chinese border.

In November, China sends troops to aid North Korea, and they press the allied troops back into South Korea, capturing Seoul.

1951

In March, the allied troops retake Seoul.

1951–1953

Armistice talks begin in July 1951, but the war continues until July 27, 1953.

1953

The Korean War ends with an armistice agreement on July 27 and a 2.5-mile-wide demilitarized zone (DMZ) is created just north of the 38th parallel, separating North and South Korea. No formal peace treaty is signed, and North and South Korea remain technically at war.

1954

Negotiations fail on a peace treaty, or any plan for reuniting North and South Korea. The United States and South Korea sign a Mutual Defense Treaty, providing for U.S. troops to remain in South Korea.

1961

North Korea signs military assistance treaties with China and the Soviet Union.

1968

North Korea seizes the USS *Pueblo*, a U.S. intelligence ship, in the Sea of Japan.

North Korean commando troops attack Seoul, and there are clashes between North and South Korea at the DMZ.

1969
North Korea downs a U.S. reconnaissance plane.

1972
North Korea approves a new constitution, making Kim Il Sung president as well as prime minister.

1974
A tunnel dug by North Korea under the DMZ is discovered, and a second tunnel is discovered in February 1975.
North Korea attempts to assassinate South Korean president Park Chung Hee.

1977
The United States plans a gradual withdrawal of troops from South Korea.

1980
Kim Jong Il, Kim Il Sung's son, is given senior posts in the Politburo, the Military Commission, and the Party Secretariat and is openly proclaimed as Kim Il Sung's successor.

1981
U.S. president Ronald Reagan ends troop withdrawals from South Korea.

1983
In October, North Korean agents attempt to assassinate South Korean president Chun Doo Hwan with a bomb. The president is not harmed, but the bomb kills seventeen members of his entourage.

1985
North Korea signs the Nuclear Non-Proliferation Treaty.

1986
The United States detects evidence that North Korea is developing nuclear weapons.

1987
In November agents of North Korea sabotage a Korean Airlines plane, killing all 115 passengers.

1988

The United States places North Korea on its list of states supporting international terrorism in January. North Korea also is under a U.S. embargo on trade and financial transactions under the Trading with the Enemy Act.

From September 17 through October 2, the Seoul Olympics are held in South Korea.

Beginning in December, the United States conducts talks with North Korea regarding missiles and other topics.

1990

Massive demonstrations are held in North Korea in support of the regime, on Kim Il Sung's seventy-eighth birthday.

1991

The Soviet Union, one of North Korea's most important allies and economic supporters, collapses, leading to increasingly serious economic problems in North Korea.

Kim Il Sung is reelected president.

1992

In January, North Korea signs an implementing agreement for the Nuclear Non-Proliferation Treaty providing for inspections. Between June 1992 and February 1993, North Korea permits the International Atomic Energy Agency (IAEA) to conduct six inspections of the country's seven declared nuclear facilities.

1993

On March 12, North Korea withdraws from the International Nuclear Non-Proliferation Treaty and refuses to allow inspections, causing a serious crisis with the United States. In May the United Nations Security Council passes a resolution urging North Korea to cooperate with the IAEA and implement the treaty. The United States begins talks with North Korea aimed at resolving the nuclear issue.

1994

In June former U.S. president Jimmy Carter holds talks with Kim Il Sung, defusing a growing crisis over North Korea's nuclear capabilities.

On July 7, North Korea announces the death of Kim Il Sung at age eighty-two. He is succeeded by his son, Kim Jong Il.

Negotiations with the United States resume after the death of Kim Il Sung, and on October 21 North Korea and the United States negotiate and sign the Framework Agreement, in which North Korea promises to halt its development of nuclear weapons in return for aid in building civilian nuclear reactors and temporary oil supplies.

1995

Floods afflict North Korea, causing agricultural losses and food shortages and requiring the country to appeal for foreign aid. Japan and South Korea donate food.

1996

Serious food shortages continue in North Korea, reaching famine proportions.

On April 16 the United States and South Korea propose four-party peace talks among the two Koreas, the United States, and China aimed at replacing the 1953 armistice agreement with a permanent peace treaty. Thereafter, a series of meetings are held between August 1997 and August 1999, but the parties are unable to agree on an agenda for the talks. The talks stall.

1997

Kim Jong Il is named general secretary of the Korean Workers' Party.

1998

The food shortages become critical because of a drought that followed the earlier floods. The government of North Korea imposes food rationing.

President Kim Dae Jung of South Korea announces a "sunshine policy," which seeks to improve relations with North Korea through negotiation and cooperation.

On August 31, North Korea launches a multistage rocket over Japan. Japan imposes sanctions on North Korea. The launch celebrates Kim Jong Il's consolidation of power in North Korea and his taking of the title of National Defense Commission chairman. Kim Il Sung is to be the eternal president of the country, even in death. North Korea openly admits that it exports missiles to a number of countries and suggests that if the United States wishes to stop the exports, it should lift its economic embargo on North Korea and compensate North Korea for the losses that would be caused by discontinuing missile exports.

1999

In September the United States agrees to lift economic sanctions against North Korea, and North Korea announces an end to missile testing. Despite this announcement, however, North Korea continues to develop long-range nuclear-capable missiles and continues to export missile technology. Tensions between North and South Korea increase due to the sinking of a North Korean ship and the arrest by North Korean officials of a South Korean tourist accused of spying.

2000

Between June 13 and 15, North Korean leader Kim Jong Il and South Korean president Kim Dae Jung meet for a summit in P'yongyang and sign a joint declaration pledging to work for reunification. Also in June, North Korea agrees to extend its ban on missile testing, and the United States thereafter relaxes economic sanctions on North Korea.

Between August 15 and 18, North and South Korea permit a reunion of 1,170 persons for the first time since they were separated by the Korean War. A second family reunion takes place for 1,220 persons between November 30 and December 2, 2000, and a third for 1,240 persons between February 16 and 18, 2001. Other attempts at economic cooperation begin, including reconnection of a railway between the North and South, development of an industrial complex by the Hyundai Group in North Korea, a flood prevention project for the Imjin River in North Korea, and other economic agreements. Social and cultural exchanges also begin between the two countries.

U.S. secretary of state Madeleine Albright visits North Korea, but no official agreement is reached on missile testing.

U.S. president George W. Bush is elected in November.

2001

In January the new U.S. Bush administration suspends diplomatic relations with North Korea and orders a review of American policy toward the country. In June, the United States proposes negotiations on nuclear and conventional weapons issues as well as North Korea's continued military presence at the DMZ, but North Korea rejects the proposal.

Official talks between North and South Korea that arose from the 2000 summit stall, and peace initiatives, such as the family reunions and other joint efforts, end. In South Korea, public support for South Korea's "sunshine policy" toward the North dissipates.

2002

On January 29 U.S. president George Bush announces in his State of the Union address that North Korea is part of an "axis of evil" (along with Iraq and Iran) that threatens the world with development of weapons of mass destruction.

Talks begin between the United States and North Korea, and on October 4 North Korea announces that it is developing nuclear weapons in violation of the 1994 Framework Agreement with the United States. North Korea demands bilateral talks with the United States and a nonaggression treaty to end the crisis.

Later in October, representatives of North and South Korea meet for the first time since talks stalled in 2001.

In November the United States and its allies cut off fuel oil promised to North Korea. Thereafter, in November and December, North Korea escalates the nuclear crisis by removing surveillance cameras from its nuclear facility, moving fuel rods to a storage site near its nuclear reactor and reprocessing plant, threatening to reopen its reprocessing plant, and ordering United Nations inspectors to leave the country.

In December South Korea votes for a successor to President Kim Dae Jung, who pursued a "sunshine policy" of reconciliation toward the North.

2003

On January 14, the United States offers to talk with North Korea and suggests that an aid package could be provided, but only if North Korea first takes steps to stop its nuclear program. North Korea rejects the offer.

In February, after U.S. surveillance shows trucks apparently moving spent nuclear fuel rods, possibly to be reprocessed into weaponry, North Korea announces that it has reactivated its nuclear facilities but promises that its nuclear activity will be limited to peaceful purposes. North Korea threatens "total war" if the United States makes a preemptive strike on its nuclear facilities.

On February 25 the new South Korean president, Roh Moo Hyun, who favors continued engagement with North Korea, takes office

For Further Research

Books

Tsuneo Akaha, *The Future of North Korea*. London: Routledge, 2002.

D. Ellsworth Blanc, ed., *North Korea, Pariah?* Huntington, NY: Novinka, 2001.

James Brady, *The Coldest War: A Memoir of Korea*. New York: Thomas Dunne, an imprint of St. Martin's Press, 1990.

Adrian Buzo, *The Making of Modern Korea*. London: Routledge, 2002.

Young Back Choi, ed., *Perspectives on Korean Unification and Economic Integration*. Cheltenham, UK: Edward Elgar, 2001.

Bruce G. Cumings, *North Korea: A Country Study*. Washington, DC: Library of Congress, 1994.

Gregory Henderson, *Korea: The Politics of the Vortex*. Cambridge, MA: Harvard University Press, 1968.

Alexandra Kura, *Rogue Countries: Background and Current Issues*. Huntington, NY: Nova Science, 2001.

Chong-Sik Lee and Se-Hee Yoo, eds., *North Korea in Transition*. Berkeley: Institute of East Asian Studies, University of California at Berkeley, 1991.

William Stueck, *Rethinking the Korean War*. Princeton, NJ: Princeton University Press, 2002.

Dae Sook Suh and Chae-Jin Lee, *North Korea After Kim Il Sung*. Boulder, CO: Lynne Rienner, 1998.

Han Woo-Keun, *The History of Korea*. Seoul: Eul-Yoo, 1970.

Periodicals

Yinhay Ahn, "North Korea in 2001: At a Crossroads," *Asian Survey*, January/February 2002.

David Albright and Holly Higgins, "North Korea: It's Taking Too Long: Inspections in North Korea Are Tied to the Reactor Deal, Which Is Far Behind Schedule," *Bulletin of the Atomic Scientists*, January/February 2002.

Bulletin of the Atomic Scientists, "Letter from Pyongyang," July/August 2002.

BusinessWeek, "The Two Koreas: What's Behind a Break in the Ice," April 15, 2002.

Victor D. Cha, "North Korea's Weapons of Mass Destruction: Badges, Shields, or Swords?" *Political Science Quarterly*, Summer 2002.

Stan Crock, *Business Week Online*, "Why Bush Must Talk to Pyongyang," October 25, 2002.

Bruce G. Cumings, "Endgame in Korea," *Nation*, November 18, 2002.

———, "Summitry in Pyongyang," *Nation*, July 10, 2000.

Hugh Deane, "Korea, China, and the United States: A Look Back," *Monthly Review*, February 1995.

Michael Duffy and Nancy Gibbs, "When Evil Is Everywhere: Has Bush Been Right All Along, or Is His World View Part of the Problem?" *Time*, October 28, 2002.

Economist (US), "Getting the Genie Back into the Bottle: North Korea's Nuclear Programme," October 26, 2002.

———, "Sunshine and Ice: The Koreas and the United States," February 9, 2002.

———, "Through the Looking Glass (Economic Aspects of North Korea)," July 10, 1999.

Kristen Eichensehr, "Broken Promises," *Harvard International Review*, Fall 2001.

Thomas H. Henrikson, "The Rise and Decline of Rogue States," *Vital Speeches*, March 1, 2001.

Donald Kirk, "Opportunity Time for the Koreas," *New Leader,* September/October 2000.

Tae-Hwan Kwak and Seung-Ho Joo, "The Korean Peace Process: Problems and Prospects After the Summit," *World Affairs,* Fall 2002.

Robert A. Manning, "The Enigma of the North," *Wilson Quarterly,* Summer 1999.

National Review, "Korea: Forty Years Ago," August 20, 1990.

——, "North Korea: Proliferation," November 11, 2002.

Thomas Omestad and Mark Mazzetti, "North Korea Breaks a No-Nukes Deal," *U.S. News & World Report,* October 28, 2002.

Phillip Park, "The Future of the Democratic People's Republic of Korea," *Journal of Contemporary Asia,* March 2001.

Progressive, "Axis to Grind," March 2002.

Scott Snyder, "North Korea's Challenge of Regime Survival: Internal Problems and Implications for the Future," *Pacific Affairs,* Winter 2000.

Jonathan Watts, "Balancing the 'Axis of Evil' in Northeast Asia," *Lancet,* September 7, 2002.

Paul Wingrove, "Who Started Korea?" *History Today,* July 2000.

Websites

Asian Info, www.asianinfo.org. This website is dedicated to introducing Asian culture and traditions to the world.

Federation of American Scientists, www.fas.org. The FAS is a nonprofit organization founded in 1945 by members of the Manhattan Project, creators of the atom bomb. The website focuses on the implications of nuclear power and weaponry for the future of humankind and it contains information about North Korea's nuclear program.

Korean News Service, www.kcna.co.jp. This is the website for the Korean Central News Agency, a state-run agency of the Democratic People's Republic of Korea. It speaks for the Workers' Party of Korea and the DPRK government.

Korea Web Weekly, www.kimsoft.com. The website includes information on Korean history, culture, economy, politics, and military.

U.S. Central Intelligence Agency (CIA), *The World Factbook 2002, North Korea*, www.cia.gov. This is a U.S. government website for the CIA, providing geographical, political, economic, and other information on the country of North Korea, as well as reports and speeches about recent political issues.

U.S. Department of Energy, *North Korea*, www.eia.doe.gov. This U.S. government website provides energy-related information about North Korea.

Washington Post, *North Korea*, www.washingtonpost.com. This website for the mass-circulation daily *Washington Post* contains up-to-date news on events in North Korea.

INDEX

Korean aggression, 113–14
Commission on Korea, 101
Committee for the Unification
    and Rehabilitation of Korea
    (UNCURK), 70
Development Programme
    (UNDP), 161
Human Rights Committee, 189
Korean elections and, 18, 70, 112
nuclear weapons and, 100, 101
post–Korean War government
    and, 70–71
Security Council, 71, 100, 113,
    114
World Food Program, 182
United States
aid for North Korean famine
    from, 163
antihegemonism against, 135–36
fighting imperialism of, 131–32
Japanese colonization and, 39,
    56–57
Korean War involvement of,
    98–100, 101–103
revising history of, 105–106
March First Movement and,
    56–57
North Korean weapons program
    and, 13, 22, 23, 211–18
occupation of, in Korea, 17–18,
    20, 66
recent policy of, toward North
    Korea, 177–78
rejection of engagement policies
    by, 202
South Korean development and,
    20
South Korean military and,
    92–93

State Department, 180
World War II and, 62–63
uranium enrichment program,
    212–18

Vandenberg, Hoyt, 100–102

Wang Kon (Koguryo general), 31
Weathersby, Kathryn, 104
West, Loraine, 157
Wilson, Woodrow, 56–57
women, discrimination against,
    190
Worker-Peasant Red Guards, 181
Workers' Party of Korea (WPK),
    131
worker's rights, 191–92
World Food Programme, 163
World War II
Japanese aggression and, 62
Japanese defeat in, 62–63
Japanese oppression of Koreans
    during, 64
Japanese surrender in, 83
Wudi (Han emperor), 28

yangban, 35, 43, 46
Yeltsin, Boris, 107
Yemaek people, 27
Yeon Hyong Muk, 200
Yi dynasty, 15–16, 34–37, 42
Yi Pom-sok, 64–65
Yi Song-gye, 15, 34
Yi Sung Yop, 125
Yi T'aewang, 46
Yonsan'gun (Choson king), 35
Yo Un-hyong, 69
Yugoslavia, 101